A Modern Chemistry Course

Modern Chemistry Series

Books by the same author in the *Modern Chemistry Series*

Calculations in Modern Chemistry
Problems in Modern Chemistry
Objective Tests in Modern Chemistry
Teachers' Guide to Assessment in Modern Chemistry
Laboratory Notes *(for* A Modern Chemistry Course)

A Modern Chemistry Course

J.C.Mathews B.Sc. F.R.I.C.

SENIOR LECTURER IN CURRICULUM DEVELOPMENT,
UNIVERSITY OF LANCASTER

FORMER HEAD OF SCIENCE AND SENIOR CHEMISTRY MASTER,
KING EDWARD VII SCHOOL, LYTHAM

HUTCHINSON EDUCATIONAL

HUTCHINSON EDUCATIONAL LTD
3 Fitzroy Square, London W1

London Melbourne Sydney Auckland
Wellington Johannesburg Cape Town
and agencies throughout the world

First published December 1964
Reprinted September 1965
Reprinted February 1966
Reprinted November 1966
Reprinted April 1968
Reprinted July 1968
Reprinted September 1968
New edition (revised and metricated) 1970
Reprinted December 1971
This edition February 1973

This book has been set in Times, printed in Great Britain
on Smooth Wove paper by Gilbert Whitehead & Co Ltd, London
and bound by Wm. Brendon, Tiptree, Essex
ISBN 0 09 115731 5

Contents

Preface

A movement for reform in the teaching of chemistry in schools has been gathering momentum over the past few years. An outstanding contribution was *Chemistry for Grammar Schools*, published by the Science Masters' Association (now the A.S.E.). This booklet appears to have influenced some of the recent changes in G.C.E. chemistry syllabuses and the need is apparent for new books which reflect the spirit of this new approach to the teaching of chemistry. *A Modern Chemistry Course* is intended to fill this need.

Briefly, the book aims to encourage investigation and understanding. Practical work forms a large part of each section and it is used to accumulate information about how matter behaves. But enthusiasm for practical work is soon tempered by a desire for explanations; the lively mind of the young beginner demands chemical concepts. Wherever possible I have tried to show that concepts arise as a result of imaginative thinking about facts, that they can be used to assist in the discovery of more facts, and that they may have to be modified as more information comes to light. At the end of most of the sections there are problems which include suggestions for additional practical investigations; there will not be time to try them all, but the hope is that the pupils will be stimulated to attempt some of them.

Concepts to which the book gives prominence include the electrical and particulate nature of matter, gram-particle units, redox reactions in terms of electron transfer, acid-base reactions in terms of proton transfer, ionic equations, the chemical bond and crystal structure, and simple reference to heats and rates of reactions. The concepts are not introduced on a once-and-for-all basis, but at intervals, so that each concept grows throughout the book to match the growth in practical work and information.

Despite the inclusion of detailed instructions for practical work and large sections on organic and industrial chemistry, the book has been kept as short as possible by a rigorous pruning of irrelevant information and by adopting a concise style. It is a book to be used as a guide through several years of work rather than as a background reader. Much information, particularly about practical work, which is of no direct interest to the pupil is contained in the separate publication, *Notes for Teachers and Laboratory Stewards*. To assist in revision, references to other parts of the book are frequent and each section ends with a summary.

Help in writing this book has come so generously from so many people that it is difficult to acknowledge it all. Over the years, my ideas on the teaching of chemistry must have been influenced by the discussion and writings of many other teachers, especially at the meetings of the Science Masters' Association and in the *School Science Review*; to all who have contributed to this steady flow of information and ideas I owe much. I am particularly indebted to the Master and Fellows of Clare College, Cambridge, whose generosity in electing me to a Visiting Fellowship gave me time to write and the opportunity to discuss much of this book. Frequent discussions with my colleagues, Mr B. L. Brown, Dr D. E. MacDuffie, and Dr C. R. Sutton, have helped me greatly; Dr MacDuffie's assistance in reading the manuscript and proofs has been invaluable. In addition, I am grateful to Mr M. G. Brown, Mr W. H. Francis, and Mr G. Raitt, for guidance and comment. Finally, my thanks go to my wife and Miss R. E. Bowker for undertaking the task of typing a difficult manuscript in its draft and final forms.

J C M

1964

Preface to the second edition

In this edition some minor corrections have been made and Experiment 16.2 has been completely replaced. The author gratefully acknowledges the work of the Nuffield Foundation Science Teaching Project as the source of the new experiment.

J C M

1968

Preface to the third edition

In this edition the text has been completely revised to take account of the work of the Nuffield Project and the revised syllabuses of the examining boards. The amount of material on kinetics, equilibria, energetics and structure, and the Periodic Table, has been increased. It has been found possible to delete sufficient material to keep the book approximately the same size. To meet the trend towards a problem solving approach to chemistry teaching, the author has left open-ended questions after some of the practical work, particularly in the new sections.

The date of publication (1970) coincides with a period of transition to the International System of units. It is not easy in 'O' level chemistry to reconcile a complete adoption of S.I. units with what is likely to be common practice in the near future. For example, it is not likely that balances will be calibrated in newtons. The author has modernized the text in the light of the very helpful publications of the A.S.E., The British Standards Institution, and the Royal Society; but he has taken the liberty of using those terms which are likely to be colloquial for many years to come. Some trivial names of chemicals have been retained, but in the main IUPAC nomenclature has been adopted.

Some new syllabuses require that the physical states of substances should be shown in equations where appropriate. In this revision the states are specified where the physical state is a significant factor in a reaction; this is specially important in ionic reactions in aqueous solutions and in equations which also specify heat of reaction. The inclusion of state symbols can be visually confusing to young readers, and where the author's intention is to emphasise some other aspect of a reaction the state symbols have been left out.

The author gratefully acknowledges his debt to the work of the Nuffield Science Teaching Project. Mr D. K. Rowley has given the author much help in reading the typescript and proofs of the revised edition and also in discussion over the past years in which we have taught together; this help has been invaluable.

J C M

Introduction

The roots of chemistry lie in the practical investigations into the nature of matter which are undertaken in the laboratory. On the results of these investigations rests the whole structure of chemical theory; and the blend of the two, observation and theory, make up the subject which we know as chemistry. The application of chemistry to the needs of mankind has resulted in a vast chemical industry producing substances which affect most parts of our lives. But it all starts in the laboratory.

The chemistry laboratory

Even a simple, school laboratory is a costly and complicated thing to build and maintain. To equip it and to ensure that it functions efficiently requires detailed organization and hard work by the laboratory and teaching staff. If the work in the laboratory is to run smoothly, and safely, your co-operation is essential. Here are some of the ways in which you can help:

Safety

If an accident happens, report it to the master in charge at once.

Do not taste any of the chemicals.

If you are instructed to smell a gas, do so cautiously. Do not look into the open end of a vessel, point it at anyone else, or hold it to your ear.

If a chemical gets on to your skin, into your eyes, or into your mouth, remove it by using plenty of water immediately.

Nothing must be taken from the laboratory.

Do not carry out unauthorized experiments.

Look carefully at the label on a bottle before using its contents.

Do not tamper with the electrical, gas, or water fittings.

Handle hot objects with care and do not put hot material into the waste boxes.

Experiments which are suitable for class work are labelled (**C**).

Experiments which are suitable for demonstration only are labelled (**D**).

Tidiness

Keep the bench tops free from chemicals and waste material.

As soon as you have finished with a reagent bottle, replace its stopper and put it back into its correct position.

Do not put insoluble material into the sinks.

Leave your apparatus clean and tidy.

Report any defects or breakages in your apparatus.

Write neat and accurate notes of your observations as soon as you have made them.

Economy in time, movement, and material

Plan your work so that you complete it in the shortest possible time.

Do not move about the laboratory unnecessarily.

Do not use more of a chemical than is necessary.

Use the apparatus which fulfils your purpose most efficiently; the use of unsuitable apparatus may lead to damage or an accident.

Do not use more gas or water than you need—both have to be paid for.

When using a specialized and expensive piece of apparatus such as a balance, make sure that you know and obey the instructions for its use.

The equipment

Size

Although there is a large variety in the sizes available, the glass apparatus suggested in this book has been standardized as far as possible in order to simplify laboratory organization and instruction. There are, however, two main sizes of apparatus, normal and semi-micro. Test tubes will serve as examples:

normal test tube—15 cm long × 1·6 cm diameter, volume about 25 cm³.

semi-micro test tube—8 cm × 1 cm diameter, volume about 5 cm³.

The quantities of materials prescribed in the experiments in this book are calculated on the assumption that tubes of approximately this size will be used. For simplicity, the two types of tube will be called test tubes and small test tubes.

Apparatus for measuring quantities

The International System of units (SI units) is now being adopted in science teaching. The SI unit of mass is the kilogramme (kg), but the gramme (g) which is 1/1000 of a kilogramme is more frequently used in school chemistry. Weight and mass are not the same thing, but weighing is a convenient way of determining the mass of substance and it is common practice to speak of weighing even though the result is expressed in grammes.

The SI unit of volume is the cubic metre (m³), but a more convenient unit in school chemistry is the cubic centimetre (cm³). The litre (l) is not an SI unit, but is commonly used when speaking of 1000 cm³. For some time you may come across the millilitre (ml) and the cc; both can be taken to be the same as the cm³. Mention of other SI units is made as they arise in the book.

For accurate measurements of the volume of liquids, burettes (p.283) and pipettes (p. 283) are used; for approximate measurements, a measuring cylinder is used. Frequently a rough guide to quantity is given by the depth to which a container is to be filled; for example, 2 cm of water in a boiling tube. Another method of approximately measuring volumes of a liquid is to deliver the liquid in drops from a teat pipette (p. 8). This is useful when doing experiments on a semi-micro scale; there are roughly twenty drops to the cubic centimetre.

Weights of substances are accurately measured on a chemical balance. For the experiments described in this book it is assumed that balances are available with which weights of substances can be measured quickly to within 0·01 g (10 milligrams). The usual instrument for handling solids is a spatula. Solid material can be scooped on to the end of the spatula and conveyed from one vessel to another (the spatula should be gently tapped to shake off superfluous solid before attempting to move it). It is convenient to have two sizes of spatula, one for normal work and the other for semi-micro work. In this book one measure means enough solid to cover the end of a normal spatula and one small measure is enough solid to cover the end of a small spatula.

Supporting and connecting apparatus

If apparatus is to be supported for long periods, retort stands and clamps are used. These are not shown in the diagrams which follow, but sometimes the best place for a clamp to be attached to an apparatus is shown by an arrow.

To allow the flow of liquids or gases from one piece of apparatus to another, tubes of glass, plastic or rubber are used. The actual joint between two pieces of apparatus is made either by using stoppers made of cork or rubber, or by using apparatus which has ground-glass joints so that one piece fits exactly into another (*figure 1*).

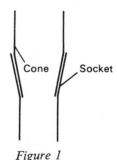

Cone   Socket

Figure 1

Sources of energy

(a) *Heat*   The most familiar source of heat is the bunsen burner, which burns a mixture of fuel gas and air. The supply of gas can be controlled by the gas tap and the supply of air by the ring of metal which alters the size of the hole at the base of the burner. When using the burner, do not close the air hole completely; lack of air causes a yellow, smoky flame with little heat. A normal bunsen flame is shown in *figure 2*. The size of the flame depends mainly on the amount of gas which is allowed into the burner, not the amount of air.

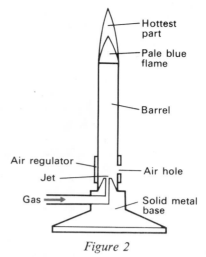

Figure 2

On occasions when a naked flame would be dangerous, water baths or electric hot plates can be used.

(b) *Electricity*   Electricity in the form of direct current (d.c.) is another important form of energy which can be used to bring about chemical change. This must not be confused with the use of electrically operated heating equipment. The two most familiar sources of direct current are either accumulators or direct current power packs. The latter is a compact piece of equipment which can be plugged into an a.c. mains supply to convert this to a d.c. supply of variable voltage.

Materials

The materials supplied for experiments are pure, unless they have been deliberately mixed with something else, and care must be taken to keep them so. Contamination of a reagent may spoil an experiment. For this reason reagents should not be returned to a bottle once they have been removed from it.

In this book, water means tap water. On the few occasions when specially purified water is required it is called purified water.

Many reagents are in solutions in water and these are of standard concentration. Most of the solutions are dilute; that is, the quantity of dissolved substance is small compared with the quantity of water. It must be remembered that there are many solvents other than water, but, for brevity, solution means a dilute solution of the substance in water.

Acids are usually available either as concentrated or dilute solutions.

Section 1
Matter and the separation of mixtures

Chemistry is the study of the substances of which things are made. The collective name for these substances is matter. Matter may be in the form of a solid, a liquid, or a gas; these are called the *three states of matter*.

The matter of which a thing is made may contain one substance or a mixture of substances. For example, water consists of a single substance; air contains a mixture of substances. Part of a chemist's work is to separate one substance from another and to identify single substances.

Pure substances

A chemist recognizes a pure substance by the constant way in which it behaves, its *properties*. Each substance has certain properties which belong to it alone; for example, copper is the only pink metal. If impurities are added to a substance, these properties are changed.

Two useful properties which are used to identify a substance are its *melting point* (the temperature at which it changes from a solid to a liquid) and its *boiling point* (the temperature at which it changes from a liquid to a gas). It is sometimes more convenient to find the temperature at which a liquid changes to a solid; this is called its *freezing point* and, under normal conditions, it is the same as the melting point.

Experiment 1.1

To determine the melting point of ice and the boiling point of water (C)

Set up the apparatus shown in *figure 3*.

Put water into the boiling tube to a depth of about 2 cm and add about an equal volume of crushed ice. Place a small flame under the tube and, stirring regularly, watch the temperature recorded by the thermometer.

Look for two temperatures which remain fairly constant despite the continued application of heat.

Experiment 1.2

To investigate the effect of dissolved solids on the boiling point of water **(C)**

After adding four measures of common salt to the water, repeat the second part of Experiment 1.

What is the difference between the boiling point of the salt solution and that of pure water?

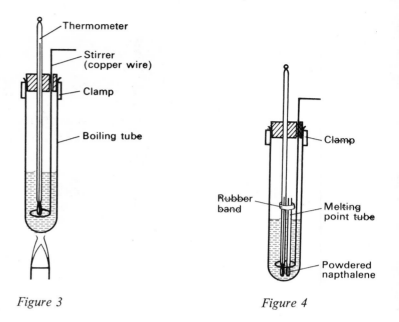

Figure 3   *Figure 4*

Experiment 1.3

To determine the melting point of (a) pure napthalene and (b) impure napthalene **(C)**

(a) Grind some pure naphthalene in a mortar; scoop some of it into the open end of the melting point tube; tap the tube to shake the powder down to the closed end. Repeat this until there is about $\frac{1}{2}$ cm of powder in the tube. Attach the tube to the thermometer and put it into the boiling tube containing liquid paraffin, as shown in *figure 4*. Take care that both the rubber band and the open end of the tube are well clear of the surface of the liquid paraffin (medicinal paraffin).

Heat the boiling tube, stirring slowly and regularly. When the temperature reaches 65°–70°C, remove the burner at intervals so that the temperature rises as slowly as possible.

(b) Record the temperature at which the white powder suddenly shrinks and forms a clear liquid. This will be the melting point of naphthalene.

Repeat this experiment using a mixture of 8 parts of naphthalene to 1 part of benzoic acid.

Is the melting point the same?

Does the melting take place as suddenly as it did for pure naphthalene?

If the members of a class compare their results for any one of these experiments, they will find that the results are not identical. Experimental error has three main causes:

(i) Human error. For example, delay in reading the thermometer when a substance is melting.
(ii) Errors in instruments. To show this, put a dozen thermometers in the same beaker of cold water.
(iii) Errors caused by the use of unsuitable apparatus.

Physical change

A physical change is one in which no new substance is formed; for example, the position or shape of a piece of wood can be changed, but the material of which it is made remains unchanged.

Most substances change from one state to another without any new substance being formed. Melting and boiling are examples of physical change, and the melting and boiling points of a substance are examples of its physical properties. Change which results in the formation of a new substance is called *chemical change* and will be discussed later.

Separation of solids from liquids

Whenever possible, physical changes are used to separate the components of a mixture; thereby the substances are not permanently changed and are easily recovered. For instance, the solid impurities which find their way into the lubricating oil of a car engine are removed by passing the oil continuously through an oil filter made of paper or gauze. This is an example of the process called *filtration*.

Experiment 1.4

To separate a mixture of sand and salt (C)

Put about 1 cm of the mixture into a test tube and half fill the tube with purified water. Shake the test tube to dissolve the salt. Fold a filter paper into a cone and set up the apparatus shown in *figure 5*.

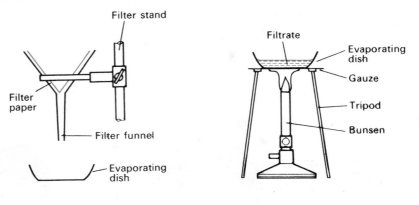

Figure 5

Figure 6

Pour the liquid contents of the test tube into the filter paper. (Hold the filter paper in place until the first few drops of liquid have moistened it sufficiently to make it settle into the filter funnel.)

Most of the sand will remain in the test tube. Add some water to the sand; shake the test tube; allow the sand to settle, pour off the water into the sink. Repeat this at least three times. This process is called washing by decantation, and it will remove the last traces of salt from the sand.

The sand can be shaken on to a filter paper and left to dry, or the tube containing the sand can be put into an oven at a temperature of about 80°–100°C.

The salt is contained in the *filtrate* (the liquid which has filtered through the filter paper) in the evaporating dish. Heat the dish, as shown in *figure 6*, so that its contents boil gently.

As the volume of liquid decreases, decrease the amount of heat applied. Continue this until dry salt is obtained.

Have you obtained all the salt and sand from the mixture? If not, how have they been lost?

Experiment 1.5

(a) To investigate the solubility of calcium carbonate and (b) to obtain pure calcium carbonate from a suspension in water **(C)**

(a) Put one small measure of powdered calcium carbonate (chalk) into a small test tube (semi-micro tube) and add purified water until the tube is a third full. Shake the tube to form a *suspension* of calcium carbonate.

Put the tube into one arm of a centrifuge and another tube, containing an equal volume of water, into the other arm. Centrifuge the suspension for 15–20 seconds. When the centrifuge has stopped, remove the two tubes. What has happened to the calcium carbonate?

With the aid of a teat pipette, draw off a few drops of the liquid from the tube containing the calcium carbonate. Compress the teat slightly before putting the pipette into the liquid. Do not draw off the liquid from the surface film; a few particles of solid calcium carbonate may still be held there (*figure 7*). Put one drop of the liquid on to a polished microscope slide. Wash the pipette with purified water and close to the first drop put one drop of purified water and one drop of tap water (*figure 8*).

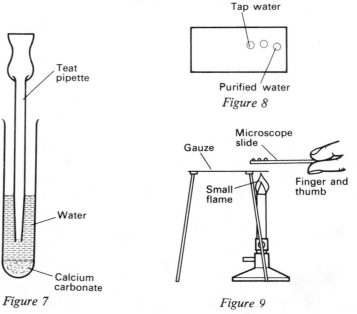

Figure 7

Figure 8

Figure 9

Hold the slide above a warm gauze (*figure 9*) until the three drops of liquid have evaporated. Hold the slide up to the light.

What does the experiment tell you about the solubility of calcium carbonate?

Why was the suspension made in purified water and not in tap water?

Why was a drop of purified water evaporated?

(b) Draw off as much water as possible from the calcium carbonate. Dry the calcium carbonate either in an oven or by laying it on a gauze and warming it gently from below with a burner.

Solution

Some solids mix with water and are distributed evenly throughout the water. Because the solid is no longer visible, it seems likely that it has been broken up into particles which are too small to be seen even with the aid of a microscope.

These solids are said to be *soluble*. They have *dissolved* in the water to form a *solution*.

Liquids other than water will dissolve solids (see Experiment 1.6). When a solution is formed, the liquid is called the *solvent* and the solid is called the *solute*.

When a solution is boiled, the solvent is removed as a vapour leaving the solute behind; this is called *evaporation*.

Dissolving and melting

These are often confused. A solid *melts* when it is heated by itself until it changes into a liquid. The liquid still consists entirely of the original substance. A solid will *dissolve* only with the aid of another substance (the solvent).

Although dissolving is often assisted by heat—for example, sugar dissolves more readily in hot water than in cold—it often takes place without the aid of heat. Under normal conditions, substances must be heated in order to melt them. Thus, common salt dissolves readily in cold water, but it must be heated to about 800°C in order to melt it.

Experiment 1.6

To make a solution of napthalene (b) to re-crystalize the napthalene (C)

(a) To each of two test tubes add one small measure of naphthalene. To one add a quarter of a tube of water and to the other a similar volume of trichloroethane. Shake both tubes. Which liquid acts as a solvent for naphthalene?

(b) Use a teat pipette to transfer one drop of the solution to a microscope slide. Look for the formation of crystals of naphthalene as the solvent evaporates.

NB: Naphthalene must be heated to 80°C in order to melt it, whereas it dissolves readily in a solvent at the temperature of the laboratory.

Experiment 1.7

The formation of crystals from a concentrated solution (C)

Add 10 cm³ of water to each of two boiling tubes. Add 6 g of powdered copper sulphate to one tube and 10 g of powdered copper sulphate to the other. Dissolve the copper sulphate by heating both tubes until the water almost boils. Cool both tubes quickly to laboratory temperature by running water from the tap on to the outside of them. Hold the tubes up to the light and look for the formation of crystals.

the other. Dissolve the copper sulphate by heating both tubes until the water almost boils. Cool both tubes quickly to laboratory temperature by running water from the tap on to the outside of them. Hold the tubes up to the light and look for the formation of crystals.

Heat the tubes again to dissolve the crystals and put them aside for a few hours so that they cool slowly to laboratory temperature. Decant the liquid from the crystals; wash them once with water; examine them and draw any regular shapes which you see in them. Take care—copper sulphate is corrosive and poisonous.

Experiment 1.7 shows that hot water will dissolve more copper sulphate than will cold water and that there is a limit to the weight of solute which will dissolve in a fixed weight of solvent.

You will notice that the particles of copper sulphate have a regular and constant shape. Many other solids, when they are slowly formed from a liquid, have a regular shape. The particles with a regular shape are called *crystals*. Copper sulphate is a *crystalline* substance, i.e. a substance which exists in the form of crystals. If the particles of a substance have no regular shape, the substance is said to be *amorphous*.

The words *concentrated* and *dilute* are used to indicate—very roughly

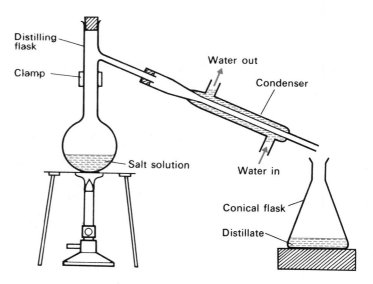

Figure 10

are called *crystals*. Copper sulphate is a *crystalline* substance, i.e. a substance which exists in the form of crystals. If the particles of a substance have no regular shape, the substance is said to be *amorphous*.

The words *concentrated* and *dilute* are used to indicate—very roughly —the relative amounts of solute contained in solutions. The proportion of solute to solvent is high in a concentrated solution and low in a dilute solution. A solution which will dissolve no more solute is said to be *saturated*.

Separation and purification of liquids

Experiment 1.8

To obtain pure water from a solution of common salt in water (D)

The steam from the boiling solution is cooled in the condenser and changes to water; the salt remains in the distillation flask.

The changing of a vapour to a liquid is called *condensation*. The whole process, liquid $\xrightarrow{heat}$ vapour $\xrightarrow{cooling}$ liquid, is called *distillation* and the liquid in the receiving vessel is the *distillate* (*figure 10*).

Experiment 1.9

To separate two immiscible liquids (C)

Put approximately 10 cm³ of trichloroethane and 50 cm³ of water into a separating funnel. Shake the liquids for about half a minute, then hold the funnel vertically to allow them to settle.

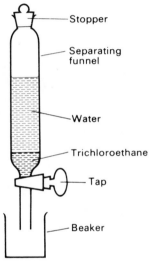

Stopper

Separating funnel

Water

Trichloroethane

Tap

Beaker

Figure 11

The liquids form two layers; they are *immiscible*.

Remove the stopper and slowly run the bottom liquid into a beaker. Try to stop the flow of liquid when the dividing line between the two reaches the tap. Run the upper liquid into another beaker.

Liquids which will mix in all proportions (miscible liquids) can often be separated by fractional distillation. An example of this is given on p. 246

Chromatography

Chromatography is a method of separating the substances in a mixture which are present in very small amounts. Many variations of this technique are now in use in analytical chemistry. Experiment 1.10 is a simple illustration of paper chromatography; it can be used to separate the components of a mixture of coloured compounds.

Experiment 1.10

To separate the coloured compounds in ink and universal indicator (C)

With a cork borer make a hole about 0·3 cm diameter in the centre of a filter paper. Roll a small strip of filter paper about 3 cm square into a plug and insert it into the hole.

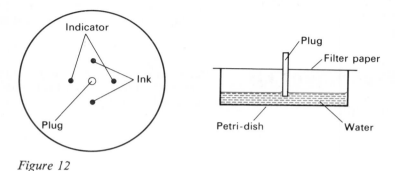

Figure 12

Put two spots of ink (Brilliant Black works well) and two spots of universal indicator on to the filter paper about 1 cm from the plug. Place the filter paper on the top of a petri-dish containing a little water.

The plug acts as a wick and water spreads to the coloured drops and then beyond to the edge of the filter paper. Examine the filter paper after about 10 minutes and notice how bands of colour are formed. These could be cut away to separate the coloured components of the two original substances.

As the water spreads across the filter paper it carries the coloured substances with it. These substances tend to stick to the fibres of the filter paper (the fibres are said to *adsorb* the substances). But some are adsorbed less firmly than others. The coloured substances which are adsorbed least firmly are carried furthest across the filter paper and eventually become completely separated.

Problems

(1) Devise an experiment to discover whether tap water contains dissolved solids.

(2) Can xylene be used as a solvent to separate sulphur from iron? (Use small quantities of xylene and a water bath to heat it)

(3) Make crystals of common salt, potassium chlorate, lead chloride, and alum. With the aid of a lens or a low-powered microscope, draw the shape of the crystals.

(4) Grind some leaves (copper beech will give good results) in a mortar with 10 cm³ of alcohol. Investigate the pigments by means of simple chromatography.

(5) Write a report on:

(i) The source and method of purification of the local water supply.

(ii) The melting and boiling points of (a) helium (b) oxygen (c) mercury (d) iron.

(iii) The separation of petrol from petroleum.
(iv) The manufacture of table salt.

Summary

(1) All things consist of either a single substance or a mixture of substances.

(2) Matter can exist in three states: solid, liquid, gas.

(3) A pure substance is identified by its properties.

(4) Two common properties used in the identification of a substance are melting point and boiling point.

(5) Melting can be brought about by heating a single substance. Solutions can only be made with the aid of a second substance, usually a liquid.

(6) Make sure that you understand the meaning of: suspension – filtrate – soluble – solute – solvent – evaporation – crystals – concentrated – dilute – saturated – condensation – distillation – miscible – immiscible.

Section 2
Air and burning

Burning is one of the most familiar and important of all chemical changes; new substances are formed and heat and light are given out.

Heat and light are forms of *energy*; unlike matter, they have no weight and no volume. The heat given out when substances burn is still our main source of domestic and industrial energy, although it may be converted into other forms of energy such as electricity.

The region in which gases burn can be seen because of the light given out. This region is called *flame*. Examples of this are: a bunsen burner flame, in which fuel gas is being burned, and a candle flame, in which vaporized wax is being burned. When a solid burns, it glows and retains a solid shape; the burning of coke is an example of this. In some fires, such as coal fires, both solids and gases are burning.

The fact that air is essential to burning is a part of everyday experience: an open domestic fire—not an electric fire—draws air into a room and causes draughts. If you open the bottom of an enclosed stove, allowing more air to enter, it burns more rapidly. Part of the technique of fire fighting is to exclude air from the burning object. This can be demonstrated in the laboratory by putting a lighted taper into a test tube (the test tube should be held with the open end downwards).

The difference between heating and burning

Experiment 2.1

The action of heat on wood in the absence of air (C or D)

Put a piece of wood, about 2 cm long and 0·5 cm wide, into a dry small test tube (semi-micro tube). Hold the tube with a test tube holder and heat it strongly at the bottom. When gas starts to come off, ignite it by holding the open end of the tube to the flame for a moment. After heating for 2–3 minutes allow the tube to cool; examine it and name its contents.

This method excludes all but a little air from the wood. The wood, although it is being heated, does not burn, but the vapour which the heat drives from it burns freely when it reaches the open air.

What is the name of the solid residue and the gas which are formed when coal is used instead of wood in Experiment 2.1?

Experiment 2.2

The action of heat on wood in air (C)

Put a piece of wood, similar to that used in Experiment 2.1, on to the edge of a gauze. Heat the wood strongly from below, removing the burner at about 10-second intervals to allow air to reach the hot wood. Is the solid residue the same as that formed in Experiment 2.1?

Repeat the experiment using the residue from Experiment 2.1.

Heating increases the energy of a substance; this is shown as a rise in temperature. Heating will only lead to burning if the substance is capable of burning and if air is present. Burning is a chemical change resulting from a reaction between the substance and air.*

Burning generates energy, but some energy is usually required to start the process. This *energy of initiation or activation* can be in various forms. Can you give examples of how heat, friction, and electricity can be used to start the process of burning?

Some substances, for example wood, can be chemically changed when heated in the absence of air, but the changes are different from those which occur when the substances are burned.

Some substances, for example water and glass, do not form new substances either when heated with air or without air. They do undergo temporary changes which are reversed when the source of heat is removed—the water boils and the glass softens; these are physical changes.

Is the whole of air used in burning?

Experiment 2.3

To determine the fraction of air used in burning (D)

Put a small piece of yellow phosphorus into an evaporating dish. Float the dish in a trough of water and place a bell jar over it. Measure the height of the air in the bell jar. Ignite the phosphorus by touching it with the end of a hot wire, then quickly replace the stopper of the jar. Measure the height of the air inside the jar when the phosphorus has stopped burning and the level of the water finally comes to rest.

Why does the volume of air increase at first?

What fraction of the air is used up by the burning phosphorus?

Light a taper; take out the stopper of the bell jar and quickly plunge the lighted end of the taper into it.

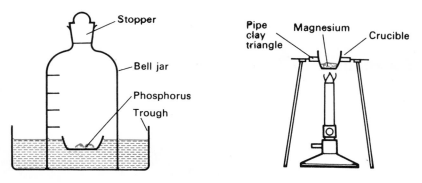

Figures 13   *Figure 14*

What is the difference between normal air and the air remaining in the bell jar?

What are the possible sources of error in the experiment?

When phosphorus burns it forms a solid which has a negligible

*The word 'burning' is sometimes used to describe reactions with gases other than air. In this section the word refers only to burning in air.

volume. What difference would you have noticed in the final volume if phosphorus had burned to form an insoluble gas?

These experiments indicate that only a part of the air, never more than one-fifth, is used up during burning and that the remaining four-fifths is a gas which does not support combustion.

What happens to the air which is used in burning?

Experiment 2.4

To measure the change in weight when magnesium burns (C or D)

Weigh a dry crucible; add 15 cm of folded magnesium ribbon and weigh again. Heat the crucible strongly on a pipeclay triangle (*figure 14*). Do not look too closely into the crucible.

After the magnesium has burned, let the crucible cool and weigh it again. You have recorded three weights:

The weight of the crucible $=$ g
The weight of the crucible and magnesium $=$ g
The weight of the crucible and ash $=$ g

Calculate (a) the weight of the magnesium (b) the weight of the ash (c) the increase in weight.

The increase in weight which takes place when a substance burns is easily measured in Experiment 2.4 because only one new substance is formed and this is solid. The increase in weight is not easy to measure when substances such as wood are burned, because some of the products are gases which are not easily collected and weighed. If, however, all the products of burning are collected, it is found that they weigh more than the original substance.

The products of combustion contain a greater amount of matter than the original substance. Unless new matter has been created, the air is the most likely source of the matter which has caused this increase in weight.

Experiment 2.5

Does burning create new matter? (D)

Weigh a dry 250 cm³ flask which is fitted with a ground-glass stopper. The stopper should be lightly greased to prevent air getting in or out of the flask. Put a small piece of phosphorus—less than 0·5 g will be enough —into the flask; put the stopper on quickly and weigh the flask again.

Observe that the phosphorus begins to smoulder. Leave the flask until the phosphorus has stopped smouldering (about 12 hours) and weigh it again. You should find that the total weight of the flask and its contents is unchanged, showing that no new matter has been created.

The amount of air used in burning phosphorus can be shown as follows: Take out the stopper to allow more air to enter the flask in place of the air which has been used in the burning. Replace the stopper and weigh the flask again.

Record your results:

The weight of the flask $=$ g
The weight of the flask and phosphorus $=$ g
The weight of the flask after burning is complete $=$ g
The weight of the flask after allowing more air to enter $=$ g

The law of conservation of mass

Experiment 2.5 illustrates this important chemical principle: the total weight of the substances before chemical change (the *reactants*) equals the total weight of the substances after chemical change (the *products*).

Chemical laws

A chemical law is a summary of the results of a large number of experiments.

Many chemists have observed that the weights of the reactants and products of many reactions are equal and this has led them to summarize their observations in the form of a concise statement (a generalization) which is called the *Law of Conservation of Mass:*
There is no change of mass during a chemical change.

It is important that you should realize the limitations of this law and of all chemical laws:
(a) Its accuracy is governed by the accuracy of the experiments. (Experiments of a much higher degree of accuracy may show slight differences between the masses of the reactants and products.)
(b) One experiment, such as Experiment 2.5, can never prove the law to be true; it simply shows that the law holds good for that particular reaction.
(c) A scientist must accept the possibility of future experiments giving results which do not conform to the law.

If experiments of high accuracy show slight defects in a law, it does not follow that the law is no longer useful to chemists. The Law of Conservation of Mass, together with other chemical laws, enables chemists to calculate the weights of substances formed as a result of chemical change. The accuracy of these calculations is quite sufficient for most of the uses to which chemists will put them.

To sum up: chemical laws summarize the results of past experiments; on the assumption that they are true until proved false, the laws can be used to predict the results of future experiments; they are usually only true within certain limits of accuracy. Keep these points in mind when studying the other chemical laws quoted in this book.

A study of the substance in the air which takes part in burning

This substance was first prepared in a reasonably pure state in the eighteenth century, and its preparation was soon followed by the explanation of the nature of burning (*combustion*) which is still accepted. The work was largely that of two men: Priestley, working in England, and Lavoisier, working in France. Until that time there had been many attempts to explain combustion, but this was the first explanation to be firmly based on observations of experiments and on correct reasoning. For this reason a study of the work of Priestley and Lavoisier is rewarding.

Priestley

Priestley strongly heated a red powder which he called calx of mercury. This substance broke up (*decomposed*) into two substances; one of the substances was mercury and the other was a gas. He also discovered that inflammable material burned much more vigorously in this gas than it did in normal air. Priestley told Lavoisier of his discovery.

Lavoisier

Lavoisier carried out an experiment in which he showed that the gas which Priestley had made was identical to that one-fifth part of air which supports combustion. A diagram of his apparatus is shown in *figure 15*.

He kept the mercury in the retort, at a temperature just lower than its boiling point, for several days. At the end of this time he observed that the volume of gas in his apparatus had been reduced by one-fifth, this being shown by a rise in the level of the mercury in the bell jar. He also observed that a red powder had been formed on the surface of the

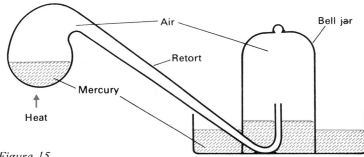

Figure 15

hot mercury in the retort. The gas remaining in his apparatus would not support combustion or life.

He collected the red powder and discovered that when it was heated to a higher temperature than that of the retort it formed mercury and Priestley's gas. This gas would support combustion and life and its volume was equal to the volume by which the air in his apparatus had been reduced. Lavoisier gave this gas its modern name of *oxygen*. The other four-fifths of the air consists mainly of a gas which we now call nitrogen.

On the basis of his observations Lavoisier arrived at the following explanation of burning and the composition of air.

(a) One-fifth of air consists of a gas which we call *oxygen*.

(b) When substances burn they combine with oxygen, forming new substances which we call *oxides*.

(c) Without oxygen, substances will not burn and animals will die.

(d) When a substance burns completely, the weight of the oxides formed equals the combined weight of the original substance and the weight of oxygen with which it has combined.

The chemical changes which took place in Preistley's and Lavoisier's experiments would now be described as follows:

(i) The heating of calx of mercury:

mercury oxide → mercury and oxygen

(ii) The heating of mercury in air:

mercury + oxygen → mercury oxide

(→ means 'forms')

Decomposition and combination

The two chemical reactions given above are examples of two very common types of reaction.

In (i) one substance (mercury oxide) breaks up into two substances (mercury and oxygen). This is called *decomposition*, i.e. *a reaction in which one substance forms two or more substances.*

In (ii) two substances (mercury and oxygen) combine to form one substance (mercury oxide). This is called *combination*, i.e. *a reaction in which two or more substances form one substance.*

The industrial preparation of oxygen

The abundance of air makes it the obvious source of oxygen. The air is made into a liquid (liquefied) by repeating the process of compressing it, cooling it, and allowing it to expand, several times. You can observe the effect of compressing a gas and then allowing it to escape slowly by using a bicycle pump with your finger over the end.

Liquid air consists mainly of nitrogen (boiling point: $-196°C$) and oxygen (boiling point: $-183°C$). The small quantities of other gases present in air will be discussed later in this section. When liquid air is allowed to evaporate, nitrogen comes off first and oxygen second. The two gases can then be collected separately and stored by compressing them into steel cylinders.

The uses of oxygen

The two natural uses of oxygen in air are to support life in the processes of breathing and respiration, and to support burning. Pure oxygen is used when it is necessary to support respiration and burning more vigorously:

(a) It is mixed with the vapours of anaesthetizing gases during surgical operations.

(b) It is used to increase the proportion of oxygen in the air supplied to patients who require treatment for defects in respiration.

(c) It is used to give an adequate supply of oxygen to high-altitude fliers and climbers.

(d) It is mixed with acetylene gas and the mixture is burned to weld or cut metals.

(e) It is used in rockets—usually in its liquid form—to make the burning of fuel more vigorous.

(f) With fuel gas it forms an inflammable mixture used for melting and shaping glass apparatus.

(g) Compressed oxygen is used in modern methods of making steel.

The laboratory preparation of oxygen

The most convenient source of oxygen for demonstration experiments in a school laboratory is an oxygen cylinder. For class experiments a convenient source is a solution of hydrogen peroxide in water. Although pure hydrogen peroxide is actually a liquid, 94% of its total weight is made up of oxygen. Half of this oxygen can be obtained by decomposing the hydrogen peroxide.

$$\text{hydrogen peroxide} \rightarrow \text{water} + \text{oxygen}$$

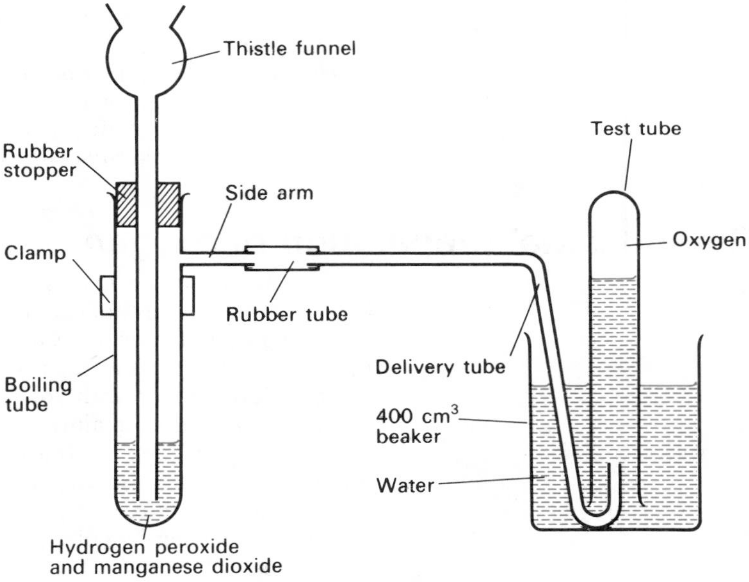

Figure 16

Experiment 2.6

To prepare, collect, and test for oxygen (C)

A convenient apparatus for preparing and collecting a small quantity of oxygen is shown in *figure 16*. Assemble the apparatus and add water to the beaker until it just covers the end of the delivery tube. Fill a test tube with water; put one finger over the end and put it upside down into the beaker; take your finger off. Provided that the end of the test tube is not lifted above the surface of the water, the water in the tube will not run out.

Remove the stopper and add one small measure of manganese

dioxide to the boiling tube. Replace the stopper and pour about 10 cm³ of hydrogen peroxide solution down the thistle funnel. After an interval of about 10 seconds put the test tube over the end of the delivery tube—take care that you do not release the water from the test tube when doing this. Why is the gas not collected immediately?

When you have filled a test tube with oxygen, put a finger or thumb over the end of the tube and remove it from the water. Light a wooden splint; blow out the flame and put the glowing end of the splint into the oxygen; remove the splint as soon as it bursts into flame. This is a method of identifying oxygen.

Chemical tests for substances

In Section 1 we discussed two properties, melting point and boiling point, by which substances could be identified. These are physical properties of the substances because they are related to physical change.

Melting points and boiling points can only be found by the use of fairly complicated apparatus and the experiments take a considerable time to perform. Chemists frequently identify a substance by means of a chemical property; this is called the *test* for the substance and the test for oxygen, given above, is an example. The characteristics of a good chemical test are:

(i) it should be easily and quickly performed.
(ii) the result should be easily observed,·
(iii) it should work only for the substance or group of substances under investigation (it should be *specific*).

Although simple chemical tests identify the presence of a substance, they do not give much information about its purity: oxygen mixed with and equal volume of nitrogen will still relight a glowing splint.

Catalysts

In Experiment 2.6 you probably noticed that when the decomposition of the hydrogen peroxide had stopped, the manganese dioxide appeared to be still present as a black suspension. Hydrogen peroxide solution will decompose slowly either at room temperature or when gently warmed, but the rate of decomposition is much greater when manganese dioxide is added to it. Furthermore, the amount of manganese dioxide required is small.

Experiment 2.7

Is there any loss of manganese dioxide during the decomposition of hydrogen peroxide? (C)

Weigh a dry small test tube; add a small measure of dry manganese dioxide and weigh again. Add hydrogen peroxide solution drop-wise until the tube is about a quarter full. When the effervescence of oxygen dies down, warm the contents of the tube gently to complete the decomposition. Centrifuge the tube for about 20 seconds.

Suck off as much liquid as possible by means of a teat pipette. Lay the tube on a gauze and dry it by warming it gently from below with a burner. Weigh the tube when it is cool.

The results obtained in Experiment 2.7 should indicate that the weight of manganese dioxide remaining at the end of the experiment equals the weight of manganese dioxide added at the beginning. It is also possible to show that the manganese dioxide has not undergone any permanent chemical change; in the decomposition of hydrogen peroxide it has acted as a *catalyst*.

Catalysts have an important place in chemistry. A full study of them is complicated, but the main characteristics of catalysts can be summarized:

(i) they increase the rate of a reaction,
(ii) they are usually effective in small quantities,
(iii) they do not appear to undergo any permanent chemical change.

Other examples and characteristics of catalysts will be found later in the book. Negative catalysts (inhibitors) are substances which decrease the rate of a reaction; they will not be discussed here.

The other gases in air

Water vapour

(The difference in meaning between the words 'vapour' and 'gas' is slight. The word vapour is used loosely to describe a gas which can also exist in the liquid form under the same conditions of temperature and pressure.) The presence of water vapour in air seems likely from the fact that water evaporates slowly even at laboratory temperature. In this form it is not visible but its presence can be shown by cooling the air.

Experiment 2.8

To show the presence of water vapour in air (**C** or **D**)

Mix crushed ice and common salt in the approximate proportion of 10:1. This is called a freezing mixture and you will find that it has a temperature which is lower than that of the melting point of pure ice. Fill a conical flask with the mixture and allow it to stand, suspended in a retort stand, for 30–40 minutes.

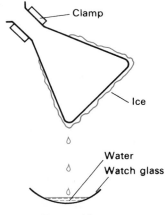

Figure 17

Scrape the ice which forms on the outside of the flask into an eva-porating dish, or empty the flask and allow the ice to melt and drip into the watch glass. Test the liquid with a piece of cobalt chloride paper; this turns from blue to pink in the presence of water. If sufficient liquid were collected in this way, it could be shown to have the properties of pure water.

The condensation of the water vapour in air shows itself in nature in the formation of cloud, fog, dew, and hoar frost.

The amount of water vapour in air varies with the conditions of climate. Air which is *exhaled* (breathed out) contains a higher propor-tion of water vapour than air which is *inhaled* (breathed in); this can be shown by breathing on to a mirror.

Carbon dioxide

This substance will be studied fully in Section 7. For the moment it is sufficient to know that it is a gas and that the chemical test for it is to bubble it through limewater, which will then form a suspension which is milky in appearance.

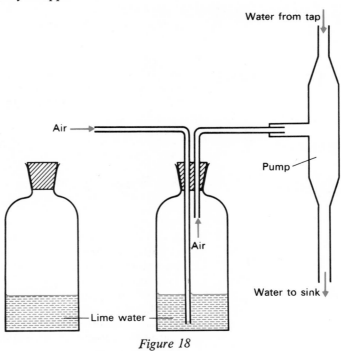

Figure 18

Experiment 2.9

To show the presence of carbon dioxide in air (**C** or **D**)

The apparatus shown in *figure 18* enables a continuous stream of air to be sucked through limewater when tap water passes through the pump. Air is passed through one bottle of limewater for about 20 minutes. A sealed bottle of limewater can be placed alongside for purposes of comparison.

Exhaled air contains a higher proportion of carbon dioxide than inhaled air (see Section 3 for an explanation of this). It follows that the proportion of carbon dioxide in air varies, particularly indoors.

The noble (inert) gases

These were the last gases in air to be discovered. The fact that they have almost no chemical properties partly accounts for their late discovery and also gave rise to their collective name.

There are six noble gases: helium, neon, argon, krypton, xenon, and radon. All except radon are found in air; argon is in the greatest proportion. Recently, some compounds, xenon tetrafluoride for example, have been made.

Atmospheric pollution

Air in places inhabited by men, particularly industrial areas, usually contains traces of other substances. Many of these substances are harmful; they pollute the air. Most of the harmful substances come from domestic and industrial fires, from petrol and diesel engines and from radioactive sources.

Living organisms

Air usually contains microscopic living particles. These include bacteria, viruses, and the spores of plants which use air to spread themselves. Some are harmful; some are not.

Problems

Investigate experimentally:

(1) The essential part which air and water play in the rusting of iron. (In scientific investigation of this type it is important that the conditions of the experiment are only changed one at a time. Thus, iron should be exposed to (i) dry air alone, (ii) air-free water alone, (iii) air and water together.)

(2) The relation between rusting and burning.

(3) The volume of oxygen which can be obtained from 10 cm^3 of hydrogen peroxide solution at laboratory temperature.

(4) The effect of (a) temperature (b) the concentration of hydrogen peroxide and (c) the weight of catalyst, on the rate of formation of oxygen from hydrogen peroxide solution.

(5) Write a report on:

 (i) Fire fighting.

 (ii) The causes of atmospheric pollution.

(iii) The harm which polluted air causes to health.

(iv) The prevention of rusting.

 (v) Materials which do not rust and can be used instead of iron.

(vi) The discovery of the noble gases.

Summary

(1) Oxygen is essential to burning in air.

(2) Burning is a chemical change, i.e. it leads to the formation of new substances.

(3) Heating in the absence of air can also lead to chemical change, but this is a different change from burning.

(4) About one-fifth of air (oxygen) is used in burning.

(5) Burning involves an increase in weight in the new substances formed and an equal decrease in weight of the air.

(6) Chemical laws are summaries or generalizations of experimental results.

(7) The Law of Conservation of Mass: There is no change in mass during a chemical change.

(8) Decomposition is a reaction in which one substance forms two or more substances.

(9) Combination is a reaction in which two or more substances form one substance. When substances burn they combine with oxygen to form new substances called oxides.

(10) A chemical test should be easily performed, easily observed, and specific.

(11) A catalyst increases the rate of a reaction, is effective in small quantities, and does not appear to change chemically.

(12) When performing a scientific investigation, change one thing at a time.

Section 3
Products of burning

Before investigating the products of burning, we must extend our knowledge of the matter which is to be burned. The study of a large number of things, such as the different forms of matter, is made easier by splitting them into smaller groups so that similar things are in the same group. This is called *classification* and it is one of the most important features of the way in which scientists work. The classification of matter into solids, liquids, and gases is one example. Another is the classification of matter into elements, compounds, and mixtures.

Elements

Section 2 contains an example of a decomposition: mercuric oxide → mercury and oxygen. In this type of chemical change one substance forms two or more substances. It follows that the products of a decomposition are simpler than the substance from which they are formed.

Table 1

Metallic elements	Non-metallic elements
sodium	carbon
magnesium	nitrogen
aluminium	oxygen
potassium	silicon
calcium	phosphorus
titanium	sulphur
chromium	chlorine
manganese	bromine
iron	iodine
copper	
zinc	
silver	
platinum	
mercury	
lead	
uranium	

Most substances can be decomposed either by straightforward heating or by more elaborate methods. It has been found, however, that a small number of substances cannot be broken down into simpler substances by chemical change; these are called *elements*. Of the 103 known elements, about 90 occur naturally in the earth and its atmosphere; the remainder have been artificially made as a result of experiments in atomic energy.

It is now known that the elements themselves are built up of even simpler forms of matter (Section 19), but these forms can only lead a separate existence under very special conditions; they cannot be seen or handled in the same way as the chemical elements.

This idea of elements is the basis of chemistry. From these few simple substances are built up all the millions of more complicated substances which make the universe.

Most of the elements can be classified into metals or non-metals and the table overpage does so for the elements (with the exception of hydrogen) which will be mentioned in this book. Hydrogen does not closely resemble any other element.

A more detailed and useful classification of the elements, called the Periodic Table, is given in Appendix B, p. 288. This will be referred to frequently throughout this book. In it the elements are further subdivided into groups, in each of which there are elements that have many properties in common.

Compounds

Compounds are substances which are composed of two or more elements combined together. The forces which hold the elements together in their combined state are often strong; energy, usually in the form of heat or electricity, has to be applied in order to overcome them and decompose the compound. The study of these forces forms a large part of modern chemistry; it is complicated, however, and only an elementary account will be given later (Sections 19 and 20).

Some compounds which have been mentioned already are:

hydrogen peroxide	a compound of hydrogen and oxygen
mercury oxide	a compound of mercury and oxygen
manganese dioxide	a compound of manganese and oxygen
sand (silica)	a compound of silicon and oxygen
naphthalene	a compound of carbon and hydrogen

A compound has properties which are not shown by any of the elements of which it is composed. The properties of the individual elements are not usually shown once they are combined together.

A compound has a constant composition. This means that the proportions, by weight, of the elements of which it is composed are fixed.

Mixtures

In a mixture, particles of different substances are brought into close contact with each other, but they are not combined with each other. The components of a mixture can usually be mixed in any proportion and they retain their original properties. A mixture, therefore, shows the properties of its components.

A mixture may contain elements, or compounds, or elements and compounds. Air is the most notable example which we have studied so far; it consists of a mixture of elements (nitrogen, oxygen, and the noble gases) and compounds (water vapour and carbon dioxide).

To distinguish between compounds and mixtures

The distinction between compounds and mixtures is not always easy to make and exceptions can be found to any general differences between the two. The following summary will act as a guide for the time being, but it should be used with caution:

Table 2

Compounds	*Mixtures*
They are single substances	They contain at least two substances
They do not show the properties of their component elements	They show the properties of their component elements or compounds
The component elements are in fixed proportions	The component elements or compounds need not be in fixed proportions
They are formed by means of a chemical change—a new substance is formed	No chemical change takes place when making a mixture—no new substance is formed
An energy change takes place when they are formed (heat is frequently given out)	No or very little energy change takes place when they are formed

Experiment 3.1

To distinguish between a mixture of iron and sulphur and a compound of iron and sulphur **(C)**

Mix iron filings and powdered sulphur in the proportion 7 to 4 by weight. Examine the mixture with a lens. Put some of the mixture into three dry small tubes to a depth of about 1 cm. Half fill the first tube with cold water and shake it. You should find that the sulphur floats and can be separated from the iron by decantation (this may have to be repeated three or four times). Notice that neither the formation of the mixture nor its separation involves a change of temperature.

To the second tube add about a quarter of a tube of dilute hydrochloric acid; warm it gently, but do not boil the acid. Hold your finger loosely over the open end of the test tube for about half a minute and then hold the end of the tube to the flame. A mild explosion will show that the gas formed is hydrogen. A similar result will be obtained if you repeat this experiment with pure iron filings.

Heat the third tube strongly at the bottom. When the mixture starts to glow red hot, remove it from the flame. You will see that the red glow continues to spread even though the original source of the heat has been removed. Let the tube cool and examine the contents at the bottom. Can you still see individual particles of iron and sulphur? Add hydrochloric acid to the tube. A gas will be evolved which, unlike hydrogen, has a remarkable smell. This gas is hydrogen sulphide; its smell can be politely described as that of rotten eggs.

Experiment 3.1 illustrates some of the differences between mixtures and compounds:

(1) When iron filings and sulphur are mixed, there is no change of energy and they can be separated without change of energy.

(2) The iron filings and sulphur could have been mixed in any proportion.

(3) The iron and sulphur retain their individual properties when mixed —the iron still reacts with hydrochloric acid to form hydrogen.

(4) The chemical change which takes place when iron combines with sulphur is started by applying heat, but, once started, it gives out is own heat; it is an *exothermic* reaction. In this it resembles the combination of substances with oxygen (burning).

(5) The compound which results from this combination—iron sulphide —has at least one property which neither iron, nor sulphur, nor a mixture of the two possesses: it gives off hydrogen sulphide when hydrochloric acid is added to it.

The burning of metallic elements

Most of the metallic elements will burn when they are heated in air. The products of burning are compounds of the elements and oxygen and are called oxides (Section 2):

$$\text{sodium} + \text{oxygen} \rightarrow \text{sodium oxide}$$
$$\text{calcium} + \text{oxygen} \rightarrow \text{calcium oxide}$$
$$\text{iron} + \text{oxygen} \rightarrow \text{iron oxide}$$

The ease with which the metallic elements burn depends principally on three things:

(i) Their reactivity. Reactivity means the readiness with which they will undergo chemical change.

(ii) Their physical state. Metals will burn more readily when they are in the form of fine wire, or powder, or thin sheets, than when they are in large pieces.

(iii) They will burn more readily in pure oxygen than they will in normal air.

Experiment 3.2

To make the oxides of sodium, calcium, and iron (D)

Fill three jars with oxygen, covering the mouth of each with a greased glass cover until it is ready for use.

Put a piece of sodium—about the size of a small pea—into a deflagrating spoon and heat it strongly. When the sodium starts to burn, put the deflagrating spoon into a gas jar of oxygen. Heat the spoon again to make sure that combustion is complete.

Repeat the experiment using a piece of calcium, and repeat again using a piece of iron wire (you may find that the calcium burns completely before there is time to get it into the gas jar).

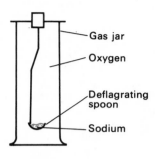

Figure 19

The burning of non-metallic elements

Experiment 3.3

To make the oxides of phosphorus and sulphur **(D)**

Fill two gas jars with oxygen, covering the mouth of each until it is ready for use.

Put a piece of phosphorus about the size of a match head into a deflagrating spoon and, without heating it, put the deflagrating spoon into a gas jar of oxygen.

Half fill a deflagrating spoon with sulphur and heat it. When the sulphur begins to burn, put the spoon into a gas jar of oxygen and leave it until the flame goes out.

Experiment 3.4

To make carbon dioxide from carbon **(D)**

Fill a gas jar with oxygen; add 20 cm³ of limewater and then cover the gas jar. Heat some powdered carbon in a deflagrating spoon until it glows red hot. Put the spoon into the gas jar and leave it there until the carbon ceases to burn. Remove the spoon and swirl the limewater. Explain what you observe.

Non-metallic elements burn to form oxides:

$$phosphorus + oxygen \rightarrow phosphorus\ pentoxide*$$
$$sulphur + oxygen \rightarrow sulphur\ dioxide$$
$$carbon + oxygen \rightarrow carbon\ dioxide$$

The burning of compounds

Elements burn to form their oxides. But what happens if we try to burn compounds in which the elements are already combined with each other? This can be investigated by using a familiar group of compounds called *hydrocarbons*.

Hydrocarbons are compounds containing hydrogen and carbon only. Carbon and hydrogen can combine in many different proportions and in many different ways; this has resulted in the existence of a large number of hydrocarbons.

All hydrocarbons are flammable. Some of them occur in large

---

* The prefixes pent- and di- refer to the ratio of the numbers of atoms of oxygen to the number of atoms of the other element in the compound: P_2O_5, SO_2, CO_2.

quantities, for example in petroleum and coal, and these are some of our most important fuels.

Experiment 3.5 uses paraffin wax—the material of which candles are made. Paraffin wax consists of a mixture of hydrocarbons and is obtained from petroleum (p. 255).

Experiment 3.5

To investigate the products of combustion of a hydro-carbon (**C** or **D**)

Assemble the apparatus shown in *figure 20*, and draw air through it for 1–2 minutes. There should be little change to either the cobalt chloride paper or the limewater.

Light the candle and continue to run the pump so that the gases from the burning candle are drawn through the apparatus. Repeat the experiment using burning sugar in a deflagrating spoon in place of the candle.

Experiment 3.5 shows that the products of combustion of a hydro-carbon are water and carbon dioxide. We shall show in the next section that water is an oxide of hydrogen.

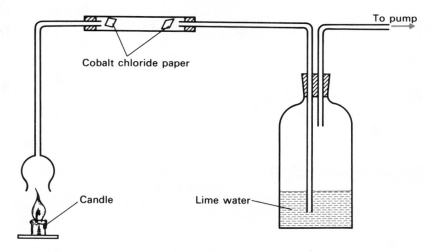

Figure 20

The importance of hydrocarbons to mankind is not that they burn to form carbon dioxide and water, but that, in doing so, energy in the form of heat and light is given out. This energy can be changed into other forms such as electrical and mechanical energy. Thus, coal and oil are burned in power stations to make electricity; petrol, which is a mixture of hydrocarbons obtained from petroleum, is burned in petrol engines to provide mechanical energy for our most common form of transport. In the domestic and industrial burning of hydrocarbons the carbon dioxide and water are not used; they are waste products.

Respiration

The process of respiration in animals consists of five main parts:

(1) Air is breathed into the lungs.
(2) Part of the air enters the blood stream.
(3) This portion of the air, together with assimilated food, reacts to provide energy for the animal.
(4) The waste products pass from the blood stream to the lungs.
(5) The waste products and the residue of the air are breathed out.

An investigation into the chemical nature of the waste products of respiration will throw light on what is happening in Part 3 of respiration.

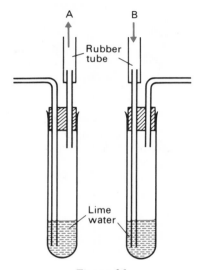

Figure 21

Experiment 3.6

To investigate the products of respiration (**C** or **D**)

Set up the apparatus shown in *figure 21*. Inhale through tube A and exhale through tube B.

Which air, inhaled or exhaled, contains the greater proportion of carbon dioxide?

An instructive experiment should not only produce a change which is clearly observed; it should also indicate the cause of the change. This can often be done by using a *control* experiment in which all the conditions are the same except one. Any difference between the results of the two experiments must, therefore, be caused by the one condition which is different. In Experiment 3.6 the action of inhaled air on limewater is the control experiment. If this control experiment had not been done, you could not be sure that exhaled air was different from inhaled air.

A fuller investigation into respiration would show that the air breathed out contains a smaller proportion of oxygen than the air breathed in (see Problem 1, p. 34). Respiration seems to consist of reactions in the body which produce energy; one of the reactants is oxygen and one of the products is carbon dioxide. This points to a process which resembles the burning of a compound containing carbon and it is interesting to note that energy-giving foods—sugar, starch, and fats—contain a high proportion of carbon.

Oxidation

The word *burning* is used to describe any combination of a substance with oxygen which results in fire. This does not adequately describe the action of oxygen in respiration because the energy so formed does not result in the high temperature and light which we associate with fire.

A word with a wider meaning is needed to describe all reactions in which oxygen combines with another substance. This word is *oxidation*. Thus, the reaction between carbon and oxygen to form carbon dioxide is an oxidation of carbon: and the carbon is said to have been *oxidized*.

Rusting is another example of an oxidation. No fire is visible, but, during rusting, iron combines with oxygen to form iron oxide.

We shall learn in Section 12 that oxidation can be given a still wider meaning.

Photosynthesis

The respiration of animals decreases the amount of oxygen in the air and increases the amount of carbon dioxide; and it would, in time, exhaust the oxygen supply if there were not another process to restore the balance. This process is photosynthesis—an essential part of the function of green plants.

Photosynthesis is a complicated process but it can be summarized as follows:

(1) Carbon dioxide and water are the reactants.
(2) Oxygen and sugar are the products (the sugar is soon changed into starch).
(3) Sunlight and chlorophyll (the green colouring matter) are essential to the process; the chlorophyll acts as a sort of natural catalyst.

The process of respiration is also complicated, but it can be summarized as a reaction between sugar and oxygen to form carbon dioxide and water.

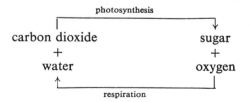

Essentially one process is the reverse of the other; as a result, the proportion of carbon dioxide and oxygen in the air remains constant. This type of balance or equilibrium which occurs in nature is called a *natural cycle*; this one is called the *carbon cycle*.

Photosynthesis will only work if energy is taken from the sun. In respiration, energy is given out in the form of animal heat and movement. The effect of the chemical reactions in this cycle, therefore, is to convert the energy of the sun into a form which animals can use; without it, life as we know it could not exist.

Problems

Investigate experimentally:

(1) The proportion, by volume, of oxygen and carbon dioxide in exhaled air.

(2) The approximate amount of heat which is given out when 1 g of candle wax is burned.

(3) The presence of sugar and starch in a growing plant.

(4) The need for carbon dioxide in photosynthesis.

(5) Write a report on:

 (i) The relative importance of coal, petroleum, and natural gas as sources of industrial and domestic energy.

(ii) The reactions which take place in a petrol engine.

Summary

(1) Elements cannot be changed into simpler substances. Most elements can be classified as metallic or non-metallic.

(2) A compound is a single substance which contains two or more elements combined together. Each compound has a constant composition and its properties are different from those of its constituent elements.

(3) A mixture contains more than one substance and can have a variable composition. It shows the properties of its components and there is little or no energy change when it is formed.

(4) Reactivity means the readiness with which a substance will undergo chemical change.

(5) Hydrocarbons are compounds of carbon and hydrogen; when they burn, they form the oxides of these two elements.

(6) A reaction in which a substance combines with oxygen is an example of oxidation.

(7) Part of the process of respiration consists of a reaction between sugar and oxygen to form carbon dioxide, water, and energy.

(8) Part of the process of photosynthesis consists of a reaction between carbon dioxide and water to form sugar and oxygen. Energy is absorbed from sunlight, and chlorophyll acts as a type of catalyst.

Section 4
Water–hydrogen–reduction

Water

Of all substances water is one of the most important and abundant. Most life cannot exist without it and life probably started in it. 70% of the world is covered by it. We drink it, wash in it, and play in it. It is familiar in all its, three states—ice, water, and steam or vapour—and it is used for both cooling and heating. It is a reactive substance and its presence or its absence plays an important part in many laboratory and industrial processes.

Our water supply is associated with another natural cycle:

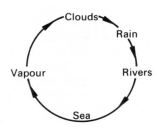

Our studies so far have led to the following information about water:

(1) Boiling point 100°C, freezing point 0°C.
(2) It is a good solvent but not the only solvent. Dissolved solids raise its boiling point and lower its freezing point.
(3) Air contains water vapour.
(4) Some compounds, e.g. hydrocarbons and sugar, form water when they burn.
(5) Cobalt chloride (blue → pink) can be used to detect the presence of water.
 6) Water should not be regarded merely as a solvent. It undergoes many chemical reactions and even its solvent properties are frequently due to chemical change.

Hydrogen

Hydrogen is a gaseous element and it is the lightest of all elements. It occurs abundantly on earth combined with other elements; the sun is largely made up of the element itself. The usual test for hydrogen in elementary chemistry is to apply a flame to a small quantity of it: in the presence of air it then explodes.

The action of metallic elements on water

Experiment 4.1

The action of sodium (D) and calcium (C) on water

Sodium is kept in oil, because it reacts quickly with air and moisture. Do not allow it to touch your skin.

Transfer a lump of sodium to a filter paper. Cut off a piece about 0·2 cm square and drop it into cold water contained in a large beaker or trough. Do not put your face near to the reacting sodium. Test the solution with red litmus paper (p. 44).

To a quarter of a test tube of cold water add one piece of calcium. Hold your thumb *loosely* on the top of the test tube for 5–10 seconds, then hold the mouth of the tube to a bunsen flame. Test the solution with red litmus paper.

What gas is evolved in the action of calcium on water? Assuming that calcium is an element, what is the only possible source of this gas?

Experiment 4.2

The action of copper and iron on water (D)

If there is any reaction between these elements and cold water it is very slow. This experiment is therefore conducted at a higher temperature using steam.

Set up the apparatus in *figure 22*. Attach it to a steam generator and pass steam until all the air has been driven out of the apparatus. Keeping a steady flow of steam, heat the copper tube strongly for one or two minutes. Can you detect any gas coming from the delivery tube?

Disconnect the steam and allow the copper tube to cool. Pour one large measure of iron filings into the bend of the tube and repeat the experiment. Collect the gas which is formed, remove it from the beaker

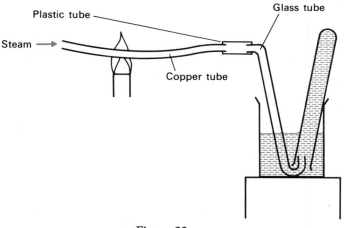

Figure 22

and put the mouth of the collecting tube to a bunsen flame. Describe what you have observed.

What gas is formed? Assuming that iron is an element, what is the source of this gas? Arrange the four elements in the order of their reactivity with water, putting the most reactive first.

Is water and element or a compound?

The reactions which take place in Experiment 4.2 can be summarized as follows:

$$sodium + water \ (cold) \rightarrow sodium \ hydroxide + hydrogen$$
$$calcium + water \ (cold) \rightarrow calcium \ hydroxide + hydrogen$$
$$iron \ (heated) + steam \rightarrow iron \ oxide + hydrogen$$

Copper has no apparent action on water. Sodium and calcium hydroxides are discussed on p. 46

These reactions indicate that water is a compound because it has been broken down to yield a simpler substance—hydrogen. They also illustrate the method of investigating the composition of a substance by *analysis*. In analysis a substance is broken down to the simpler substances which compose it.

The synthesis of water

Another method of investigating the composition of a substance is to synthesize it. *Synthesis* is the use of simple substances to make a more complicated substance.

Experiment 4.3

What is formed when hydrogen burns? **(D)**

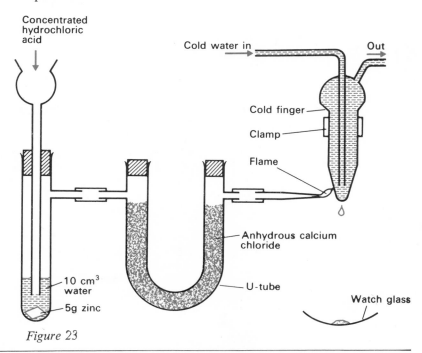

Figure 23

Set up the apparatus shown in *figure 23*. Hydrogen–oxygen mixtures explode when they are ignited and for this reason the amount of glass in the apparatus is kept to a minimum.

The reaction between the zinc and hydrochloric acid produces hydrogen. The calcium chloride is a *drying agent* which removes water vapour from the hydrogen. The cold finger acts as a simple condenser.

Run in the concentrated hydrochloric acid so that a steady flow of hydrogen is maintained. WARNING: *It is important that all the air should be swept from the apparatus before an attempt is made to light the jet of hydrogen; if this is not done, a serious explosion can result.* Collect a sample of the hydrogen in a test tube (*figure 24*) and apply a light to it. This method of collecting hydrogen is made possible by the fact that hydrogen is much lighter than air; it is called *upward delivery displacing air*. If the hydrogen burns quietly, it is safe to light the jet; if it explodes, continue to take samples until the hydrogen does burn quietly.

A liquid will form on the outside of the cold finger. Allow one or two drops to fall on to a slide and test them with cobalt chloride paper or anhydrous copper sulphate; the latter changes from white to blue in the presence of water.

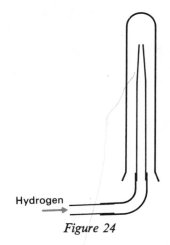

Hydrogen

Figure 24

Experiment 4.3 shows that water is the product of the burning of hydrogen. It is a compound of hydrogen and oxygen, or, to give it a name which is rarely used, it is hydrogen oxide.

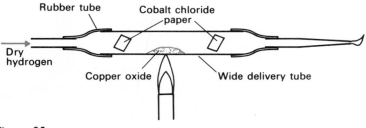

Rubber tube   Cobalt chloride paper

Dry hydrogen

Copper oxide   Wide delivery tube

Figure 25

Experiment 4.4

How does hydrogen react with copper oxide? **(D)**

The apparatus for generating dry hydrogen (*figure 23*) is connected to a delivery tube containing copper oxide and two pieces of cobalt chloride paper, as shown in *figure 25*. Air is swept from the apparatus by a stream of hydrogen which is then lit at the jet. The copper oxide is then heated for about 15 seconds.

Describe the changes which you observe in the copper oxide and in the two pieces of cobalt chloride paper. Why are *two* pieces of the paper used?

Reduction

The reaction which takes place in Experiment 4.4 must be:

copper oxide+hydrogen → copper+water

Oxygen was removed from copper oxide and copper remained. When a metal is formed from its oxide by the removal of the oxygen, the oxide is said to have been *reduced*. This change is an example of reduction and it is the reverse of oxidation. We shall learn later that reduction, like oxidation, has a wider meaning.

The hydrogen in this reaction has removed the oxygen and is therefore called a *reducing agent*. Note that the hydrogen itself has been oxidized because it has combined with oxygen to form water.

The action of heat on water

We have shown that water is a compound by combining the elements hydrogen and oxygen. Energy in the form of heat and light was given out during this combination. Can water be decomposed back into its elements by applying energy to it?

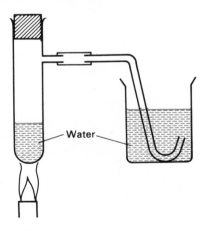

Figure 26

Experiment 4.5

(C)

Heat a quarter of a boiling tube of water until it boils gently. Test the steam, using both a glowing and a lighted splint, for the presence of oxygen and hydrogen. Hold a piece of cobalt chloride paper in the steam.

Set up the apparatus shown in *figure 26*. Boil the water gently in the boiling tube until the air has been swept from the apparatus. Remove the flame and watch the movement of the cold water.

The difference between water and steam

When water is boiled it does not decompose into its elements. It changes into a gas which has the same essential properties as liquid water and which changes back into the same liquid when the source of heat is removed.

Experiment 4.5 illustrates that steam occupies a much greater volume than the same weight of water. Thus, when the steam cools and condenses into water, a partial vacuum is created and this in turn causes the sucking back which you observed in this experiment.

In Section 2 we showed that air contains water vapour. It seems that water has the power to disperse itself into a much larger volume; it then becomes an invisible gas. This power to disperse itself is assisted by heat. In Section 8 we shall discuss a possible explanation of this phenomenon.

The presence of air in water

When you heated water slowly in a boiling tube you may have seen small bubbles of gas being formed and clinging to the side. This happens before the water is hot enough to boil and form bubbles of steam; these small bubbles consist of air which has been dissolved in the water. The solubility of gases, unlike that of solids, is less in hot than in cold water.

The dissolved air in water, although it is small in quantity, is important because it is the only source of oxygen available to creatures which live in water. An investigation into the amount and composition of dissolved air is suggested in Problem 4, p. 43

Water as a solvent

Water is widely used as a solvent. It is convenient, cheap, and can dissolve many substances. Many of the chemical reactions which we shall study take place in solution in water (*aqueous* solution). You have only to look round the laboratory to see that many reagents are used in aqueous solution.

Because of its powers as a solvent, water found in nature is rarely pure. Rain water is the purest natural water; it remembles distilled water and dissolves only a little gas as it falls through the air. Stream, spring, and river water contain small quantities of solids dissolved during their contact with soil and rock. In sea water the dissolved solids have accumulated and they are an important source of minerals. Most of the dissolved solids in sea water are compounds of the elements sodium, magnesium, calcium, potassium, and chlorine. The remainder consists of traces of the compounds of many elements; some, such as bromine, can be extracted profitably; others, such as gold and silver, cannot.

There are many types of substance which do not dissolve in water but which do dissolve in other liquids. Hydrocarbons and fats are examples of these (see Experiment 1.6, p. 9).

Water in the air, drying agents

When salt is put into water it rapidly disperses itself throughout the liquid and no individual particles of salt can then be seen. In a similar way water can dispersd itself into the air and cannot then be seen. We have already shown (Section 2) how the water vapour can be removed from the air by cooling it. Experiment 4.6 is designed to investigate the power of some chemicals to do the same thing.

Experiment 4.6

The action of calcium chloride and sodium hydroxide on air (C)

Put a piece of sodium hydroxide and a piece of calcium chloride on to watch glasses and leave them exposed to the air. Look for traces of moisture after 10 minutes and again after 24 hours.

Experiment 4.6 shows that sodium hydroxide and calcium chloride can remove water from the air in sufficient quantities to form a solution. Solid substances which do this are called *deliquescent* and the phenomenon is known as *deliquescence*.

Some liquids, for example alcohol and concentrated sulphuric acid, also absorb water vapour from the air. These liquids are said to by *hygroscopic*. The word is also used to describe solids such as copper oxide which absorb water from the air but do not form a solution with the water. Hygroscopic and deliquescent substances can be used as drying agents for removing water vapour from gases (p. 37).

Hydrates (water of crystallization)

Experiment 4.7

To investigate the action of heat on washing soda (hydrated sodium carbonate) (C)

Put about 1 cm of crystals of washing soda into a dry test tube and insert a piece of cobalt chloride paper into the mouth of the tube. Heat gently in the position shown in *figure 27*.

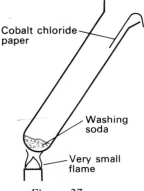

Cobalt chloride paper

Washing soda

Very small flame

Figure 27

It appears that sodium carbonate crystals give off water when they are heated, although in appearance the crystals are dry. The remaining powder is still sodium carbonate but it contains no water; it is therefore called *anhydrous* sodium carbonate.

The water which is given off when a crystal is heated is sometimes called water of crystallization. Crystals which contain water of crystallization are said to be *hydrated*.

hydrated sodium carbonate $\xrightarrow{\text{heat}}$ anhydrous sodium carbonate + water

NB: Not all crystals contain water of crystallization.

Experiment 4.8

To investigate the composition of hydrated copper sulphate (C)

Put a small crucible on to a pipeclay triangle and heat it gently to dry it. When it is cool enough to handle, weigh it. Fill the crucible a third full with powdered copper sulphate crystals and weigh it again. Heat the crucible with a 5 cm bunsen flame for 5 minutes, allow it to cool and weigh it again.

You will have observed that the blue powder has changed to white anhydrous copper sulphate. This alone is not enough to show that all the water has been driven off. Heat the crucible for another 5 minutes; cool it and weigh it again. This should be repeated until the weight is constant, showing that all the water has been driven off.

Calculate the % of water in hydrated copper sulphate as follows:

weight of crucible $= A$g
weight of crucible + crystals $= B$g
weight of crucible + anhydrous copper sulphate $= C$g
weight of crystals $= (B-A)$g
weight of water $= (B-C)$g

% of water in hydrated copper sulphate $= \dfrac{B-C}{B-A} \times 100$

Add a few drops of water to the cool anhydrous copper sulphate and note the return of the characteristic blue colour of hydrated copper sulphate.

Hydrated copper sulphate appears to be a compound formed by reaction between anhydrous copper sulphate and water:

anhydrous copper sulphate + water $\rightarrow$ hydrated copper sulphate

This is an example of a *reversible* reaction, because

hydrated copper sulphate $\xrightarrow{\text{heat}}$ anhydrous copper sulphate + water

A reversible reaction is one in which the products can themselves react to re-form the original substances. Another example is to be found in the action of heat on mercury oxide (p. 19).

Problems

Investigate experimentally:
(1) The action of magnesium on water. Investigate the effect of (a) the physical state of the magnesium—ribbon and powder, (b) the temperature of the water, (c) the purity of the water—tap and distilled. How

does the reactivity of magnesium with water compare with that of sodium, calcium, iron, and copper?

(2) The percentage by weight of dissolved solids in sea water, river water, and tap water.

(3) The maximum weights of potassium nitrate which will dissolve in 100 g of water at temperatures ranging from room temperature to 100°C at 10°C intervals. Plot a graph of these weights against temperature.

(4) The volume of dissolved air per cm³ of tap water and the percentage of oxygen in this air.

(5) Write reports on:

  (i) The pollution of river water.

  (ii) The pollution of sea water.

  (iii) The composition of the dissolved solids in sea water and their commerical uses.

  (iv) The production of purified water for laboratory use.

  (v) The use of water in the production of energy (electric – hydro-electric – locomotive – domestic).

Summary

(1) Water is a compound of hydrogen and oxygen.

(2) Some metallic elements displace hydrogen from water or steam.

(3) Copper has no apparent action on water.

(4) The order of reactivity of four metallic elements with water is sodium, calcium, iron, copper.

(5) The test for hydrogen is that it explodes when ignited.

(6) There are two main ways of determining the composition of a compound—decomposition (analysis) and formation (synthesis).

(7) Hydrogen burns to form water.

(8) Reduction is the removal of oxygen from a compound.

(9) Hydrogen is a reducing agent.

(10) There is no apparent decomposition of water when it is heated.

(11) When a liquid changes to a gas there is a large increase in volume.

(12) Some solids combine with water to form hydrates.

(13) A reversible reaction is one in which the products can react to form the original substances.

Section 5
Acidic and basic solutions (1)–salts

Acidic solutions

You will have noticed reagent bottles labelled 'acids'. There are probably four of these acidic solutions available to you:

hydrochloric acid, sulphuric acid, nitric acid, and acetic acid.

It is important that you realize that these are dilute solutions of substances which in the pure state may have very different appearance and properties. For example, hydrochloric acid is the aqueous solution of an invisible gas, hydrogen chloride.

Many substances change colour when treated with acidic solutions; these are called *indicators*. An indicator commonly used is litmus, made by the oxidation of certain lichens. It can be used either as a solution or as litmus paper, which is made by soaking paper in litmus solution and allowing it to dry.

Basic (alkaline) solutions

There are probably three basic solutions available to you:

sodium hydroxide, calcium hydroxide (limewater), and ammonium hydroxide.

The substances which dissolve to form such solutions are called *bases* or *alkalis*. The simplest test for a basic solution is its action on red litmus paper.

Experiment 5.1

To investigate the action of acidic and basic solutions on plant colouring matter (C)

Put four drops of litmus solution into a test tube; add two drops of an acidic solution and shake to mix them. Add four drops of a basic solution slowly, shaking the tube continually. Record the colour changes.

Grind a handful of petals from a brightly coloured plant with 5 cm³ of water and 5 cm³ of alcohol in a mortar with a pestle. Repeat the experiment described above, using the coloured aqueous extract from the petals instead of the litmus solution. Record the colour changes.

Both types of solution cause colour changes in plant pigments:

acidic solutions change blue litmus to red
basic solutions change red litmus to blue

Experiment 5.2

The action between acidic and basic solutions **(C)**

Put 25 cm³ of dilute hydrochloric acid into a 100 cm³ beaker; add 25 cm³ of dilute sodium hydroxide solution and mix them by stirring. Notice the rise in temperature; this is an indication that a chemical change has taken place.

Test the solution with blue litmus paper. If necessary add a few more drops of hydrochloric acid until the solution has an acidic action on litmus paper. This ensures that no sodium hydroxide remains. Transfer two drops of the solution to a clean microscope slide or watch glass and evaporate to dryness by holding it above a hot gauze.

Acidic and basic solutions react readily together to form substances which are called *salts*. The salt formed by the action between sodium hydroxide and hydrochloric acid is called common salt or sodium chloride.

Water is also formed as a result of the action between acidic and basic solutions, but its formation is not easy to demonstrate because of the water already present.

Experiment 5.3

To investigate the action on litmus of solutions of oxides **(D)**

Pour 10 cm³ of litmus solution into each of four boiling tubes. To the first add one small measure of sodium oxide. To the second add one small measure of calcium oxide. To the third add one small measure of phosphorus pentoxide. Bubble sulphur dioxide gas for a few seconds into the fourth tube.

Oxides which react with water to form acidic solutions are *acidic oxides* and are usually the oxides of non-metallic elements:

sulphur dioxide + water → sulphurous acid solution
phosphorus pentoxide + water → phosphoric acid solution

Oxides which react with water to form basic solutions are *basic oxides* (*bases*) and are usually the oxides of metallic elements. The oxide is changed into a hydroxide by this process:

sodium oxide + water → sodium hydroxide solution
calcium oxide + water → calcium hydroxide solution

Basic oxides which are soluble in water are also called *alkalis* and their solutions are said to be *alkaline*.

Insoluble acids and bases

Some oxides of non-metallic elements are insoluble in water and have no action on litmus. They can still be classified as acidic oxides, however, if they are capable of reacting with a base to form a salt. Thus silicon dioxide (sand) is an acidic oxide because it reacts with bases to form salts called silicates.

Similarly, some oxides of metallic elements are insoluble in water. They do not react with water to form hydroxides and have no reaction with litmus. They can still be classified as basic oxides (bases) if they react with an acid to form a salt. Thus copper oxide is a basic oxide because it can form a salt—copper sulphate—when it reacts with sulphuric acid:

copper oxide + sulphuric acid → copper sulphate + water

Experiment 5.4

To prepare hydrated copper sulphate from copper oxide (C)

Heat 25 cm³ of dilute sulphuric acid almost to boiling point in a beaker on a tripod and gauze. Add one measure of copper oxide to the acid and boil gently for about one minute. If any of the copper oxide remains unchanged, filter it off and collect the filtrate in an evaporating dish. Heat the evaporating dish on the tripod and gauze until the solution of copper sulphate is reduced to about half of its original volume. Allow the solution to stand for about 24 hours.

Decant the solution from the copper sulphate crystals. Dry the crystals between filter papers and examine their shape and colour.

The naming of salts

The name of a salt has two parts. The first part is derived from the name of a metallic element or a base:

sodium hydroxide → sodium salts
ammonium hydroxide → ammonium salts
copper oxide → copper salts

(Ammonium is not a metal. Its nature and that of ammonium hydroxide are discussed in Section 17.)

The second part of the name of a salt is derived from the name of an acid:

hydrochloric acid	→ chlorides
sulphuric acid	→ sulphates
nitric acid	→ nitrates
carbonic acid (or carbon dioxide)	→ carbonates
silicic acid (or silicon dioxide)	→ silicates
acetic acid	→ acetates
sulphurous acid	→ sulphites
nitrous acid	→ nitrites

Most acids whose names end in *-ic* form salts whose names end in *-ate* (hydrochloric acid is an exception to this). Most acids whose names end in *-ous* form salts whose names end in *-ite*. Thus, the names of salts are derived from the names of the bases and acids from which they can be formed:

sodium hydroxide	+ sulphuric acid	→ sodium sulphate	+ water
copper oxide	+ nitric acid	→ copper nitrate	+ water
ammonium hydroxide	+ hydrochloric acid	→ ammonium chloride	+ water
calcium hydroxide	+ carbonic acid	→ calcium carbonate	+ water

The action of acids on metallic elements

Experiment 5.5

To investigate the action of iron, magnesium, and copper on dilute hydrochloric, sulphuric, and acetic acids (C)

Put one small measure of iron filings into a small tube and add eight drops of dilute hydrochloric acid. Warm gently, if necessary, to complete the reaction, but do not boil. Test for hydrogen. Suck some of the liquid into a teat pipette and put one drop on to a microscopic slide. By holding the slide over a warm gauze (see *figure 9*, p. 8), evaporate the liquid until crystals begin to form.

Repeat the experiment using the other metals and acids.

The reactivity of metals with acids varies. You will have discovered that magnesium is more reactive than iron and iron more reactive than copper. In the reactions which do take place, a salt and hydrogen are formed:

iron	+ hydrochloric acid	→ iron chloride	+ hydrogen
iron	+ sulphuric acid	→ iron sulphate	+ hydrogen
magnesium	+ hydrochloric acid	→ magnesium chloride	+ hydrogen
magnesium	+ sulphuric acid	→ magnesium sulphate	+ hydrogen
magnesium	+ acetic acid	→ magnesium acetate	+ hydrogen

Nitric acid also reacts with metals to form salts, but hydrogen is not evolved when it does so.

The action of acids on carbonates

Carbonates are the salts of carbonic acid which is the acid formed when carbon dioxide reacts with water.

Experiment 5.6

To investigate the action of sulphuric and acetic acids on copper carbonate (C)

Put one small measure of copper carbonate into a test tube. Pour lime-water into another tube so that it is ready to test for carbon dioxide.

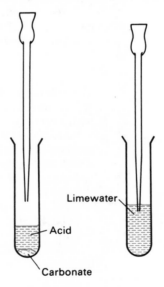

Figure 28

Add four or five drops of dilute sulphuric acid to the copper carbonate. Note the evolution of gas. Remove a sample of this gas by sucking some into a teat pipette and then blow the gas through the surface layer of the limewater.

Put one drop of the solution which results from the action of the acid on the carbonate on to a microscope slide and evaporate it slowly until crystals form. Examine the crystals with the aid of a lens or a low-powered microscope and compare their shape and colour with those of copper sulphate prepared in Experiment 5.4. Repeat the experiment using acetic acid.

It appears that salts can be made by the action of acids on carbonates, which are themselves salts of carbonic acid. These reactions can be explained by assuming that carbonic acid is a weaker acid than sulphuric acid and acetic acid, and that stronger acids have the power to displace carbonic acid from carbonates. The carbonic acid then decomposes into carbon dioxide and water:

copper carbonate + sulphuric acid → copper sulphate + carbonic acid
$$\downarrow$$
carbon dioxide + water

copper carbonate + acetic acid → copper acetate + carbonic acid
$$\downarrow$$
carbon dioxide + water

pH scale and universal indicator

The relative acidity and alkalinity of solutions is specified quantitatively by a scale known as the *pH scale*. Acidic solutions have a pH less than 7, and the lower the pH the greater the acidity. Alkaline solutions have a pH greater than 7 and the higher the pH the greater the alkalinity.

Pure water marks the dividing line between acidity and alkalinity, having a pH of 7; it is said to be *neutral*. The pH of a solution can be determined by using a universal indicator which gives a range of colours according to the pH of the solution to which it is added.

Experiment 5.7

To investigate the action of acidic and basic solutions on universal indicator (C or D)

The solutions of acids and bases which are kept in the reagent bottles will be too concentrated for this experiment; they must first be diluted with twenty times their own volume of water.

Pour 10 cm³ of universal indicator solution (diluted according to the maker's instructions) into each of five boiling tubes. Put the tubes into a rack with a piece of white paper behind them.

Tube 1   add two drops of diluted hydrochloric acid solution
Tube 2   add two drops of diluted acetic acid solution
Tube 3   contains indicator and water only
Tube 4   add two drops of diluted ammonium hydroxide solution
Tube 5   add two drops of diluted sodium hydroxide solution

Shake the boiling tubes and compare the colours with those given on the maker's standard chart to determine the pH values.

Repeat the experiment with other acids: sulphuric, nitric, carbonic, and boric acids, and arrange them according to their strength. The boric acid solution should be saturated, and the carbonic acid solution can be made by blowing directly into the indicator solution.

The relative strengths of acids and bases

A strong acid will form a solution of lower pH than will a weak acid, provided that the concentrations of the solutions are comparable (see molar solutions p. 78). Thus Experiment 5.7 provides a rough measure of the relative strengths of acids and bases.

	↑	hydrochloric, sulphuric, and nitric acids
strongest acids		acetic acid
		carbonic acid
		boric acid

(water)

strongest bases		ammonium hydroxide
	↓	sodium and potassium hydroxides

Problems

(1) The substance A is a magnesium salt. Add dilute sulphuric acid to it and identify the gas given off. Evaporate some of the resulting solution to form the crystals B. What are the chemical and common names of A and B?

(2) Put some of the substance C, which is a sodium salt, into a boiling tube, add about a quarter of a tube of dilute sulphuric acid and heat nearly to boiling point. Smell the vapour cautiously. What is C?

(3) Investigate the pH of solutions of substances such as soap, salt, baking powder, and lemon juice.

Summary

(1) Acidic and basic (alkaline) solutions can be distinguished by the use of indicators. Litmus is red with an acidic solution and blue with a basic solution.

(2) Acidic and basic solutions react to form a salt plus water.

(3) Soluble oxides of metals form basic solutions. Soluble oxides of non-metals form acidic solutions.

(4) Insoluble oxides of metals can form salts when treated with acids. They can, therefore, be classified as bases.

(5) The first part of the name of a salt is derived from a metallic element or a base; the second part is derived from an acid.

(6) Some metallic elements react with acids to form a salt plus hydrogen.

(7) Carbonates are the salts of carbonic acid. They will react with acids stronger than carbonic acid to form a new salt plus water and carbon dioxide.

(8) Strong acids will normally displace weaker acids from salts of weaker acids.

(9) Relative acidity and alkalinity of solutions can be measured on a pH scale by the use of universal indicator. An acidic solution has a pH less than 7. An alkaline solution has a pH greater than 7. A neutral solution has a pH of 7.

Section 6
Electrical energy and chemical change

We have studied many reactions in which heat energy has caused chemical change. Electrical energy is equally important in causing chemical change and will be studied in this section.

The metallic elements are said to be good conductors of electricity because they can transfer electrical energy from one place to another with very little loss. This movement of electricity does not itself cause chemical change in the metal, but if some of the electrical energy is changed into heat energy the heat may cause chemical changes such as the burning of the metal.

Most non-metallic elements are not good conductors of electricity. Some forms of carbon, particularly graphite, are exceptions to this.

Can compounds conduct electricity?

Experiment 6.1

Do sodium chloride and calcium chloride conduct electricity? **(D)**

Fill a small crucible one-third full with sodium chloride. Insert two steel rods (*figure 29*) and connect them through an ammeter (reading up to 3 amp) and a 4 volt source of direct current (d.c.). The two steel rods

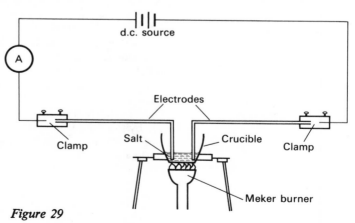

Figure 29

which connect the sodium chloride to the source of electricity are called *electrodes*; that connected to the positive terminal is called the *anode* and that connected to the negative terminal is called the *cathode*.

Melt the sodium chloride by heating it with a Meker burner (this gives a higher temperature than a normal burner). Switch on the electricity and note the current.

Remove the burner and allow the salt to solidify. What happens to the current?

When the crucible is cold, fill it up with distilled water. What happens to the current?

Repeat the experiment with calcium chloride (a normal burner will suffice).

Experiment 6.2

Do water, concentrated sulphuric acid, and alcohol conduct electricity? **(D)**

Fill a dry U-tube with concentrated sulphuric acid to the level shown in *figure 30*. Insert two electrodes made of platinum foil about 1 cm square.

Connect the two electrodes to a 10 volt source of d.c. and an ammeter. Switch on the electricity. Does the ammeter register any current?

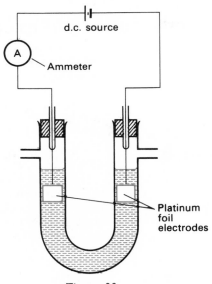

Figure 30

Repeat the experiment with purified water and with alcohol. If the same U-tube and electrodes are used, they must be well rinsed with the new liquid before starting each experiment.

Do solutions of compounds in water conduct electricity?

You will have deduced from Experiments 6.1 and 6.2 that, although water and solid sodium chloride separately do not conduct electricity, a mixture of the two is a good conductor. Experiment 6.3 will show whether water has a similar effect when mixed with sulphuric acid or alcohol.

Experiment 6.3

Do aqueous solutions of sulphuric acid and alcohol conduct electricity (D)

Use the same apparatus and procedure as that given in Experiment 6.2. The *conductance* (ability to carry an electric current) of dilute sulphuric acid can be measured first, followed by that of a 10% solution of alcohol in purified water.

The results of Experiments 6.1, 6.2 and 6.3 can be summarized as follows:

(1) *Good conductors:* molten sodium chloride and calcium chloride; solutions of sodium chloride, calcium chloride, and sulphuric acid, in water.

(2) *Poor conductors and non-conductors;* solid sodium chloride and calcium chloride, water, alcohol, concentrated sulphuric acid and a solution of alcohol in water.

(The use of higher voltages and more sensitive meters would show that some of these compounds—water, for example—do conduct electricity slightly; they are very poor conductors rather than non-conductors.)

Can electricity cause chemical change?

The effect of electrical energy on molten sodium and calcium chlorides is to form sodium and calcium metals at the cathode; the metals give off flashes of light as they reach the air and burn. The sodium and calcium chlorides must have undergone decomposition.

Chemical change brought about by an electric current is called *electrolysis.*

Experiment 6.4

The products of electrolysis of a solution of copper chloride in water (D)

The apparatus can be the same as that used in Experiment 6.2. Use a 25% solution of copper chloride and a 10 volt source of d.c.

Hang a piece of moist litmus paper (either colour) in the top of the anode compartment. As the electrolysis proceeds, notice that this litmus paper becomes bleached. This shows that the gaseous element chlorine is given off at the anode.

Switch off the current and examine the deposit of copper on the cathode.

Experiment 6.5

The products of electrolysis of a solution of sulphuric acid in water (C or D)

Set up the apparatus shown in *figure 31* and fill the U-tube to a point 2 cm below the side arms with a dilute solution of sulphuric acid. Connect the electrodes to an ammeter and a 10 volt source of d.c. Note the formation of gas at both electrodes.

Allow 2 or 3 minutes for the air to be swept from the apparatus and then collect the gases in test tubes. Compare the volumes of the two gases. Test the anode gas with a glowing splint and the cathode gas with a lighted taper.

Experiments 6.4 and 6.5, give us further information about the products of electrolysis at cathodes and anodes:

	Cathode	*Anode*
aqueous copper chloride →	copper	+ chlorine
aqueous sulphuric acid →	hydrogen	+ oxygen

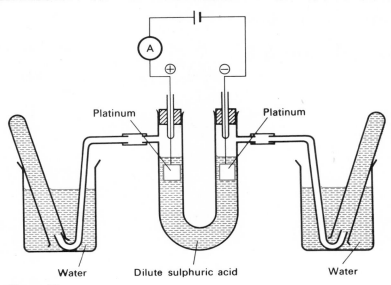

Figure 31

Note that the products of electrolysis of aqueous sulphuric acid are hydrogen and oxygen in the ratio 2:1 by volume. These are the products which one would expect from the decomposition of water.

Electrolytes

These are compounds which conduct electricity when they are in the liquid state or when they are dissolved in water.

Experiments 6.4 and 6.5, indicate that when electricity flows through an electrolyte, metallic elements or hydrogen are formed at the cathode and non-metallic elements are formed at the anode. The experiments also indicate that electrolytes can be classified into:

(*A*) Those which are conductors of electricity when they are in the liquid state *and* when they are dissolved in water.
(*B*) Those which are conductors of electricity only when they are in certain solvents such as water.

Compounds which do not conduct electricity are called *non-electrolytes*. Here are some examples of electrolytes and non-electrolytes:

Table 3

Electrolytes		Non-electrolytes
A Many salts and oxides of metals	*B* Hydrochloric, nitric and sulphuric acids	Alcohol, sugars, hydrocarbons

Can chemical change produce electricity?

Heat can produce chemical change and chemical change can produce heat. In this section we have shown that electricity can produce chemical change; let us now see if chemical change can produce electricity.

Experiment 6.6

Can the action of metals on acids produce electricity? (**C** or **D**)

Connect a weighed piece of copper foil (about 10 cm²) to the positive terminal of an ammeter by means of a crocodile clip and wire. Connect a weighed piece of zinc of similar size to the other terminal. Suspend

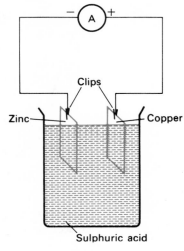

Figure 32

both pieces of metal in a solution of sulphuric acid so that they face each other (*figure 32*). Note the current which flows.

After about 10 minutes disconnect the pieces of metal; wash them, dry them and weigh them.

Experiment 6.6 shows that the zinc has undergone a chemical change but the copper has not. You will also have observed that a gas is evolved at both the copper and the zinc; this is hydrogen. If you repeat the experiment with various metals—lead can be used in the place of copper and magnesium ribbon in the place of zinc—you will find that the current produced varies with the reactivity of the metals. This will be discussed in more detail in Section 19.

Problems

(1) Devise an experiment to show which is the better conductor of electricity, a 5% solution of sodium hydroxide in water or a 5% solution of sodium hydroxide in alcohol.

Summary

(1) In general, metallic elements are better conductors than non-metallic elements.
(2) Electrolytes are compounds which conduct electricity when in the liquid state or when dissolved in water.
(3) There are two main types of electrolyte:

(*A*) Those which are good conductors both when they are in the liquid state *and* when they are dissolved in water.

(*B*) Those which are good conductors only when they are dissolved in certain solvents such as water.

(4) Non-electrolytes are compounds which do not conduct electricity either when they are in the liquid state or when they are dissolved in water.

(5) Electrolysis is chemical change brought about by an electric current. Metals and hydrogen are formed at the cathode (negative electrode); non-metals are formed at the anode (positive electrode).

(6) Chemical change can produce an electric current.

C

Section 7
Carbon and carbon compounds (1)

Although small quantities of the element carbon occur naturally, most of it occurs in compounds. Compounds of carbon, chiefly with the elements hydrogen, oxygen, and nitrogen, are very numerous. (The number of carbon compounds which have been identified exceeds a million.) Most of the compounds of which living things—both plant and animal—are composed contain carbon, and for this reason the study of carbon compounds is usually called organic chemistry.

The detection of carbon

Both carbon and carbon compounds can be detected by oxidizing them to carbon dioxide. This can be done by burning them, but a surer method is to heat them with an oxidizing agent such as copper oxide. If hydrogen is also present in the compound, it will be oxidized to water at the same time.

Experiment 7.1

To test for carbon (C)

Put one small measure of dry copper oxide into a dry small tube. Add half a small measure of powdered carbon (charcoal) and then another small measure of copper oxide. Shake the tube to mix them. Have ready a teat pipette and half a small tube of limewater.

Heat the first tube until the contents glow red. Withdraw some of the resulting gas by means of the teat pipette (p. 47) and discharge it into the surface of the limewater.

Experiment 7.2

To test for carbon and hydrogen in compounds (C)

Repeat Experiment 7.1 using sugar instead of charcoal. You will observe drops of liquid which condense on the colder part of the tube. These can be shown to contain water by touching them with cobalt chloride paper or anhydrous copper sulphate.

Copper oxide contains neither carbon nor hydrogen. The sugar, therefore, must have contained the carbon and hydrogen and these were converted into carbon dioxide and water during the reaction.

You can get an idea of the range of carbon compounds by applying Experiment 7.2 to such substances as motor oil, bread, meat, starch, and coal.

The various forms of carbon

The element carbon occurs naturally as either diamond or graphite. In properties which do not involve a chemical change (physical properties), diamond and graphite are unlike each other: they have different crystal shapes (p. 205); diamonds are hard—graphite is soft; diamonds are transparent—graphite is black. Pure diamond and graphite, however, contain nothing but carbon: equal weights of the two will burn to form equal weights of carbon dioxide.

Different forms of the same element are called *allotropes* or *allotropic forms*. The allotropes of carbon other than diamond and graphite were at one time classified as *amorphous* (non-crystalline or without shape), but it now seems likely that they are various forms of graphite. Here is a summary of the manufacture and uses of some of the forms of carbon:

Diamond is the hardest of all natural substances. Its crystal shape is an octahedron. It is used for cutting and drilling other hard substances, and as a gem stone.

Graphite is very soft. Its crystals consist of small flat hexagons. It is used as a lubricant, as a moderator in nuclear reactors, and, when mixed with clay, in pencil leads.

Coke is made by heating coal in retorts in the absence of air. There are different types of coke, depending on the quality of the coal from which it is made and the temperature at which it is heated. It is used as a fuel and as a reducing agent in the smelting of ores.

Charcoal is made by heating wood in the absence of air. For centuries it was used in smelting, but it has now been replaced by coke. Its power to adsorb certain substances makes it useful in some purification processes; its use in gas masks is one example of this (Experiment 7.3).

Animal charcoal is made by heating bones in the absence of air. It can be used for removing coloured impurities from solutions (Experiment 7.4).

Lampblack is made by burning hydrocarbons with a restricted supply of air. A sample is readily made by holding a cold test tube in a candle flame. It is used in printer's ink, and is mixed with the rubber used to make tyres.

Sugar carbon is made by heating sugar in the absence of air. It can also be made by the action of concentrated sulphuric acid on sugar (p. 127). If a spoonful of sugar is heated very gently, it chars slightly; the product is caramel, used for colouring and flavouring.

Coal is a complex mixture of compounds of carbon; it contains some free carbon.

Experiment 7.3

The adsorption of gases by charcoal (D)

Put two drops of liquid bromine into a 250 cm³ flask fitted with a ground-glass stopper. Replace the stopper and allow the liquid bromine to vaporize. Notice the orange-brown colour of the bromine vapour.

Remove the stopper and quickly add one measure of granulated charcoal. The pieces of charcoal should be about the size of a match head. Shake the flask for half a minute. Notice that it no longer contains bromine vapour.

Remove the stopper. Put the charcoal into a dry test tube and heat it in a bunsen flame. Notice that the heat drives bromine vapour out of the charcoal.

Experiment 7.4

To decolourize brown sugar
(C)

Put four measures of brown sugar into a boiling tube. Add one-third of a tube of water and warm and shake the tube until the sugar dissolves. Divide the solution into two equal parts.

Keep one part as a control and add half a measure of powdered decolourizing charcoal to the other. Shake the tube containing the charcoal for about 2 minutes and then filter the contents. Compare the colour of the filtrate with that of the original solution.

The experiment can be repeated with very dilute solutions of various dyes: litmus, universal indicator, and rhodamine B all work well.

Carbon dioxide

Our work on carbon dioxide so far can be summarized as follows:
(1) It is the product of the oxidation of carbon or compounds containing carbon.
(2) It turns limewater milky.
(3) It is an essential starting material in the process of photosynthesis.
(4) It dissolves in water to form carbonic acid, which is a weak acid.
(5) It can be displaced from salts of carbonic acid (carbonates) by the action of a stronger acid.

Experiment 7.5

To prepare and collect carbon dioxide, and to investigate some of its properties (C)

Set up the standard apparatus for the preparation and collection of gases shown in *figure 16* (p. 20). Put two or three marble chips (calcium carbonate) into the boiling tube. Slowly pour dilute hydrochloric acid down the thistle funnel until it reaches a depth of one inch.

Note the rapid formation of bubbles of gas; this is called *effervescence*. Do not collect this gas immediately, because it will be mixed with air. After about 2 minutes invert a test tube full of water over the end of the delivery tube. Collect three test tubes full of carbon dioxide in this way.

Dilute nitric acid can be used instead of hydrochloric acid and any other carbonate can be used instead of calcium carbonate. Washing soda (hydrated sodium carbonate) can be used: it reacts with nitric hydrochloric, sulphuric, and acetic acids, but does not give such a steady flow of carbon dioxide as does marble.

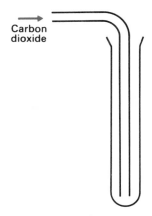

Carbon
dioxide

Figure 33

Carbon dioxide is heavier than air; it can be collected by delivering it downwards directly into a test tube (*figure 33*). It displaces air from the test tube, whereas in the first method it displaces water from the test tube; but in collecting a colourless gas by this method, it is not easy to tell when the tube is full.

Put one finger tightly over the end of one of the test tubes of carbon dioxide and remove the tube from the beaker. Put a lighted taper into the carbon dioxide.

Remove another test tube of carbon dioxide from the beaker and transfer it to a beaker containing a similar volume of water. Add one test tube of sodium hydroxide solution to the second beaker. Compare the rate at which carbon dioxide dissolves in the water in the first beaker with the rate at which it dissolves in the sodium hydroxide solution in the second beaker (*figure 34*).

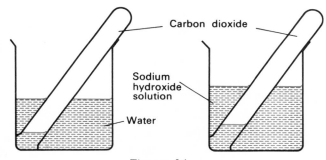

Figures 34

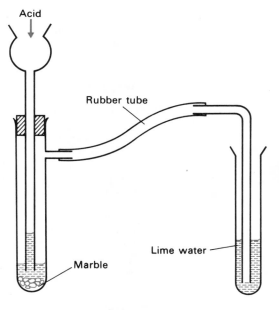

Figure 35

Experiment 7.6

To investigate the action between carbon dioxide and alkaline solutions (calcium and sodium hydroxides) (C)

Assemble the apparatus shown in *figure 35*. Add dilute hydrochloric or nitric acid a little at a time to the gas generator and pass the resulting carbon dioxide into a quarter of a tube of limewater (calcium hydroxide solution). Note that the white precipitate which is first formed dissolves to form a clear solution when treated with more carbon dioxide.

Repeat the experiment using 3 cm³ of a dilute solution of sodium hydroxide instead of limewater. Even when the carbon dioxide is generated as slowly as possible, you will observe that much of it is bubbling through the sodium hydroxide solution without reacting. A more efficient way of reacting gases with liquids is shown in *figure 36*.

After treating the solution with carbon dioxide for about 10 minutes,

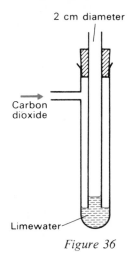

2 cm diameter

Carbon dioxide

Limewater

Figure 36

test it for the presence of carbonate. This is done by adding an equal volume of dilute nitric acid and testing the resulting gas with limewater (p. 47).

We can now add to our knowledge of carbon dioxide:

(1) It is colourless and heavier than air.
(2) It does not burn, neither does it support combustion.
(3) It is more readily soluble in solutions of alkalis than it is in water.
(4) It reacts with solutions of alkalis to form carbonates (salts of carbonic acid).
(5) There are two types of carbonates (a) normal carbonates (b) bicarbonates.*

When carbon dioxide reacts with alkalis it first forms normal carbonates, but an excess of the gas converts the carbonates into bicarbonates. Thus the white precipitate of calcium carbonate, which is formed when carbon dioxide reacts with calcium hydroxide solution, reacts with excess carbon dioxide to form calcium bicarbonate. Beacuse calcium bicarbonate is soluble, a clear solution is finally formed.

* Bicarbonates will later be called hydrogen carbonates (p. 122).

The reaction of carbon dioxide with a solution of sodium hydroxide is similar: sodium carbonate and then sodium bicarbonate are formed. Both salts are soluble in water, but sodium bicarbonate is less soluble than sodium carbonate. If a precipitate is formed in the second part of Experiment 7.6, it is likely to be sodium bicarbonate.

$$\text{an alkali} + \text{carbon dioxide} \rightarrow \text{a normal carbonate} + \text{water}$$
$$|$$
$$+ \text{excess carbon dioxide}$$
$$\downarrow$$
$$\text{a bicarbonate}$$

To distinguish between sodium carbonate and sodium bicarbonate

In appearance there is little difference between sodium carbonate and sodium bicarbonate; both can be obtained as white powders. Furthermore, if a few drops of a solution of an acid are added, both effervesce and yield carbon dioxide.

Experiment 7.7

To investigate the action of heat on sodium carbonate and bicarbonate (C)

Bring one-third of a small boiling tube of water almost to boiling point. Add one small measure of powdered sodium carbonate and test for carbon dioxide. Repeat the experiment with sodium bicarbonate.

Boil the sodium bicarbonate solution until no more carbon dioxide is evolved (2 or 3 minutes). Add a few drops of nitric acid solution. Note the effervescence of a gas which can be shown to be carbon dioxide by the usual test.

Experiment 7.7 indicates that sodium bicarbonate readily decomposes in hot water, whereas sodium carbonate does not. Furthermore, two of the products of decomposition of sodium bicarbonate are carbon dioxide and sodium carbonate.

Calcium bicarbonate behaves similarly. If you heat a solution of calcium bicarbonate you will observe the evolution of bubbles of gas and the formation of a precipitate of insoluble calcium carbonate.

Carbon monoxide

Experiment 7.8

To investigate the action of carbon dioxide on heated carbon (D)

Pack granulated charcoal loosely into the middle 15 cm of a silica tube. The charcoal can be held in place by two loose plugs of asbestos.

Assemble the apparatus shown in *figure 37* and pass carbon dioxide to sweep out the air. Adjust the flow of carbon dioxide to about one bubble per second through the first bottle of sodium hydroxide solution. Heat the middle portion of the silica tube strongly in a furnace for 15 minutes. Double the rate of flow of carbon dioxide and start to collect the resulting gas over water. Apply a lighted taper to the mouth of a gas jar full of the gas.

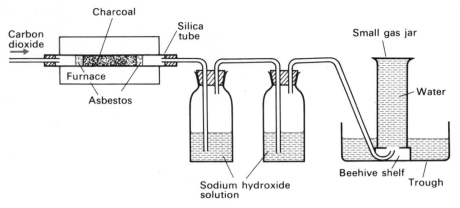

Figure 37

The gas which is collected in Experiment 7.8 burns readily and is obviously different from carbon dioxide. A likely explanation of its formation is that the hot carbon has removed some of the oxygen (reduction) from the carbon dioxide to form a gas (carbon monoxide) which contains a smaller proportion of oxygen:

carbon dioxide + carbon → carbon monoxide
(reduced)   (oxidized)

When carbon monoxide burns, with its characteristic blue flame, it combines with oxygen to re-form carbon dioxide:

carbon monoxide + oxygen → carbon dioxide

Petrol engines, in which hydrocarbons are exploded with a limited supply of air, contain carbon monoxide in their exhaust gases. As carbon monoxide is very poisonous exhaust fumes are dangerous in confined spaces. Carbon monoxide sometimes occurs in coal mines and is also the poisonous component of coal gas.

The reducing properties of carbon and carbon monoxide

In the last experiment carbon reduced carbon dioxide to carbon monoxide. In Experiment 7.1, at the beginning of this section, carbon was oxidized to carbon dioxide; at the same time copper oxide was reduced to copper by the carbon:

carbon + copper oxide → copper + carbon dioxide
(oxidized)   (reduced

Carbon monoxide is also a reducing agent. When passed over heated copper oxide, it reduces the copper oxide to copper; at the same time the carbon monoxide is oxidized to carbon dioxide:

carbon monoxide + copper oxide → copper + carbon dioxide
(oxidized)   (reduced)

It appears that in a reaction between two substances if one is oxidized (gains oxygen) the other must be reduced (loses oxygen).

The production of metals by reduction of oxides

The reducing powers of carbon and carbon monoxide are used in smelting ores. The large-scale production of metals involves heating the oxides of the metal with carbon, usually in the form of coke (p. 57). Iron, lead, and zinc are all produced in this way. If a blast of hot air is passed into the oxide and coke mixture, some of the coke is converted into carbon monoxide which then reduces the oxide of the metal:

$$\text{iron oxide} + \text{carbon monoxide} \rightarrow \text{iron} + \text{carbon dioxide}$$
$$\text{lead oxide} + \text{carbon monoxide} \rightarrow \text{lead} + \text{carbon dioxide}$$

If air is not passed into the oxide and coke mixture, the actual reducing agent is the coke itself:

$$\text{zinc oxide} + \text{carbon} \rightarrow \text{zinc} + \text{carbon monoxide}$$

The production of metals in this manner is illustrated in the following experiment.

Experiment 7.9

The reduction of lead oxide to lead (C)

With a penknife drill a conical hole, about 1 cm diameter and 1 cm deep, into a carbon block. Fill it almost to the top with litharge (lead monoxide) and add a thin layer of sodium carbonate (the sodium carbonate melts and prevents the lead oxide from being blown out of the hole).

Have ready a bunsen flame about 8 cm high and with just sufficient air intake to remove the yellow colour from it. Rest the tip of a blowpipe on the top edge of the burner and blow through the flame. This produces a small hot flame which can be concentrated on to a small area.

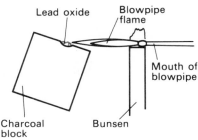

Figure 38

Direct the tip of the blowpipe flame at the lead oxide, tilting the carbon block through about 30° (if you tilt it too far the molten lead will fall on to the bench). Blow steadily—with practice you will find that you can blow continuously through your mouth while breathing in and out through your nose—until a bead of lead forms in the bottom of the hole.

Add two or three drops of water to stop the carbon from smouldering. Probe out the lead when it is cool and test it by marking paper with it.

The actual reducing agent in this experiment is probably carbon monoxide, formed by the action of the blowpipe flame on the carbon.

Problems

(1) Investigate and write an account of the uses of carbon dioxide and carbonates in fire extinguishers.

(2) Investigate the action which takes place when a mixture of powdered carbon and lead oxide (3:1 by volume) is heated in the bottom of a small, dry, hard-glass test tube.

(3) Investigate and write an account of the manufacture and uses of coke.

(4) Draw a diagram to illustrate the production of coal gas and list some of the by-products of the process.

Summary

(1) Carbon and carbon compounds yield carbon dioxide when oxidized by heating with copper oxide. If hydrogen is present in the compound, water is formed at the same time.

(2) Carbon is a reducing agent; it can remove the oxygen from some oxides of metals to form the metals themselves.

(3) Allotropes are different forms of the same element. They have different physical properties, but their chemical properties are similar.

(4) Carbon dioxide reacts with alkalis to form carbonates and bicarbonates, the salts of carbonic acid.

(5) Both carbonates and bicarbonates yield carbon dioxide when treated with an acid, but bicarbonates readily decompose to form carbon dioxide and the normal carbonates.

(6) Hot carbon reduces carbon dioxide to carbon monoxide.

(7) Carbon monoxide burns to form carbon dioxide.

(8) Carbon and carbon monoxide are used industrially to reduce oxides of metals to metals.

(9) In a reaction between two substances, if one is oxidized the other is reduced.

Section 8
The particulate nature of matter

Chemical theories

In the preceding sections we have accumulated facts about matter, mainly by the observation of experiments. We have also classified some of the substances and types of change, because classification makes the study of them easier. But facts and their classification have never been the end of scientific investigation; we also seek to explain them. Such an explanation is called a *theory*.

A theory is a mental picture which helps us to understand what we observe. A good theory is a useful tool to a scientist; it not only helps him to explain what he has observed, it also helps him to predict further observations. It is in this way that most scientific progress is made.

It is important that you realize that theories are mental pictures; they are not observed facts. They must be judged not so much by whether they are true or false, but by whether they work or do not work in their task of explaining our observations and predicting further observations. For this reason we must be critical of theories, and prepared to modify or even discard them if they do not fit new facts which experiments bring to light.

How is matter constructed?

The first step in answering this question is to decide whether a substance is all one piece (continuous) or whether it is made up of small separate particles (discontinuous). The following experiments, together with other evidence, will help us to decide which is the more likely explanation of the structure of matter:

Experiment 8.1

To investigate the diffusion of hydrogen sulphide (D)

Take the lid off a gas jar full of hydrogen sulphide in one corner of the laboratory. Note the time it takes for the smell of the gas to reach each pupil. (Hydrogen sulphide is poisonous, but this quantity in a large laboratory will cause no ill effects).

Gases appear to have the power to move rapidly without any outside assistance. This spontaneous movement is called *diffusion*. By this process gases easily spread throughout volumes much larger than their original one. They are then said to be *dispersed*.

Experiment 8.2

To investigate the diffusion of bromine **(D)**

Smear grease thinly round the lip of a gas jar. Put two drops of bromine on to the centre of a gas jar cover and cover it immediately with the inverted gas jar. Observe the diffusion of the bromine throughout the gas jar.

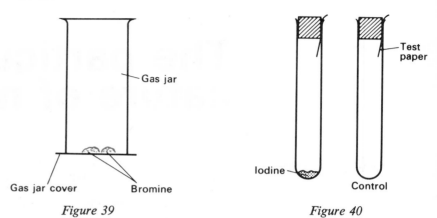

Figure 39

Figure 40

Experiment 8.3

To investigate the diffusion of iodine **(C)**

Put two dry test tubes into a test tube rack. Hold a strip of filter paper, moistened with starch solution, in the mouth of one of the tubes with the aid of a cork. This acts as a control experiment. Do likewise with the other tube, having first added a crystal of iodine.

Look for the appearance of a blue colour on one of the strips of filter paper (iodine forms a blue colour with starch and this is used as a test for iodine).

Experiments 8.1, 8.2, and 8.3, indicate that small amounts of substances can disperse themselves throughout very large volumes of air. This in turn indicates that there is space in air into which particles of diffusing substances can move. Experiment 8.5 will indicate that a similar dispersion is possible throughout a liquid.

We have observed earlier that heat speeds up diffusion. Thus water, when heated, rapidly diffuses in the form of water vapour over a much larger volume.

Experiment 8.4

To compare the rate of diffusion of air with those of (a) hydrogen and (b) carbon dioxide **(C** or **D)**

(a) Fit a porous pot with a rubber bung through which runs a delivery tube. Drape a polythene bag over the pot, which is then clamped vertically with the end of the delivery tube about 1 cm below the surface of a beaker of water (*figure 41*).

Prepare hydrogen by adding about 3 cm of dilute hydrochloric acid to about 30 cm of magnesium ribbon in the usual gas preparation apparatus. Allow a few seconds for the air to be swept from the apparatus and then, with a rubber tube, deliver the hydrogen upwards into the polythene bag.

Watch the water level in the tube attached to the porous pot during this operation and again when the source of hydrogen is removed.

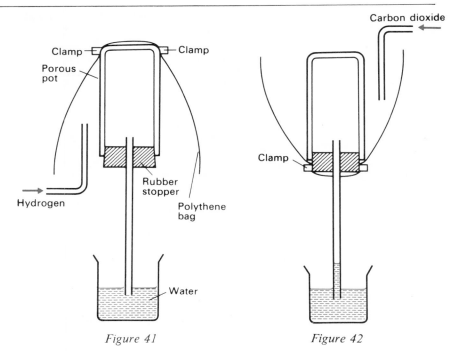

Figure 41   Figure 42

Experiment 8.4 (a) indicates:

(i) Gases can diffuse through a porous pot.

(ii) Hydrogen diffuses into the pot more rapidly than air diffuses out of it; hence pressure builds up inside the pot and gas escapes through the delivery tube.

(iii) When the source of hydrogen is removed, hydrogen inside the pot diffuses out more rapidly than air diffuses in; hence pressure decreases inside the pot and the water level rises in the tube.

(b) Fit the polythene bag to the porous pot so that the mouth of the bag is uppermost. If the polythene is thin enough, a small hole can be pierced in it by the end of the delivery tube to enable this rearrangement to be made (*figure 42*).

Prepare carbon dioxide by adding 3 cm of dilute hydrochloric acid to one or two marble chips in the usual gas preparation apparatus. Deliver the carbon dioxide downwards into the polythene bag and watch the water level in the tube attached to the porous pot. Remove the source of carbon dioxide and again watch the water level. Explain your observations.

Experiment 8.5

To investigate the dispersion of dichlorofluorescein **(C)**

Weigh a dry watch glass; add one small measure of dichloroflourescein and weigh again. Pour 5 cm³ of aqueous sodium hydroxide into a measuring cylinder, make the volume up to 100 cm³ with water and use this solution to wash the dichlorofluorescein into a 250 cm³ beaker. Stir until the dichlorofluorescein dissolves.

Pour 10 cm³ of the aqueous dichlorofluorescein into the measuring cylinder, and empty and rinse the beaker. Pour 10 cm³ of solution back into the beaker and add 90 cm³ of water. The new solution has a concentration one-tenth of that of the former one. If this process is repeated four times, the colour of the dichlorofluorescein can still be seen.

Assuming that there are approximately 20 drops to the cm³, calculate the weight of dichlorofluorescein in one drop of the final solution.

The kinetic theory of matter

Some facts

Here is a summary of the evidence which comes from our experiments in this and previous sections:

(1) Many substances can exist as solids, liquids, and gases: for example, water can exist as ice, water, and steam.

(2) Solids have a greater resistance to penetration by other material than liquids have. Gases offer little resistance to penetration.

(3) A rise in temperature assists the change of solids to liquids and liquids to gases.

(4) Gases occupy a much greater volume than the same weight of liquid or solid.

(5) Some substances disperse themselves spontaneously. This movement is called diffusion.

(6) Gases of high density diffuse more slowly than those of lower density.

The theory

The facts listed above can be explained if the following assumptions are made about the nature of matter:

(1) Matter consists of small separate particles.

(2) The particles are continuously moving.

(3) The speed of the particles increases with temperature.

(4) The speed of lighter particles is greater than the speed of heavier particles at the same temperature.

(5) The particles are attracted to each other with a force which is greatest when they are closest together.

(6) The particles are closest together in solids and furthest apart in gases.

These six assumptions form part of *The Kinetic Theory of Matter*.

For the moment the smallest particle which can exist on its own under normal conditions will be called a *molecule*. Later (Sections 9 and 10), we shall learn that there are different types of particles and that the name 'molecule' can only be properly applied to some of them.

The theory in action

Let us see if the theory can explain some of our observations.

(1) *The Action of Heat on Water*

As the temperature of water rises, the molecules move more quickly and further apart. Vapour is formed because some of the molecules gain sufficient energy to overcome the attraction of neighbouring molecules and break free from the liquid.

(2) *All Gases mix completely with Each Other*

In a gas the distance between molecules is great compared with their size, so there is very little attraction between them; therefore, the movement of each molecule is almost independent. If a second gas is introduced, there is plenty of space into which its molecules can move and hence mix completely (*figure 43*).

(3) *The Vapour Pressure of Liquids*

If a few drops of water are introduced into a barometer tube (*figure 44*), the level of the mercury drops and then remains steady.

The distance through which the mercury drops is much greater than would be expected from the weight of the small quantity of water on top of the mercury. The Kinetic Theory of Matter gives us the following explanation:

Some of the water molecules have sufficient energy to escape from the surface of the water and to form a vapour. The momentum of the molecules of water vapour in the space above the mercury causes a pressure which forces the level of the mercury down. The distance through which the mercury drops is a measure of the vapour pressure of water.

The vapour pressure soon remains constant, and this indicates that the number of water vapour molecules remains constant. It appears that water molecules are moving from the vapour to the liquid at the same rate as they move from the liquid to the vapour, so that the actual number in the vapour remains constant. This sort of situation is called an *equilibrium*.

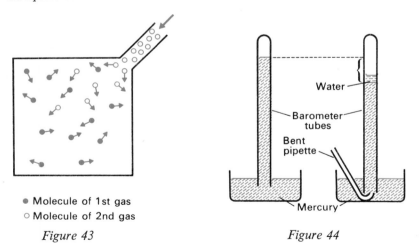

● Molecule of 1st gas
○ Molecule of 2nd gas

Figure 43

Figure 44

The Brownian movement

When smoke is brightly illuminated and viewed under a microscope, the position of each smoke particle can be seen because of the bright speck of light reflected from it (this is why a beam of light can be seen in a smoky atmosphere but not in a clear one). Each particle of smoke appears to be moving. This movement, called the Brownian movement, is random—it is not steady or predictable.

The Brownian movement can be explained by assuming that each particle of smoke is being bombarded by molecules of air. Although the smoke particle is much bigger than the molecules, it is small enough to be moved by them if at any one moment the momentum of the colliding molecules is greater in one direction than in another.

The Brownian movement can also be demonstrated by using a very fine suspension of a solid in a liquid.

Problems

(1) In Experiment 8.1 what factors other than spontaneous diffusion could have caused the dispersion of the hydrogen sulphide?
(2) In Experiment 8.2 what difference in the observations would have been likely if the air in the gas jar had been under reduced pressure?

Summary

(1) Theories are used to help us to understand what is observed and to predict further observations. As our observations extend, the theories may have to be altered to make them agree with new facts.
(2) Diffusion is the spontaneous movement of particles of matter. It can result in the matter being dispersed through a larger volume.
(3) The less dense a gas, the more quickly if diffuses.
(4) The energy of particles increases with temperature.
(5) Gases occupy a much greater volume than the same weight of liquid or solid.
(6) The Kinetic Theory of Matter helps us to understand the nature of matter; it is summarized on p. 68
(7) For the moment, the smallest particles which can exist on their own will all be called molecules.

Section 9
Atoms–gram atom–formulae– valency–gram formula–equations

Atoms

The word 'atom' was first used in its modern sense by John Dalton (1766–1844), who explained his experimental work (on the combining weights of elements) by what is now known as Dalton's Atomic Theory. This resulted in a great step forward in chemistry and, although it has had to be modified because of more recently discovered facts, it remains one of the most famous and useful of all chemical theories. The details of Dalton's own experimental work will not be given here.

Dalton called the smallest particle of an element an *atom*. He assumed that all atoms of the same element were identical and that the smallest particles of compounds consisted of small whole numbers of atoms combined together.

Symbols

A *chemical symbol* represents one atom of an element; for example,

H represents one atom of hydrogen,
O represents one atom of oxygen,
Fe represents one atom of iron.

Whenever possible, the symbol for one atom of an element is the first letter of the name of the element. Some elements have the same initial letter, so, to avoid confusion, the first two letters are used, e.g. Co (cobalt), or the first two letters of the Latin name of the element, e.g. Cu (*cuprum* = copper).

A list of chemical symbols is given in Appendix C.

Molecules of compounds

As all compounds consist of two or more elements combined together the smallest particle of a compound must always contain at least two different atoms combined together.

Atoms and molecules of elements

The atoms of some elements can exist singly, uncombined with any other atoms. But the atoms of other elements do not exist singly under normal conditions; they combine with each other and the resulting particles are called molecules of the element.

Elements whose atoms exist singly are said to be *monatomic*.

Elements whose molecules contain two atoms are said to be *diatomic*.

The number of atoms in one molecule of an element is called the *atomicity* of the element.

Figure 45 represents helium which is monatomic, and *figure 46* represents hydrogen which is diatomic.

● 1 Atom or molecule
of helium

○ 1 Atom of hydrogen

◌◌ 1 Molecule of hydrogen

Figure 45   *Figure 46*

Hydrogen, oxygen, nitrogen, chlorine, bromine, and iodine are examples of diatomic elements. Under normal conditions, single atoms of these elements can only exist when they are combined with at least one atom of another element.

An experiment basis for the theory of atomicity will be given in Section 16. Meanwhile, an elementary knowledge of atomicity is necessary so that molecules of elements can be correctly represented in chemical equations (p. 80).

Atomic weights of elements

The Units

The gram is too large for convenient use when measuring the weights of atoms. On this scale a hydrogen atom would weigh about $1 \cdot 7 \times 10^{-24}$ g.

A more convenient unit would be the weight of a hydrogen atom. If we call the weight of a hydrogen atom 1, then the weight of a carbon atom on this scale would be 12, because the weight of a carbon atom $= 12 \times$ the weight of a hydrogen atom.

(The hydrogen atom as an accurate standard of atomic weight has been abandoned. The unit of atomic weight is now one-twelfth of the weight of the principal isotope of carbon (p. 183). This is about the same as the weight of a hydrogen atom; therefore approximate atomic weights will be the same on both the hydrogen and the carbon standard.)

More recently (F. W. Aston, 1936) the mass spectrograph (*figure 47*) has been developed to compare the weight of atoms without recourse to chemical reactions.

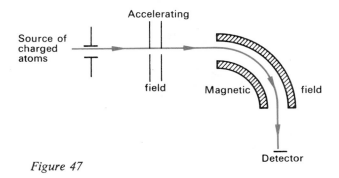

Figure 47

Briefly, the mass spectograph changes atoms into electrically charged particles called ions. The ions are accelerated in a tube at low pressure by an electrical field and the beam of ions is then deflected by a magnetic field onto a detector. The magnetic force required to deflect the ions will depend on the electrical charge and the mass of the ions. By measuring the magnetic force the relative weights of atoms can be determined.

A list of approximate atomic weights is given in Appendix C.

The Avogadro number

Suppose that there are N atoms of oxygen in 16 g of oxygen, N being a very large number.

Each atom of oxygen weighs 16 (atomic weight) and N atoms weigh 16 g.

Similarly an atom of magnesium weighs 24; therefore, N atoms of magnesium weigh 24 g.

Therefore, the number of atoms of oxygen in 16 g of oxygen = the number of atoms of magnesium in 24 g of magnesium.

This number is called the *Avogadro Number* or the Avogadro Constant and is approximately 6×10^{23}. It is given the symbol N_A.

Another way of saying this is:

$$\frac{\text{Weight of } N_A \text{ atoms of magnesium}}{\text{Weight of } N_A \text{ atoms of oxygen}} = \frac{24}{16} = \frac{\text{weight of 1 atom of magnesium}}{\text{weight of 1 atom of oxygen}}$$

To take a simple analogy, if you compare the weight of one sphere made of polystyrene with another made of lead, the ratio will be the same as if you compared the weights of an equal number—say 100—of each type. So it is with atoms and other small particles.

Gram-atom (g-atom)

A fundamental part of the work of chemists is to determine the numbers of atoms of each element which combine to form a compound. For example, it is important to know how many atoms of magnesium combine with each atom of oxygen to form magnesium oxide.

It is impossible to work with individual atoms, but it is possible—and very useful—for chemists to have a unit of quantity for all elements in which there is an equal number of atoms. The number which has been chosen is N_A, the Avogadro Number, and the weight in grams of N_A atoms of an element is called a **gram-atom** (g-atom). Thus:

$$N_A \text{ atoms of magnesium weigh 24 g} = 1 \text{ g-atom of Mg}$$
$$N_A \text{ atoms of oxygen weigh 16 g} = 1 \text{ g-atom of O}$$
$$N_A \text{ atoms of carbon weigh 12 g} = 1 \text{ g-atom of C}$$
$$N_A \text{ atoms of hydrogen weigh 1 g} = 1 \text{ g-atom of H}$$

Notice that the ratio of the weights of 1 g-atom of elements is the same as the ratio of their atomic weights.

Combining weights and empirical formulae

The weights of elements which are combined with each other in compounds can be determined by experiment. For example, an experiment similar to Experiment 2.4 (p. 16), but more accurately performed, could show results such as:

$$\text{Weight of magnesium} = 0\cdot192 \text{ g}$$
$$\text{Weight of magnesium oxide} = 0\cdot300 \text{ g}$$
$$\therefore \text{ Weight of oxygen} = 0\cdot108 \text{ g}$$

$$\therefore 0\cdot192 \text{ g of magnesium is combined with } 0\cdot108 \text{ g of oxygen}$$
$$\text{But 1 g-atom of magnesium weighs 24 g}$$
$$\text{And 1 g-atom of oxygen weighs 16 g}$$

$$\therefore 0\cdot192 \text{ g of magnesium} = \frac{0\cdot192}{24} \text{ g-atom of magnesium}$$

$$= 0\cdot008 \text{ g-atom Mg.}$$

$$\text{and } 0\cdot108 \text{ g of oxygen} = \frac{0\cdot108}{16} \text{ g-atom of oxygen}$$

$$= 0\cdot008 \text{ g-atom O.}$$

$$\therefore 0\cdot008 \text{ g-atom Mg is combined with } 0\cdot008 \text{ g-atom O}$$
$$\text{This ratio in g-atoms is } 1 : 1.$$
$$\therefore N_A \text{ atoms of Mg are combined with } N_A \text{ atoms of O.}$$
$$\therefore 1 \text{ atom of Mg is combined with 1 atom of oxygen.}$$

This simple ratio of numbers of atoms of each element in a compound is shown as the **Empirical Formula** of the compound. Thus, the empirical formula of magnesium oxide is MgO.

If you do Experiment 2.4 yourself, experimental error is likely to lead to a ratio which is not exactly a whole number of atoms; for example, you might get:

$$1\cdot1 \text{ g-atoms Mg combined with } 1\cdot0 \text{ g-atoms O.}$$

Provided that it can be attributed to experimental error, a ratio such as this may be converted to the nearest simple whole number, which in this case is 1:1. It appears that in most compounds atoms combine in simple whole number ratio with each other.

The limitations of the use of empirical formulae

(1) An empirical formula does not necessarily show the *actual* number of atoms in one molecule of a compound. Thus water has the empirical formula H_2O, but this would still be so if a molecule of water contained 4 atoms of hydrogen and 2 atoms of oxygen (H_4O_2). Further experimental evidence is needed before we can decide the actual number of atoms contained in one molecule. For many purposes, however, one molecule of a compound can be represented by its empirical formula.

(2) An empirical formula does not indicate any change in an atom after it has combined. We shall learn in Section 10 that, in fact, atoms are often considerably changed by combination with other atoms; in particular they may acquire an electrical charge.

(3) The fact that the empirical formula of a compound can be calculated does not necessarily mean that molecules of the compound actually exist. Many compounds are not made up of molecules (p. 183).

Valency

By experimental determination of the ratio of g-atoms of elements in compounds, it can be shown that an atom of one element can combine with more than one atom of another element; for example:

(1) In water 1 atom of oxygen is combined with 2 atoms of hydrogen (H_2O).

(2) In carbon dioxide 1 atom of carbon is combined with 2 atoms of oxygen (CO_2).

(3) In methane (natural gas) 1 atom of carbon is combined with 4 atoms of hydrogen (CH_4).

If we say that a hydrogen atom has a combining capacity of 1, then an oxygen atom has a combining capacity of 2 because it can combine with 2 hydrogen atoms. Similarly, a carbon atom has a combining capacity of 4 because it can combine with 2 oxygen atoms or 4 hydrogen atoms.

The combining capacity of an atom is called its *valency*.

Appendix D shows the valencies of the common elements. Turn to the Periodic Table (Appendix B) and try to deduce a relationship between the valency of an element and the group in which it occurs.

The prefixes *mono-*, *di-*, *tri-*, *tetra-*, etc. are sometimes used to denote valency. Thus a trivalent element has a valency of 3.

Multiple valency

We have established that a knowledge of combining weights and atomic weights can lead us to the ratio of the atoms of each element in a compound. Here are examples of a general method by which this calculation can be done:

Example 1 A compound on analysis was found to contain 28 g of iron to 35·5 g of chlorine by weight. Calculate its empirical formula.

	Iron	*Chlorine*
(divide by atomic weights)	$\dfrac{28}{56}$	$\dfrac{35·5}{35·5}$
Ratio of g-atoms =	$\frac{1}{2}$:	1
=	1 :	2

$\therefore$ Empirical formula of compound = $FeCl_2$

Example 2 A compound on analysis was found to contain $18\frac{2}{3}$ g of iron to 35·5 g of chlorine by weight. Calculate its empirical formula.

	Iron	*Chlorine*
(divide by atomic weights)	$\dfrac{18\frac{2}{3}}{56}$	$\dfrac{35\cdot5}{35\cdot5}$
Ratio of g-atoms $=$	$\frac{1}{3}$:	1
$=$	1 :	3

$\therefore$ Empirical formula of compound $=$ $FeCl_3$

The figures quoted in Examples 1 and 2 indicate that some elements can have more than one combining weight. It follows, since their atomic weights are constant, that they have more than one combining capacity (valency).

Iron is an example of one of these elements. It can show a valency of either two or three. The compounds in which iron shows a valency of two are called iron (II) compounds, and those in which it shows a valency of three are called iron (III) compounds. Mercury and copper also can show more than one valency; in mercury (I) and copper (I) compounds they show a valency of one, and in mercury (II) and copper (II) compounds they show a valency of two.

A general method for constructing empirical formulae of simple compounds

It is important to realize that all empirical formulae are derived from a practical determination of the composition of compounds. However, there is neither the time nor the necessity to repeat this practical work. The empirical formulae of simple compounds, particularly those formed between metallic and non-metallic elements, can be deduced from the valencies given in Appendix D.

Example The formula of aluminium oxide
   [metallic]   1 atom of aluminium, Al, has a valency $= 3$
   [non-metallic] 1 atom of oxygen, O, has a valency $= 2$
               2 atoms of aluminium, Al_2, have a valency $= 3 \times 2 = 6$
               3 atoms of oxygen, O_3, have a valency $= 2 \times 3 = 6$
   $\therefore$ The combining capacity of Al_2 = the combining capacity of O_3
       $\therefore$ The simplest formula of aluminium oxide $= Al_2O_3$

NB: (1) The total valency of each part is the LCM of the individual valencies of the the two elements. Thus, 6 is the LCM of 2 and 3.
   (2) The small number at the base of a symbol refers to that symbol only.
   (3) The metallic part is placed first in the formula.

For practice, construct the formulae of (a) sodium oxide (b) calcium chloride (c) aluminium bromide.

Radicals

Many compounds contain a common group of atoms. For example, SO_4 represents a group of atoms, composed of one sulphur atom and four oxygen atoms, which occurs in all sulphates: sodium sulphate (Na_2SO_4), copper sulphate ($CuSO_4$), sulphuric acid (H_2SO_4), and many others. Because they all contain a common group, all sulphates have some properties in common (see the test for sulphates, p. 130).

These groups of atoms, which are called *radicals*, are found only in compounds; they do not have a separate existence under normal conditions. But because they combine with a definite number of other atoms they do have a valency; for example, the sulphate radical has a valency of two because it can be combined with two hydrogen atoms which have a valency of one each.

With the exception of the ammonium radical (NH_4), all the radicals which we shall study form the non-metallic part of a compound. Appendix D gives the valency and the composition of the common radicals.

The construction of empirical formulae of compounds containing radicals

The main thing to remember is that radicals are to be regarded as single units whose composition does not vary. For this reason, if a radical is to be shown as doubled or trebled it must be contained in brackets. For example: $(OH)_2$ $(NH_4)_2$ $(SO_4)_3$.

Example 1   The formula of zinc nitrate

[metallic]   1 atom of zinc, Zn, has a valency = 2
[non-metallic]   1 nitrate radical, NO_3, has a valency = 1

$\therefore$ 2 nitrate radicals, $(NO_3)_2$, have a valency = $1 \times 2 = 2$
$\therefore$ The combining capacity of Zn = the combining capacity of $(NO_3)_2$
$\therefore$ The simplest formula of zinc nitrate = $\underline{Zn(NO_3)_2}$

Example 2   The formula of ammonium sulphate

[metallic]   1 ammonium radical, NH_4, has a valency = 1
[non-metallic]   1 sulphate radical, SO_4, has a valency = 2
$\therefore$ 2 ammonium radicals, $(NH_4)_2$, have a valency = $1 \times 2 = 2$
$\therefore$ The combining capacity of $(NH_4)_2$ = the combining capacity of SO_4
$\therefore$ The simplest formula of ammonium sulphate = $\underline{(NH_4)_2SO_4}$

For practice, construct the formulae of (a) sodium sulphate (b) ammonium chloride (c) zinc carbonate (d) aluminium hydroxide.

Formula weights

The sum of the weights of the atoms shown in a formula is called the *formula weight*.

Example 1   The formula weight of aluminium chloride

$$Al \qquad Cl_3$$
$$27 + (3 \times 35 \cdot 5)$$
$$27 + 106 \cdot 5$$
$$\therefore \text{ Formula weight} = \underline{133 \cdot 5}$$

Example 2   The formula weight of ammonium sulphate

$$(NH_4)_2 \qquad SO_4$$
$$2[14+(4\times 1)]+32+(4\times 16)$$
$$2[18] \qquad +32+64$$
$$36 \qquad +32+64$$
$$\therefore \text{ Formula weight} = \underline{132}$$

For practice, work out the formula weights of (a) aluminium oxide (b) sodium hydroxide (c) aluminium sulphate (d) ammonium carbonate (e) copper nitrate.

Gram formula (g-formula)

An empirical formula shows the composition of the smallest possible unit of a substance and its weight is called the formula weight.

The weight of Avogadro's number (N_A) of these units is called 1 gram-formula (1 g-formula) of the substance. Thus:

Table 4

	Formula weight	1 g-formula
water (H_2O)	18	18 g
carbon dioxide (CO_2)	44	44 g
sodium chloride (NaCl)	58·5	58·5 g
copper sulphate ($CuSO_4$)	160	160 g

Molar solutions

Many chemical reactions are performed in solution and it is usually convenient to know the concentration of a solution in terms of the number of g-formulae of the solute per unit volume of solution.

A molar solution is one which contains 1 g-formula of solute per litre of solution. For example:

A molar solution of sodium chloride (NaCl) contains 58·5 g/l. This can be abbreviated to M NaCl.

The number of g-formulae of solute per litre of solution is known as the *molarity** of the solution:

A solution containing $\frac{1}{10}$ g-formula of solute per litre is said to be one-tenth molar (M/10 or 0·1 M). A solution containing 2 g-formulae of solute per litre is said to be two molar (2 M).

Example 1   Calculate the molarity of a solution containing 11·7 g of sodium chloride (NaCl) per litre.

1 g-formula of sodium chloride is 58·5 g

$$11\cdot 7 \text{ g of sodium chloride} = \frac{11\cdot 7}{58\cdot 5} \text{ g-formula} = \frac{1}{5} \text{ g-formula}$$

$\therefore$ Solution contains $\frac{1}{5}$ g-formula per litre

$\therefore$ Solution is $\underline{\text{M}/5 \text{ NaCl}}$ (0·2 M NaCl)

* 'Molarity' and 'molar' are derived from the term 'mole', explained on p. 186

Example 2   Calculate the molarity of a solution containing 6·25 g of copper sulphate crystals ($CuSO_4.5H_2O$) in 250 cm³.

$$\text{Formula weight of } CuSO_4.5H_2O = 64+32+(4\times16)+(5\times18)$$
$$= 250$$

$$1 \text{ g-formula of copper sulphate crystals} = 250 \text{ g}$$

$$6\cdot25 \text{ g of copper sulphate crystals} = \frac{6\cdot25}{250} \text{ g-formula}$$

$$= \frac{1}{40} \text{ g-formula}$$

$\therefore$ Solution contains $\frac{1}{40}$ g-formula in 250 cm³

$\therefore$ Solution contains $\frac{1}{40} \times 4$ g-formula in 1 litre

$$= \tfrac{1}{10} \text{ g-formula in 1 litre}$$

$\therefore$ Solution is M/10 or 0·1 M

Example 3   Calculate the weight of sulphuric acid in 250 cm³ of M/4 H_2SO_4 solution.

$$\text{Formula weight of sulphuric acid} = 2+32+64 = 98$$
$$1 \text{ g-formula of sulphuric acid} = 98 \text{ g}$$

$$\therefore \tfrac{1}{4} \text{ g-formula of sulphuric acid} = \frac{98}{4} \text{ g} = 24\cdot5 \text{ g}$$

$\therefore$ 1 litre of M/4 H_2SO_4 solution contains 24·5 g of sulphuric acid

$$\therefore 250 \text{ cm}^3 \text{ of M/4 } H_2SO_4 \text{ solution contains } \frac{24\cdot5}{4} \text{ g}$$

$$= 6\cdot125 \text{ g}$$

The dilute solutions of laboratory reagents are made up to a known (standard) molarity. In the instructions for experiments in this book the following concentrations of solutions are assumed:

hydrochloric acid	2 M HCl
nitric acid	2 M HNO_3
acetic acid	2 M $CH_3.COOH$
sulphuric acid	M H_2SO_4
sodium hydroxide	2 M NaOH
ammonium hydroxide	2 M NH_4OH
sodium carbonate	M Na_2CO_3
silver nitrate	M/20 $AgNO_3$

(Can you think of any reason why the molarity of sulphuric acid should be half that of the other acids?)

Experiment 9.1

To make a molar solution of sodium carbonate for use in the laboratory (C)

Calculate the weight of sodium carbonate (Na_2CO_3) contained in 250 cm³ of a molar solution and, using a dry 250 cm³ beaker as a container, weigh exactly this amount of sodium carbonate.

Fill another 250 cm³ beaker about two-thirds full of water and slowly, with continuous stirring, add the sodium carbonate to the water. Wash

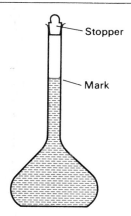

Figure 48

the remaining grains of sodium carbonate into the solution with a little water.

Pour the solution through a filter funnel into a 250 cm³ graduated flask (*figure 48*). Rinse the remaining drops of solution on the beaker and filter funnel into the flask with small quantities of water. Make the solution up to the mark on the neck of the flask by adding more water. Put the stopper into the flask and invert it several times, holding the stopper in position, to mix the solution.

Chemical equations

The overall results of a chemical change can be represented by the symbols or formulae of the substances which are put into a reaction and of those which are produced. The commonest type of equation is one in which the compounds are represented by their empirical formulae. This can be called a *formal equation*.

The elements hydrogen, oxygen, nitrogen, chlorine, bromine, and iodine are represented as diatomic molecules when they are not combined with other elements (p. 72). The accepted method of representing a diatomic molecule is to put a small $_2$ at the base and to the right of the symbol: H_2, O_2, N_2, Cl_2, Br_2, I_2. Do not write 2H etc.; this represents two separate atoms of hydrogen (H + H), whereas H_2 represents two atoms joined together. All other elements are regarded as monatomic and are represented by a single symbol.

Example $$2H_2 + O_2 \rightarrow 2H_2O$$

This equation indicates:

(1) Hydrogen combines with oxygen to form water.
(2) Two molecules of hydrogen combine with one molecule of oxygen to form two molecules of water or the same ratio in g-molecules.
(3) The molecules of hydrogen and oxygen contain two atoms each.
A molecule of water contains two atoms of hydrogen combined with one atom of oxygen.

(4) (a) The weight of hydrogen = the weight of four atoms of hydrogen = $4 \times 1 = 4$.
   (b) The weight of oxygen = the weight of two atoms of oxygen = $2 \times 16 = 32$.
   (c) The weight of water = 2 (the weight of two atoms of hydrogen + the weight of one atom of oxygen) = $2[(2 \times 1) + 16] = 2[18] = 36$.

Thus, 4 parts by weight of hydrogen combine with 32 parts by weight of oxygen to form 36 parts by weight of water.

The determination of an equation by experiment

You will notice in Table 4 that the ratio of the g-formulae of the substances is the same as the ratio of their formula weights. Thus if we can discover the ratio of numbers of g-formulae of each substance which takes part in a reaction, we can construct an equation by writing the formulae of the substances in the same ratio.

Experiment 9.2

To determine the equation for the dehydration of hydrated copper sulphate (C)

Revise Experiment 4.8 on p. 42. Repeat this experiment, this time recording your results in g-formula units instead of g units. Assume the formula for anhydrous copper sulphate ($CuSO_4$) and the formula for water (H_2O).

Specimen results

Weight of crucible	= 4·94 g
Weight of crucible + hydrated copper sulphate	= 5·85 g
Weight of crucible + anhydrous copper sulphate	= 5·52 g

∴ Weight of anhydrous copper sulphate = $(5·52 - 4·94)$ g = 0·58 g
Weight of water = $(5·85 - 5·52)$ g = 0·33 g
1 g-formula of $CuSO_4$ = $(64 + 32 + 64)$ g = 160 g
1 g-formula of H_2O = $(2 + 16)$ g = 18 g
∴ Ratio of g-formulae of $CuSO_4$: g-formulae of H_2O

$$= 0·58/160 \quad : \quad 0·33/18$$
$$= 0·0036 \quad : \quad 0·018$$
$$= 1 \quad : \quad 5$$

It follows that the composition of hydrated sulphate is 1 part $CuSO_4$ to 5 parts H_2O. The formula for hydrated copper sulphate is, therefore, $CuSO_4.5H_2O$ and the equation for its decomposition is:

$$CuSO_4.5H_2O \rightarrow CuSO_4 + 5H_2O$$

Similar investigations can be carried out on other salt hydrates.
N.B. It is important to realize that equations are derived from practical determinations of quantities of reactants and products. The mere construction of a balanced equation, as shown below, does not ensure that the reaction can take place in the quantities given in the equation. However, there is neither the time nor the necessity to repeat all the practical work: some simple equations can be derived by the application of the following rules.

Some rules for constructing equations

(i) Write the reaction in words:

e.g., magnesium combines with oxygen to form magnesium oxide.

(ii) Write the symbols for the elements and the correct empirical formulae for the compounds:

$$Mg + O_2 \rightarrow MgO$$

(iii) Check that the valencies in the formulae balance:

$$Mg \text{ has valency} = 2, \quad O \text{ has valency} = 2$$

(iv) Check that the elements hydrogen, oxygen, nitrogen, chlorine, bromine, and iodine have been represented as diatomic molecules—H_2, O_2, N_2, Cl_2, Br_2, I_2—if they are not combined with any other element.

(v) Balance the equation. The numbers of atoms of each element must be the same on both sides of the equation (the law of conservation of mass, p. 17):

$$2Mg + O_2 \rightarrow 2MgO$$

N.B. A number in front of a formula means that the whole formula is doubled or trebled, etc. A number at the base of a symbol means that that symbol alone is doubled or trebled, etc.

Here are some examples of the construction of chemical equations step by step:

Example 1

(i) Sodium + oxygen $\rightarrow$ sodium oxide

(ii) $\quad$ Na $\quad + \quad O_2 \quad \rightarrow \quad\quad Na_2O$

(iii) Valency of $Na_2 = 2 \times 1 = 2$

Valency of $O = 2 \quad\quad \therefore Na_2O$ is correct.

(iv) Oxygen is represented by O_2 when it is not combined with another element.

(v) There are two oxygen atoms on the left; therefore, on the right Na_2O must be doubled ($2Na_2O$). There are now four sodium atoms on the right; therefore, four sodium atoms must be shown on the left (4Na).

Balanced equation: $4Na + O_2 \rightarrow 2Na_2O$.

Example 2

(i) Iron + chlorine $\rightarrow$ iron (III) chloride

(ii) Fe $\quad + \quad Cl_2 \quad \rightarrow \quad\quad FeCl_3$

(iii) Valency of Fe = 3

Valency of $Cl_3 = 3 \times 1 = 3 \quad\quad \therefore FeCl_3$ is correct.

(iv) Chlorine is represented by Cl_2 when it is not combined with another element.

(v) There are two chlorine atoms on the left and three on the right. As it would be incorrect to represent free chlorine on the left as either Cl_3 or $3Cl$, a balance of chlorine atoms can only be obtained by showing six chlorine atoms on each side. This is done by writing $3Cl_2$ on the left and $2FeCl_3$ on the right.

$2FeCl_3$ means that the whole formula is doubled. There are now two iron atoms on the right; therefore two iron atoms must be shown on the left (2Fe).

Balanced equation: $2Fe + 3Cl_2 \rightarrow 2FeCl_3$

Example 3

  (i) Copper oxide + nitric acid $\rightarrow$ copper nitrate + water

  (ii) CuO + HNO_3 $\rightarrow$ $Cu(NO_3)_2 + H_2O$

 (iii) Valency of $Cu = 2$ Valency of $O = 2$

     $\therefore$ CuO is correct.

     Valency of $H = 1$ Valency of $NO_3 = 1$

     $\therefore$ HNO_3 is correct.

     Valency of $Cu = 2$ Valency of $(NO_3)_2 = 1 \times 2 = 2$

     $\therefore$ $Cu(NO_3)_2$ is correct.

  (iv) —

  (v) When balancing radicals in an equation, regard them as single units, e.g. (NO_3), not as individual atoms. There are two nitrate radicals on the right and one on the left. As it would be incorrect to alter the formula HNO_3, two nitrate radicals can only be shown on the left by doubling the whole formula $(2HNO_3)$. The numbers of the other atoms now balance.

     Balanced equation: $CuO + 2HNO_3 \rightarrow Cu(NO_3)_2 + H_2O$

Further information which may be included in chemical equations

(1) *The physical state of the substances* is often shown by writing (s) (l) (g) or (aq) at the base of a formula. These symbols represent respectively: solid, liquid, gas, aqueous solution. For example:

$$3Fe(s) + 4H_2O(g) \rightarrow Fe_3O_4(s) + 4H_2(g)$$

(Solid iron reacts with steam to form a solid oxide of iron and gaseous hydrogen.)

$$NaOH(aq) + HCl(aq) \rightarrow NaCl(aq) + H_2O(l)$$

(Aqueous solutions of sodium hydroxide and hydrogen chloride react to form an aqueous solution of sodium chloride and water.)

(2) *The physical condition* necessary to bring about a chemical change can be shown:

$$CaCO_3 \xrightarrow{heat} CaO + CO_2$$

(Calcium carbonate, when heated, decomposes to calcium oxide and carbon dioxide.)

(3) *A reversible reaction* is shown $\rightleftharpoons$, for example:

$$2HgO \rightleftharpoons 2Hg + O_2$$

Mercury (II) oxide can decompose to form mercury and oxygen; mercury and oxygen can combine to form mercury (II) oxide.

This further information is not always included in a chemical equation. It is only shown if needed to emphasize one aspect of a reaction. For example, if we are discussing the reversible nature of chemical reactions we should write:

$$CaCO_3 \rightleftharpoons CaO + CO_2$$

for the decomposition of calcium carbonate. But if we merely wanted to indicate that calcium oxide can be manufactured by the decomposition of calcium carbonate, we should write:

$$CaCO_3 \rightarrow CaO + CO_2$$

Limitations of the use of formal chemical equations

Devices such as models, diagrams, equations, etc. make the study of scientific matters easier. For example, if we wish to explain the working of a car engine, models, sketches, and blue-prints of the engine could well be easier to understand than a study of the engine itself. So it is with formal chemical equations. They represent in a concise manner some aspects of a chemical change, but to represent other aspects we may have to use a different type of equation. On page 96 and 106 the use of ionic equations will be explained. These represent some of the electrical changes which take place during a chemical reaction. In other words, we shall use whichever device suits our purpose best, provided that it is based on experiment and observation.

The use of chemical equations to calculate reacting weights

The most useful information which can be obtained from a formal chemical equation is the relative weights of the reactants and the products.

In order to do this it must be assumed that the reaction which the equation represents is the only one which takes place; if the reaction is reversible or if a secondary reaction takes place, calculations based on the equation alone may not be accurate.

Method
(1) From the equation, calculate the weights of those substances about which information is given or required.
(2) Construct a statement of the reacting weights, putting at the end the substance about which information is required.
(3) The units of weight which are used do not matter provided they are the same throughout the statement.

Example 1 Calculate the weight of magnesium oxide formed when 3 g of magnesium are burned in oxygen.

$$2Mg + O_2 \rightarrow 2MgO$$
$$(2 \times 24) \qquad 2[24 + 16]$$
$$48 \qquad\qquad 80$$

$\therefore$ 48 g of magnesium form 80 g of magnesium oxide

$\therefore$ 1 g of magnesium forms $\dfrac{80}{48}$ g of magnesium oxide

$\therefore$ 3 g of magnesium form $\dfrac{80}{48} \times 3$ g

$$= \underline{5\ g} \text{ of magnesium oxide}$$

Example 2 Calculate the weight of calcium carbonate which must be heated in order to make 7 tonnes* of calcium oxide.

$$CaCO_3 \quad \rightarrow CaO + CO_2$$
$$40 + 12 + (3 \times 16) \quad 40 + 16$$
$$100 \quad\quad 56$$

∴ 56 tonnes of calcium oxide are formed from 100 tonnes of calcium carbonate

∴ 7 tonnes of calcium oxide are formed from $\dfrac{100}{56} \times 7$ tonnes

$$= \underline{12 \cdot 5 \text{ tonnes of calcium carbonate}}$$

Example 3 Calculate the weight of copper oxide which will react with a solution containing 3·6 g of sulphuric acid.

$$CuO + \quad H_2SO_4 \quad \rightarrow CuSO_4 + H_2O$$
$$64 + 16 \quad (2 \times 1) + 32 + (4 \times 16)$$
$$80 \quad\quad 98$$

∴ 98 g of sulphuric acid react with 80 g of copper oxide

∴ 3·6 g of sulphuric acid react with $\dfrac{80}{98} \times 3 \cdot 6$ g

$$= \underline{2 \cdot 9 \text{ g}} \text{ of copper oxide}$$

Example 4 Calculate the weight of hydrogen formed together with 3·2 g of magnesium sulphate, when magnesium reacts with dilute sulphuric acid.

$$Mg + H_2SO_4 \rightarrow \quad MgSO_4 \quad + \quad H_2$$
$$24 + 32 + (4 \times 16) \quad (2 \times 1)$$
$$120 \quad\quad 2$$

∴ 120 g of magnesium sulphate are formed together with 2 g of hydrogen

∴ 3·2 g of magnesium sulphate are formed together with $\dfrac{2}{120} \times 3 \cdot 2$ g

$$= \underline{0 \cdot 053 \text{ g}} \text{ of hydrogen}$$

Problems

(1) An element X has an atomic weight of 65 and a combining weight of 32·5. Write the formulae for the oxide, chloride, hydroxide, nitrate, sulphate, and carbonate of X.

(2) Calculate the empirical formulae of compounds of the following composition by weight:
(a) Mg 25·3%, Cl 74·7%
(b) Ca 40%, C 12%, O 48%
(c) K 44·8%, S 18·4%, O 36·8%
(d) Mg 9·8%, S 13·0%, O 26%, H_2O 51·2%
(3) (a) Calculate the weight of magnesium chloride formed when 12·0 g of magnesium react with excess chlorine.

* 1 tonne = 1000 kilogrammes

(b) Calculate the weight of calcium oxide formed when 2·0 g of calcium are burned in oxygen.

(c) Calculate the weight of magnesium which, when it is burned in oxygen, will form 10 g of magnesium oxide.

(d) Calculate the weight of oxygen required to change 4·6 g of sodium into sodium oxide.

(4) Weigh accurately about 0·1 g of potassium permanganate. Dissolve it by shaking it vigorously with 100 cm³ of water. Dilute it by known amounts until the colour is only just visible. Calculate (a) the g-formula weight of potassium permanganate ($KMnO_4$) (b) the number of particles represented by $KMnO_4$ which are contained in your original potassium permanganate (c) the number of particles of $KMnO_4$ which are contained in one drop of your final solution (Avogadro's number $= 6 \times 10^{23}$).

(5) Calculate the number or fraction of g-formulae in (a) 66 g of carbon dioxide (b) 8 g of sulphur dioxide (c) 6·3 g of nitric acid (d) 513 g of sugar ($C_{12}H_{22}O_{11}$).

(6) Calculate the weight of (a) 2 g-formulae of sodium chloride (b) 0·5 g-formula of anhydrous sodium sulphate (c) 0·1 g-formula of sodium hydroxide (d) 0·05 g-formula of silver nitrate.

(7) Calculate the molarity of the following solutions: (a) 4 g of sodium hydroxide in 1 litre (b) 12·6 g of nitric acid in 1 litre (c) 8 g of sodium hydroxide in 250 cm³ (d) 4·25 g of silver nitrate in 250 cm³.

(8) Calculate (a) the weight of hydrated sodium sulphate ($Na_2SO_4 . 10H_2O$) in 1 litre of a 0·1 M solution (b) the weight of calcium chloride in 200 cm³ of a 2 M solution (c) the weight of sulphuric acid in 250 cm³ of a 0·125 M solution (d) the weight of hydrated barium chloride ($BaCl_2 . 2H_2O$) in 1 litre of a 0·2 M solution.

Summary

(1) An atom is the smallest particle of an element.

(2) A symbol represents one atom of an element.

(3) The atoms of some elements combine with each other to form larger particles called molecules.

(4) Atomicity in the number of atoms contained in one molecule of an element.

(5) The unit for the approximate weights of atoms or molecules is the weight of one hydrogen atom.

(6) A g-atom is the weight of Avogadro's number (N_A) of atoms of an element.

(7) An empirical formula represents the simplest ratio of the atoms of the component elements of a compound.

(8) Valency is the combining capacity of an atom compared with that of an atom of hydrogen, which is said to have a valency of one.

(9) In an empirical formula the valency of the metallic part equals the valency of the non-metallic part.

(10) A radical is a group of atoms which exists, with the same composition, in many compounds. It can be allocated a valency. It does not have a separate existence.

(11) A formula weight is the sum of the atomic weights in a given formula.

(12) A molecular weight is the weight of a molecule—for most purposes formula weight and molecular weight are taken to be the same.

(13) A g-formula is the weight of Avogadro's number (N_A) of particles of a compound, assuming that the particle is that which is represented by the empirical formula.

(14) A molar solution contains 1 g-formula of the solute per litre of solution.

(15) In a formal equation compounds are represented by their empirical formulae; elements are represented by a single symbol, with the exception of hydrogen, oxygen, nitrogen, chlorine, bromine and iodine, which are represented as diatomic molecules (H_2, O_2, N_2, Cl_2, Br_2, I_2).

(16) Rules for constructing equations:
  (i) Write the equation in words.
 (ii) Write the symbols for the elements and the empirical formulae for the compounds.
(iii) Check that the valencies in the formulae balance.
 (iv) Check that diatomic elements are shown as such, if they are not combined with any other element.
  (v) Balance the equation.

(17) A number in front of a formula applies to the whole formula. A number at the base of a symbol applies to that symbol only.

D

Section 10
The electrical nature of matter (1)

Before starting this section you should read Section 6 again. There we learned that chemical change can be brought about by an electric current, and that in this process of electrolysis metallic elements were formed at the cathode (negative electrode) and non-metallic elements were formed at the anode (positive electrode).

In this section we shall study the quantities of elements formed during electrolysis. We shall then use these facts to form a theory about the electrical nature of matter; in this we shall be assisted by the atomic theory expounded in Section 9.

Make sure that you understand the use of the following units:

(i) The *ampere* (amp). This is a unit of electrical *current*.
(ii) The *coulomb*. This is a unit of a *quantity* of electricity. If one amp flows for one second, one coulomb of electricity has passed through the conductor.

$$\text{the number of coulombs} = \text{amps} \times \text{seconds}$$

At first the investigation will be confined to those compounds which conduct electricity both when they are molten and when they are dissolved in water.

Experiment 10.1

To investigate the relation between the weight of copper* formed at a cathode and the quantity of electricity passed (C)

Two strips of thin clean copper sheet, approx. 2 cm × 10 cm, can be used as electrodes. Scratch an A on the anode and a C on the cathode in order to avoid confusion later. Put the anode on to a filter paper (also marked A) and the cathode on to another filter paper (marked C). Determine the combined weight of each electrode and its filter paper. By means of a crocodile clip attach each electrode to a length of wire.

Into a 250 cm³ beaker pour 200 cm³ of 10% solution of copper sulphate crystals in dilute sulphuric acid. Place the two electrodes into the beaker so that they are about 3 cm apart, facing each other, and each submerged to about half its depth. Do not wet the crocodile clips. Clamp the electrodes in this position (*figure 49*). Connect the electrodes through an ammeter (this should be capable of reading up to 0·3 amp) and to a 2 volt source of d.c. electricity.

Switch on the electricity and look at the reading on the ammeter; switch off quickly. The current should be between 0·15 and 0·25 amp.

* From copper (II) salts only.

If it is greater than 0·25 amp, move the electrodes further apart; switch on and off again. Adjust again if necessary until the current is between

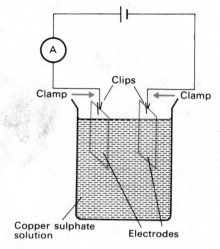

Figure 49

the two limits. The opposite adjustment can be made if the current is too low. The current can also be decreased or increased by raising or lowering the electrodes. Once you have a satisfactory current, note the time and do not alter the position of the electrodes again.

After the current has been flowing for between 45 and 75 minutes, switch it off and note the exact time for which it has flowed.

Carefully unclamp the cathode, holding it by the end which has not been submerged (observe the pink colour of the deposited copper). Dip the electroplated end first into a beaker of water and then into a beaker of acetone. Hold the cathode in the air for a few seconds until the acetone has evaporated (*acetone is inflammable and should be used with care*). Put the cathode on to its filter paper and determine their combined weight. Repeat the process with the anode.

You should find that the cathode has gained weight due to the copper deposited on it and that the anode has lost the same weight due to copper being dissolved from it.

The experiment should be repeated, by you or by other pupils, using different currents and different times.

Specimen results

Weight of cathode + filter paper   = 2·27 g
Weight of cathode + filter paper after electrolysis = 2·52 g
∴ Weight of copper deposited   = 0·25 g
Time = 1 hr (3600 seconds)
Current = 0·20 ampere
∴ Quantity of electricity passed = 0·20 × 3600
                                    = 720 coulombs

∴ The weight of copper deposited by one coulomb $= \dfrac{0·25}{720}$ g

$\qquad\qquad\qquad\qquad\qquad\qquad\qquad\qquad\qquad = 0·000\,34$ g

If in the last experiment the number of coulombs passed through the solution was doubled by increasing the current or the time or both, the weight of copper deposited would also be doubled. By using various quantities of electricity and other electrolytes it can be shown that *the weight of an element produced in electrolysis is proportional to the number of coulombs of electricity which have been passed through the electrolyte.* This generalization is known as *Faraday's First Law of Electrolysis.*

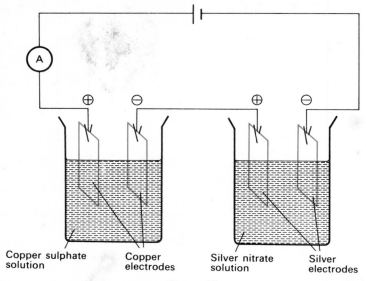

Copper sulphate solution   Copper electrodes   Silver nitrate solution   Silver electrodes

Figure 50

Experiment 10.2

To compare the quantities of electricity required to deposit one gram-atom of different elements (**C** or **D**)

The circuit and general procedure is the same as that for Experiment 10.1, except that two electrodes made of silver gauze are connected in series with the copper electrodes (*figure 50*). This ensures that the same quantity of electricity flows through the whole circuit. (All the electrodes should be about 2 cm × 10 cm.) The silver electrodes are immersed in a 10% solution of silver nitrate in distilled water.

Weigh all four electrodes on their respective filter papers before and after electrolysis. The silver deposit should not exceed about 0·6 g (0·2 amp for about 45 minutes will give this amount); even under these conditions the silver deposit is more easily knocked off than the copper deposit and it must be handled carefully.

Specimen results

Weight of copper cathode	= 2·45 g
Weight of copper cathode after electrolysis	= 2·61 g
∴ Weight of copper deposited	= 0·16 g
Weight of silver cathode	= 3·16 g
Weight of silver cathode after electrolysis	= 3·70 g
∴ Weight of silver deposited	= 0·54 g

Time = 40 minutes
Current = 0·2 ampere

$\therefore$ Quantity of electricity passed = 480 coulombs

1 g-atom of copper = 64 g (approx.)

1 g-atom of silver = 108 g

0·16 g of copper is produced by 480 coulombs

$\therefore$ 64 g (1 g-atom) of copper is produced by $480 \times \dfrac{64}{0·16}$ coulombs

$$= \underline{192\,000\ \text{coulombs}}$$

0·54 g of silver is produced by 480 coulombs

$\therefore$ 108 g (1 g-atom) of silver is produced by $\dfrac{480}{0·54} \times 108$ coulombs

$$= \underline{96\,000\ \text{coulombs}}$$

The quantity of electricity required to form one atom of an element by electrolysis

Experiment 10.2 shows that it takes twice as much electricity to form 1 g-atom of copper from a copper (II) salt as it does to form 1 g-atom of silver from a silver salt by electrolysis. But 1 g-atom of copper and 1 g-atom of silver contain an equal number of atoms (Avogadro's number (N_A)—see Section 9).

$\therefore$ The amount of electricity required to produce 1 atom of copper by electrolysis

$$= \frac{192\,000}{N_A}\ \text{coulombs}$$

And the amount of electricity required to produce 1 atom of silver by electrolysis

$$= \frac{96\,000}{N_A}\ \text{coulombs}$$

$\therefore$ In electrolysis it takes twice as much electricity to produce one atom of copper as it does to produce one atom of silver.

If we call the amount of electricity required to produce 1 atom of silver e, then the amount required to produce one atom of copper = $2e$. e, of course, will be very small and, since no atom can be produced by anything less than this quantity of electricity, e can be regarded as an atom of electricity.

The Faraday

More accurate experiments show that the amount of electricity required to produce 1 g-atom of an element is always 96 500 coulombs or a simple multiple of this. 96 500 coulombs is called *1 faraday*.

Table 5 shows the quantity of electricity which must be passed in order to produce 1 g-atom and 1 atom of some common elements:

Table 5

Metallic elements	To liberate 1 g-atom	To liberate 1 atom
silver	1 faraday	e
sodium	1 faraday	e
copper	2 faradays	$2e$
zinc	2 faradays	$2e$
aluminium	3 faradays	$3e$
hydrogen	1 faraday	e
Non-metallic elements chlorine	1 faraday	e
oxygen	2 faradays	$2e$

Can you suggest a relationship between these quantities and the position of the elements in the Periodic Table (Appendix B)?

The theory of electrolysis

The evidence

(1) Some compounds, particularly those formed by the combination of metallic elements with non-metallic elements, conduct electricity when they are molten or dissolved in water.

(2) During the electrolysis of these compounds, metallic elements are produced at the negative electrode and non-metallic elements are produced at the positive electrode.

(3) The weight of an element formed by electrolysis is proportional to the quantity of electricity which has passed.

(4) The quantity of electricity which must be passed in order to produce 1 g-atom of an element is 1 faraday or a simple multiple of this quantity.

(5) The quantity of electricity which must be passed in order to produce 1 atom of an element is 1 faraday $\div$ Avogadro's number, or a simple multiple of this quantity.

The theory

(1) Some compounds, particularly those formed by the combination of metallic elements with non-metallic elements, when molten or dissolved in water consist of charged particles. We shall call these particles *ions*.

(2) These ions are free to move (*figure 51*); the positive ions move towards the cathode (negative electrode); the negative ions move towards the anode (positive electrode).

(3) As metallic elements are formed at the cathode, we can assume that the ions of metallic elements are positively charged.

(4) Similarly the ions of the non-metallic elements are negatively charged.

(5) At an electrode ions can lose their charge (they can be *discharged*) and form atoms.

(6) In order to become discharged, positive ions must receive one or more negative charges from the cathode. This unit of negative charge we shall call the *electron*. The electron can be regarded as an atom of electricity (the symbol e^- will be used).

Example 1 Two electrons are required to form 1 atom of copper during electrolysis. Therefore, the copper (II) ions carry two positive charges each (Cu^{2+}).

The action at the cathode can be shown by the equation:

$$Cu^{2+} + 2e^- \rightarrow Cu$$
$$\text{(solution)} \quad \text{(from cathode)} \quad \text{(metal)}$$

Example 2 One electron is required to form one atom of silver during electrolysis. Therefore, silver ions carry one positive charge each ($Ag+$).

$$Ag^+ + e^- \rightarrow Ag$$
$$\text{(solution)} \quad \text{(from cathode)} \quad \text{(metal)}$$

(7) In order to be discharged, negative ions must give up one or more negative charges, i.e. one or more electrons, to the anode.

Example 1 In order to form one atom of chlorine (half a molecule) during electrolysis, one unit of electricity must be passed. Therefore, the ions of chlorine (chloride ions) must carry one negative charge (Cl^-).

The action at the anode:

$$Cl^- \rightarrow \tfrac{1}{2}Cl_2 + e^-$$
$$\text{(gas)} \quad \text{(to anode)}$$

Example 2 In order to form one atom of oxygen (half a molecule) during electrolysis, two units of electricity must be passed. Therefore,

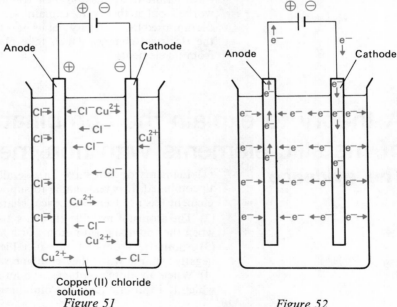

Copper (II) chloride solution

Figure 51   *Figure 52*

the ions of oxygen (oxide ions) must carry two negative charges (O^{2-}).

The action at the anode:

$$O^{2-} \rightarrow \tfrac{1}{2}O_2 + 2e^-$$
$$\text{(gas)} \quad \text{(to anode)}$$

(8) There must be a steady movement of positive ions towards the cathode and negative ions towards the anode, otherwise the electrolysis would stop as soon as the ions closest to the electrode had been discharged (*figure 51*).

Example The electrolysis of copper (II) chloride:

The function of anodes and cathodes

An anode receives electrons from the electrolyte (the function of the anode is different in Experiments 10.1 and 10.2).

A cathode gives electrons to the electrolyte (*figure 52*).

Electrons enter the electrolyte at the cathode and leave the electrolyte at the anode. The electrons entering the electrolyte may not be the ones which leave it, but, if we assume all electrons to be identical, the overall effect is a flow of electrons through the electrolyte, and in this way the electrical circuit is completed between the cathode and the anode.

The relation between ionic charge and valency

Table 5 shows that the number of units of charge on an ion is the same as the valency of the element. Thus copper, in copper (II) compounds, has a valency of two and the copper (II) ion has two positive charges; silver in silver compounds has a valency of one and the silver ion has one positive charge.

This is the first evidence we have of a connection between the electrical nature of atoms and their combining capacity (valency). We have worked out a theory to explain what happens when a compound is decomposed by electricity; let us now try to work out a theory to explain the electrical changes which take place when a compound is formed from its elements.

A theory to explain the combination
of metallic elements with non-metallic elements

The evidence

(1) Elements do not have an overall electrical charge when they are uncombined. It is reasonable to suppose, therefore, that an atom of an element has no overall electrical charge.

(2) The atoms of metallic elements appear to acquire a positive charge when they combine with atoms of non-metallic elements.

(3) Similarly, atoms of non-metallic elements appear to acquire a negative charge when they combine with atoms of metallic elements.

(4) When an atom combines, the number of units of electrical charge which it acquires equals its combining capacity (valency).

The theory

(1) It is reasonable to suppose that what happens when two elements combine is the reverse of what happens when the resulting compound is decomposed by electrolysis.

(2) In electrolysis, a positive ion in a compound gains one or more electrons to become an electrically neutral atom (p. 92),

e.g. $$Na^+ + e^- \rightarrow Na$$

Therefore, an atom of a metallic element appears to give up one or more electrons, forming a positive ion, when it combines with a non-metallic element,

e.g. $$Na \rightarrow Na^+ + e^-$$

(3) In electrolysis, a negative ion in a compound gives up one or more electrons to become an electrically neutral atom,

e.g. $$Cl^- \rightarrow \tfrac{1}{2}Cl_2 + e^-$$

Therefore, an atom of a non-metallic element appears to receive one or more electrons, forming a negative ion when it combines with a metallic element.

$$\tfrac{1}{2}Cl_2 + e^- \rightarrow Cl^-$$

(4) *To sum up, atoms of metallic elements appear to give electrons to atoms of non-metallic elements when they form a compound together.*

Therefore, in compounds formed between metallic and non-metallic elements, the valency of a metallic atom equals the number of electrons it gives, and the valency of a non-metallic atom equals the number of electrons it receives.

Here are some examples:

Example 1   When sodium (valency 1) combines with chlorine (valency 1) to form sodium chloride, one atom of sodium gives one electron to one atom of chlorine:

$$Na \rightarrow Na^+ + e^-$$

$$\tfrac{1}{2}Cl_2 + e^- \rightarrow Cl^-$$

These two equations can be combined:

$$Na + \tfrac{1}{2}Cl_2 \rightarrow Na^+Cl^-$$

Example 2   When magnesium (valency 2) combines with oxygen (valency 2) to form magnesium oxide, each magnesium atom gives 2 electrons to each oxygen atom:

$$Mg \rightarrow Mg^{2+} + 2e^-$$
$$\tfrac{1}{2}O_2 + 2e^- \rightarrow O^{2-}$$
$$Mg + \tfrac{1}{2}O_2 \rightarrow Mg^{2+}O^{2-}$$

Example 3   When calcium (valency 2) combines with chlorine (valency 1) to form calcium chloride, each calcium atom gives two electrons and two chlorine atoms receive one of these electrons each:

$$Ca \rightarrow Ca^{2+} + 2e^-$$
$$Cl_2 + 2e^- \rightarrow 2Cl^-$$
$$Ca + Cl_2 \rightarrow Ca^{2+}(Cl^-)_2$$

Elements (usually metals) which tend to lose electrons and form positive ions are said to be *electropositive*. Elements (usually non-metals) which tend to gain electrons and form negative ions are said to be *electronegative*.

Structure of solid ionic compounds

Solid compounds are not good conductors of electricity and cannot be electrolysed; but this does not rule out the possibility that they consist of ions. In Section 8 we decided that some of the physical properties of solids could be explained by assuming that they consisted of individual particles closely packed and held together by forces which were greater the nearer the particles were together. It is possible that the type of compound which we have been studying in this section consists of ions, even when it is in the solid state; and that the solid cannot be electrolysed, simple because the ions are held tightly together and are not free to move.

Further evidence is to be found in their melting and boiling points (see Table 6). Compounds such as sodium chloride which conduct electricity when they are in the liquid state have much higher melting and boiling points than substances such as water, ethanol, and hydrogen chloride which do not conduct electricity when they are in the liquid state.

This implies that the particles in sodium chloride are much more difficult to separate than the particles in water and ethanol; therefore, the particles in sodium chloride are held together by much greater forces. These forces could be the strong electrostatic forces between positively charged sodium ions and negatively charged chloride ions in solid sodium chloride. This type of bond between combined particles is called the *electrovalent (or ionic) bond*.

Table 6

	Melting point	Boiling point
sodium chloride	804°C	1413°C
calcium chloride	772°C	1600°C
calcium oxide	2572°C	2850°C
water	0°C	100°C
ethanol (alcohol)	−117°C	78°C
hydrogen chloride	−112°C	−84°C

Ionic equations

Ionic equations can be used to represent reactions in which ions form part of the reactants or the products. For example, the combination of magnesium and oxygen can be represented by a formal equation:

$$2Mg + O_2 \rightarrow 2MgO$$

or by an ionic equation:

$$Mg + \tfrac{1}{2}O_2 \rightarrow Mg^{2+}O^{2-}$$

In an ionic equation the sum of the electrical changes must balance. Instead of the conventional representation of diatomic elements, single symbols, e.g. O, or half a single formula, e.g. $\tfrac{1}{2}O_2$, can be used to avoid a lot of tedious doubling of the numbers of particles.

The change which takes place in a single particle, for example the formation of a magnesium ion from a magnesium atom, can be shown by an ionic half-equation:

$$Mg \rightarrow Mg^{2+} + 2e^-$$

The choice of which type of equation to use must be governed by the type of information you wish to convey. If it is simply a matter of calculating reacting weights, then a formal equation will do; but if it is necessary to show the ionic nature of a reactant or a product, then an ionic equation should be used. Further examples will be found in the following section.

Some limitations of the theory of compound formation

(1) Many compounds do not conduct electricity under any normal conditions and some only conduct electricity when they are dissolved in certain solvents such as water. It is therefore unlikely that these compounds, when they are pure, contain ions and the theory of compound formation just worked out cannot be applied to them.

(2) We have assumed that the ions of a compound when it is dissolved in water are the same as they are when the compound is on its own. In fact, this is rarely true; most simple ions react with water molecules to form larger and more complex ions. For example, the simple oxide ion (O^{2-}) and the simple hydrogen ion (H^+) do not exist in aqueous solution; they are combined with the water molecules:

$$O^{2-} + H_2O \rightarrow 2OH^-$$
$$H^+ + H_2O \rightarrow H_3O^+$$

Simple ions after they have combined with water molecules are said to be hydrated.

OH^- is called a hydrated oxide ion, or, more commonly, a *hydroxide ion*.

H_3O^+ is called a hydrated hydrogen ion, or, more commonly, a *hydronium ion*.

Problems

(1) In Experiment 10.2 no element was formed at the anodes; instead, the silver and copper anodes decreased in weight and presumably went into solution. Remembering that the function of an anode is to acquire electrons, work out a theory to explain the dissolution of these two anodes.

(2) You are provided with two strips of the divalent metal A, an aqueous solution of the sulphate of A, an ammeter and a 2 volt d.c. source. Adopt a procedure similar to that of Experiment 10.1 to determine the atomic weight of A.

(3) Write an account of the use of electroplating in industry.

(4) Investigate the conditions necessary to produce a smooth, coherent deposit of silver on a copper cathode.

(5) 0·000 082 g of oxygen are formed by passing one coulomb of electricity. Calculate the weight of oxygen formed by a current of 0·80 amp flowing for one hour.

(6) A current of 2·6 amp flowing for 4 minutes produces 0·206 g of copper. Calculate the weight of copper produced by a current of 2·4 amp flowing for 12·5 minutes.

(7) For how long must a current of 0·50 amp flow in order to form 1 g of silver by electrolysis (1 faraday = 96 500 coulombs)? Calculate to the nearest hour.

(8) For how long must a current of 0·90 amp flow in order to form 6·35 g of copper by electrolysis? Calculate to the nearest hour.

(9) The metallic element X has an atomic weight of 52. During an electrolysis of one of its compounds, 1·04 g of X were formed by passing a current of 0·1 amp for 10·5 hours. Calculate the charge on an ion of X and write the formula for its chloride.

(10) During an electrolysis of a solution of a salt of the divalent element Y, 0·88 g of Y were formed by passing a current of 0·2 amp for 4 hours. Calculate the atomic weight of Y.

(11) Use the Periodic Table of the elements to help you to suggest the charge on the ions of the following elements: (a) lithium (b) barium (c) sulphur (d) iodine (e) fluorine (f) aluminium.

(12) Construct ionic equations for the following reactions: (a) potassium + oxygen → potassium oxide (b) calcium + oxygen → calcium oxide (c) magnesium + chlorine → magnesium chloride (d) aluminium + oxygen → aluminium oxide (e) potassium + bromine → potassium bromide.

Summary

(1) Quantity of electricity is measured in coulombs (amps × seconds) Faraday's First Law of Electrolysis states: The weight of an element produced in electrolysis is proportional to the quantity of electricity which has been passed.

(2) The quantity of electricity required to produce 1 g-atom of an element by electrolysis is 1 faraday (96 500 coulombs) or a simple multiple of 1 faraday (Faraday's Second Law).

(3) The quantity of electricity required to produce 1 atom of an element by electrolysis is 1 electron (96 500 ÷ Avogadro's number) or a simple multiple of 1 electron.

Since no atom can be produced by anything less than 1 electron, the electron is regarded as the smallest unit of electricity. It is said to be a negative charge and is given the symbol e^-.

(4) Ions of metallic (electropositive) elements are positively charged and move towards the cathode; ions of non-metallic (electronegative) elements are negatively charged and move towards the anode.

(5) The number of charges on an ion equals the valency of the element.

(6) An electric current can be regarded as a flow of electrons. During electrolysis, electrons pass to the electrolyte from the cathode and from the electrolyte to the anode. A cathode gives electrons, an anode receives them.

(7) When some compounds are formed, atoms of metallic elements appear to give electrons to atoms of non-metallic elements. Compounds formed in this way are made up of positive and negative ions. These compounds conduct electricity when molten and they usually have

higher melting and boiling points than compounds which do not conduct electricity when molten. The ions in an ionic compound are said to be held together by an electrovalent bond. Note: The work in this section does not offer an explanation of the formation of compounds which do not conduct electricity when molten.

(8) Ionic equations are useful representations of reactions in which one or more of the reactants or products is ionic.

(9) The hydroxide ion (OH^-) is the hydrated form of the oxide ion (O^{2-}), and the hydronium ion (H_3O^+) is the hydrated form of the hydrogen ion (H^+).

Section 11

Chlorides of metals–hydrogen chloride–acids (2)– ionic equations

The element chlorine does not occur naturally, but the compounds it forms with metals (chlorides) are abundant. The best known chloride is sodium chloride (common salt). In this section we shall study the compounds which chlorine forms with metals and with hydrogen, going on to study the element itself in Section 12.

Experiment 11.1

To investigate the action of (a) aqueous sulphuric acid and (b) concentrated sulphuric acid on some chlorides of metals **(C)**

(a) Put one small measure of sodium chloride into a small test tube. Add a quarter of a tube of dilute sulphuric acid. Is any gas evolved?
(CAUTION: Never directly smell a gas which is being given off. Hold the reaction vessel about a foot away from your face and waft some of the gas towards your nose with your hand.)
(b) Repeat the experiment using potassium chloride, ammonium chloride, and calcium chloride.

Repeat the experiment again, this time modifying it by using five drops of concentrated sulphuric acid instead of dilute sulphuric acid. Test the gas which is evolved with dry blue litmus paper and then with wet blue litmus paper. Blow across the top of the test tube. Smell the gas carefully.

(CAUTION: Concentrated sulphuric acid contains very little water and it can react violently when water is added to it. When washing the tubes after this experiment, first pour excess acid into a large beaker or into a sink containing water. If you get any acid on any part of your body or clothes, wash it off at once with plenty of water).

Experiment 11.1 indicates:
(1) Dilute sulphuric acid has no apparent action on chlorides of metals.
(2) Concentrated sulphuric acid reacts with chlorides of metals to form a gas. This gas is called hydrogen chloride.

(3) Hydrogen chloride is invisible. It has a distinctive smell and it forms a mist when it mixes with moist air.

(4) Dry hydrogen chloride has little action on dry litmus paper, but it turns wet litmus paper from blue to red. Therefore it appears that hydrogen chloride forms an acidic solution with water.

The action of concentrated sulphuric acid on sodium chloride can be represented by the equation:

$$NaCl + H_2SO_4 \rightarrow NaHSO_4 + HCl$$
$$\text{(sodium hydrogen sulphate)}$$

Work out equations for the action of concentrated sulphuric acid on the other chlorides.

Solutions of hydrogen chloride

Experiment 11.2

To prepare solutions of hydrogen chloride **(D)**

Set up the apparatus shown in *figure 53*. Drip the concentrated sulphuric acid on to the ammonium chloride at the rate of about one drop per

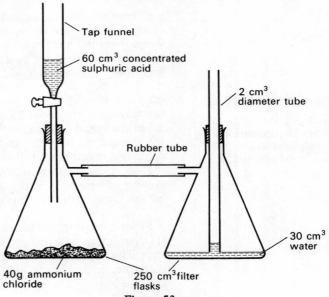

Tap funnel

60 cm³ concentrated sulphuric acid

2 cm³ diameter tube

Rubber tube

30 cm³ water

40g ammonium chloride

250 cm³ filter flasks

Figure 53

second. If the solvent is water, solution takes place quickly (1 cm³ of water can dissolve 444 cm³ of hydrogen chloride at 12°C) and the resulting solution is called hydrochloric acid. Later you will investigate the properties of hydrochloric acid and the properties of a solution of hydrogen chloride in toluene (a liquid hydrocarbon).

Experiment 11.3

To investigate the effect of electricity on solutions of hydrogen chloride **(C or D)**

Set up the apparatus for electrolysis shown in *figure 54*. A solution made by mixing equal volumes of concentrated hydrochloric acid and water can be used as the electrolyte (concentrated hydrochloric acid contains about 36% hydrogen chloride and 64% water by weight).

Connect the electrodes to a 6 volt d.c. source and note the current. Test the gas which is evolved at the anode with wet litmus paper

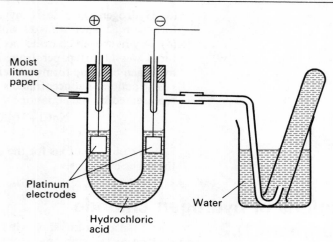

Figure 54

(chlorine bleaches moist litmus).

After waiting for about five minutes, to give time for the air to be swept from the apparatus, collect the gas evolved at the cathode in a test tube and test it for hydrogen. Repeat the experiment using a solution of dry hydrogen chloride in dry toluene.

Experiment 11.4

To investigate the action of solutions of hydrogen chloride on (a) magnesium (b) calcium carbonate **(C)**

(a) Pour about 5 cm³ of a saturated solution of hydrogen chloride in dry toluene on to about 2 cm of magnesium ribbon in a dry test tube. What change, if any, can be observed?

(b) Decant the solution on to a piece of marble (calcium carbonate) contained in another dry tube.

Decant the solution into a small tap funnel. Add about an equal volume of water and shake the mixture for two or three minutes. Run off the lower layer, which is aqueous, and use it to repeat (a) and (b).

From Experiments 11.3 and 11.4 the following can be deduced:

(1) A solution of hydrogen chloride in water is a good conductor of electricity. Hydrogen is formed at the cathode and chlorine at the anode; therefore, hydrochloric acid appears to contain hydrogen ions and chloride ions.

$$\text{At the cathode: } H^+_{(aq)} + e^- \rightarrow \tfrac{1}{2}H_{2(g)}$$
$$\text{At the anode: } \quad Cl^-_{(aq)} \rightarrow \tfrac{1}{2}Cl_{2(g)} + e^-$$

(2) A solution of hydrogen chloride in dry toluene does not conduct electricity; therefore it does not contain ions.

(3) A solution of hydrogen chloride in dry toluene does not react with magnesium or calcium carbonate.

(4) When a solution of hydrogen chloride in toluene is shaken with water, the hydrogen chloride appears to move from the toluene to the water, and the resulting aqueous solution reacts with both magnesium and calcium carbonate:

$$Mg + 2HCl_{(aq)} \rightarrow MgCl_{2(aq)} + H_2$$
$$CaCO_3 + 2HCl_{(aq)} \rightarrow CaCl_{2(aq)} + H_2O + CO_2$$

Does hydrogen chloride consist of ions?

Hydrogen chloride appears to be in the form of hydrogen ions and chloride ions when it is dissolved in water but not when it is dissolved in some other solvents, of which toluene is an example. Furthermore, it can be shown, although not in a school laboratory, that pure liquid hydrogen chloride is not a good conductor of electricity; its ability to carry an electric current is about the same as that of pure water.

It appears, therefore, that hydrogen chloride itself does not consist of ions, but that when it dissolves in water ions are formed. As water is also a non-conductor, these ions must be a product of a reaction between hydrogen chloride and water. This reaction can be represented by the equation:

$$HCl \ + \ H_2O \ \rightarrow \ H_3O^+ \ + \ Cl^-$$

| 1 hydrogen chloride molecule | 1 water molecule | 1 hydrated hydrogen ion | 1 chloride ion |

The hydrated hydrogen ion (the hydronium ion) behaves in most respects as if it were a simple hydrogen ion. For this reason, the formation of ions from hydrogen chloride is frequently shown by the simple equation:

$$HCl_{(g)} + (aq) \rightarrow H^+_{(aq)} + Cl^-_{(aq)}$$

You must remember, however, that this equation does not indicate the essential part which the water plays in the formation of the ions.

Ionization and ionizing solvents

The formation of ions from a substance which in the pure state is not ionized is called *ionization*. A solvent which brings this about is called an *ionizing solvent*. Water is the commonest of these solvents, and the only one discussed in this book; but there are many others, for example, concentrated sulphuric acid and liquid ammonia.

A definition of an acid

(A definition is a precise description of a group of things, which distinguishes it from all other things.) So far, acids have been recognized simply by the action of their aqueous solutions on certain indicators, but the pure dry acid may have no action on indicators. The work in thi section leads to a more useful definition of an acid:

An acid is a compound which can give hydrogen ions. Thus, hydrogen chloride is an acid because it gives hydrogen ions to water:

$$\begin{cases} HCl \quad\quad \rightarrow H^+ + Cl^- \\ \\ H_2O + H^+ \rightarrow H_3O^+ \end{cases}$$

The resulting solution is commonly called hydrochloric acid but, historically, this name arose simply because the solution had an acid or sour taste.

The so-called acidic properties of aqueous solutions, for example the reaction with indicators, metals, bases and carbonates, are caused by the presence of the hydrated hydrogen ions (H_3O^+). For this reason, acidic solutions show many similar reactions and they can be represented in the equations for these reactions by H_3O^+ or H^+. For example, the reactions of aqueous hydrochloric acid and aqueous sulphuric acid on magnesium can both be represented:

$$Mg_{(s)} + 2H^+_{(aq)} \rightarrow Mg^{2+}_{(aq)} + H_{2(g)}$$

The formulae of acids

If a molecule of an acid is capable of giving a hydrogen ion, it must itself contain hydrogen. A molecule of an acid consists of hydrogen combined with a non-metallic atom or radical. Here are the formulae of some other common acids:

hydrobromic acid	HBr
hydriodic acid	HI
nitric acid	HNO_3
sulphuric acid	H_2SO_4
acetic acid	$CH_3.COOH$

If there is more than one hydrogen atom per molecule of an acid, it does not follow that all the hydrogen atoms can be changed into hydrogen ions. Sulphuric acid can ionize in two stages to give two hydrogen ions from each molecule (p. 127), but acetic acid can give only one (p. 250).

$$H_2SO_4 \quad \rightarrow \quad 2H^+ \quad\quad SO_4^{2-}$$
1 molecule of → 2 hydrogen + 1 sulphate
sulphuric acid   ions   ion

$$CH_3COOH \quad \rightarrow \quad H^+ \quad + CH_3.COO^-$$
1 molecule of → 1 hydrogen + 1 acetate
acetic acid   ion   ion

The action of hydrochloric acid on alkalis

Alkalis are bases which are soluble in water (p. 45). The common alkalis are sodium, potassium, calcium and ammonium hydroxides. In aqueous solution they consist of ions (ammonium hydroxide is not fully ionized, see p. 158).

Acidic and alkaline solutions react together to form salts and water; for example, solutions of hydrochloric acid and sodium hydroxide react to form sodium chloride and water:

(i) $HCl + NaOH \rightarrow NaCl + H_2O$

But sodium hydroxide, hydrochloric acid, and sodium chloride consist of ions in aqueous solution; equation (i) can therefore be written:

(ii) $H^+_{(aq)} + Cl^-_{(aq)} + Na^+_{(aq)} + OH^-_{(aq)} \rightarrow Na^+_{(aq)} + Cl^-_{(aq)} + H_2O_{(l)}$

Since chloride and sodium ions are common to both sides, they can be cancelled and the equation written:

(iii) $H^+_{(aq)} + OH^-_{(aq)} \rightarrow H_2O_{(l)}$

The reaction between aqueous solutions of acids and alkalis, therefore, is really a reaction between hydrogen and hydroxide ions. This is true no matter which acids and alkalis are used, and can be illustrated by another example—the reaction between nitric acid and potassium hydroxide to form potassium nitrate and water:

(i) $$HNO_3 + KOH \rightarrow KNO_3 + H_2O$$

(ii) $$H^+_{(aq)} + NO_3^-_{(aq)} + K^+_{(aq)} + OH^-_{(aq)} \rightarrow K^+_{(aq)} + NO_3^-_{(aq)} + H_2O_{(l)}$$

(iii) $$H^+_{(aq)} + OH^-_{(aq)} \rightarrow H_2O_{(l)}$$

The ions of the salt which results from the reaction between an acid and a base will remain independent of each other until evaporation of the water increases their concentration sufficiently to cause them to separate out together as a solid.

Ionic precipitation
Experiment 11.7

The test for chloride ions in aqueous solution (C)

Put four drops of aqueous sodium chloride into a small tube. Add four drops of dilute nitric acid followed by four drops of aqueous silver nitrate. Divide the resulting suspension into three parts. Note the action on the suspension of (a) six drops of ammonium hydroxide solution (b) five drops of sodium thiosulphate (hypo) solution (c) exposure to light for about ten minutes. Repeat the experiment with various other chlorides, including aqueous hydrogen chloride.

The white precipitate formed in Experiment 11.7 is silver chloride. Silver chloride is insoluble in water, but it dissolves readily in ammonium hydroxide solution or sodium thiosulphate solution.

(i) $$AgNO_3 + HCl \rightarrow AgCl + HNO_3$$

With the exception of the precipitate of silver chloride, all the substances represented in the equation are in solution and are in the form of ions.

Therefore, the equation can be written:

(ii) $$Ag^+_{(aq)} + NO_3^-_{(aq)} + H^+_{(aq)} + Cl^-_{(aq)} \rightarrow AgCl_{(s)} + H^+_{(aq)} + NO_3^-_{(aq)}$$

or, cancelling those ions which are common to both sides:

(iii) $$Ag^+_{(aq)} + Cl^-_{(aq)} \rightarrow AgCl_{(s)}$$

The reaction between solutions of sodium chloride and silver nitrate is really a reaction between the two ions, chloride and silver, to form a precipitate of silver chloride. Since all aqueous solutions of chlorides contain the chloride ion, this reaction serves as a test for chloride ions in aqueous solution (the nitric acid is present merely to prevent the precipitation of other insoluble silver salts, for example silver carbonate).

This type of reaction is called an *ionic precipitation* and it can be represented by an ionic equation of which equation (iii) is an example. The reaction will only take place between ions if the resulting substance is insoluble and it is a convenient method for preparing some insoluble compounds. The only other common, insoluble chlorides are those of lead (II), mercury (I) and copper (I).

Experiment 11.8

To investigate the action of light on silver chloride (C)

Soak a filter paper in M NaCl solution and then dry it. Drop spots of silver nitrate solution on to the dry filter paper and observe the formation of silver chloride. Cover one or two of the spots of silver chloride with a coin and leave the filter paper in the light for three or four minutes. Remove the coins and compare the colour of the spots of silver chloride.

When silver chloride is exposed to light it decomposes. The silver, so formed, causes the darkening of the precipitate of silver chloride which you observed in the last experiment. This is the second chemical change we have studied which is caused by light energy—the first was photosynthesis (p. 33). This effect of light on silver salts is the basis of photography.

Construction of ionic equations

The action of metals and alkalis on aqueous solutions of acids, and the precipitation of silver chloride, have served as an introduction to ionic equations. Ionic equations can obviously only be used in reactions in which ions are concerned. The commonest types of reaction for which ionic equations can serve a useful purpose are:

(1) Electrolysis.
(2) The combination of metallic elements with non-metallic elements.
(3) Oxidation and reduction.
(4) Reaction between metals and acids.
(5) Reaction between bases and acids.
(6) Ionic precipitation and precipitation of metals.

There are, of course, many other reactions for which ionic equations could be used; but for work at this level, their use is best confined to those reactions listed above.

You will find that the use of ionic equations can be much easier than the use of formal equations, but, until you have had more experience, a method of deriving an ionic equation from a formal equation may be useful.

It can be done in the following stages:

(1) Write a balanced formal equation—for example:

$$Zn + H_2SO_4 \rightarrow ZnSO_4 + H_2$$
$$\text{zinc} + \text{dilute} \rightarrow \text{zinc sulphate} + \text{hydrogen}$$
$$\text{sulphuric acid} \quad \text{solution}$$

(2) Show those substances which are in the form of ions under the conditions of the experiment as ions. These substances are usually *acids, alkalis, and salts, in aqueous solution.*

$$Zn_{(s)} + 2H^+_{(aq)} + SO_4^{2-}_{(aq)} \rightarrow Zn^{2+}_{(aq)} + SO_4^{2-}_{(aq)} + H_{2(g)}$$

N.B. Many salts and many oxides of metals are in the form of ions in the solid state. It is conventional, however, in elementary chemistry not to represent solid compounds as ions in equations.

(3) Cancel those ions which are common to both sides of the equation:

$$Zn_{(s)} + 2H^+_{(aq)} \rightarrow Zn^{2+}_{(aq)} + H_{2(g)}$$

Some explanations

Our knowledge of the nature of hydrogen chloride and hydrochloric acid can be used to explain some of the other reactions studied in this section.

(1) *Dilute sulphuric acid and chlorides*
When sodium chloride and aqueous sulphuric acid are mixed in aqueous solution, the mixture contains the ions: Na^+, Cl^-, H^+, and SO_4^{2-}.* No hydrogen chloride is apparent because water is present, so the hydrogen and chloride ions remain in solution and do not form hydrogen chloride.

(2) *Concentrated sulphuric acid and chlorides*
The relative acidic strengths of sulphuric acid and hydrogen chloride are about the same. They both ionize almost completely when dissolved in water. There must therefore be some other reason why hydrogen chloride can be displaced from its salts by concentrated sulphuric acid.

The explanation lies in the different boiling points of the two acids.

Hydrogen chloride (boiling point $-83°C$) is a gas at laboratory temperature, whereas sulphuric acid (boiling point $356°C$) is a liquid at laboratory temperature; hydrogen chloride is said to be more volatile than sulphuric acid. Even if the reaction between a chloride of a metal and concentrated sulphuric acid were reversible:

$$NaCl_{(s)} + H_2SO_{4(l)} \rightleftharpoons NaHSO_{4(s)} + HCl_{(g)}$$

the reaction right → left is unlikely to take place, because the hydrogen chloride, being given off as a gas, loses contact with the sodium hydrogen sulphate. Other examples of the effect of physical properties of substances on the course of chemical reactions can be found on pp. 132 and 158.

(3) *The evolution of hydrogen chloride from concentrated hydrochloric acid*
Concentrated hydrochloric acid continuously gives off hydrogen chloride gas. This indicates that the reaction between hydrogen chloride and water is reversible:

$$HCl_{(g)} + H_2O_{(l)} \rightleftharpoons H_3O^+{}_{(aq)} + Cl^-{}_{(aq)}$$

Problems

(1) Investigate the nature of the gas formed at the anode during the electrolysis of dilute hydrochloric acid. Use the bench dilute acid first. Repeat the experiment using a solution made by mixing the bench acid with an equal volume of water.
(2) Write an account of the uses of silver salts in photography.
(3) Perform the following tests on the substance A: (a) the action of heat in a dry tube (b) the action of water (c) the action of concentrated sulphuric acid (d) the action of dilute nitric acid and silver nitrate solution on an aqueous solution of A (e) the electrolysis of an aqueous solution of A.

Record your observations.

* Hydrogen sulphate ion (HSO_4^-) will also be present.

What can you infer about the nature of A?

Construct equations for the reactions which have taken place.

Repeat the tests with the substance B. (A and B are not chlorides)

(4) 50 cm³ of 2 M hydrochloric acid and 2 g of magnesium oxide react completely with each other. Calculate (a) the fraction of a g-formula of hydrogen chloride present in the acid solution and (b) the fraction of a g-formula represented by 2 g of magnesium oxide. (c) Determine the simplest whole number ratio of g-formulae in which the two substances react and hence deduce a possible equation for the reaction.

Summary

(1) Hydrogen chloride is formed when concentrated sulphuric acid reacts with chlorides of metals.

(2) Hydrogen chloride dissolves readily in water, the resulting solution is called hydrochloric acid.

(3) Water acts as an ionizing solvent, reacting with hydrogen chloride to form hydrated hydrogen ions (hydronium ions) and chloride ions:

$$H_2O_{(l)} + HCl_{(g)} \rightarrow H_3O^+_{(aq)} + Cl^-_{(aq)}$$

As a result, hydrochloric acid is a good conductor of electricity and many of its properties are those of the hydrogen and chloride ions.

(4) Hydrogen chloride, when it is pure or when it is in solution in non-ionizing solvents does not consist of ions. As a result, its properties differ from those of its aqueous solution.

(5) An acid is a compound which can give hydrogen ions.

(6) Hydrochloric acid reacts with some metals to form chlorides and hydrogen; it reacts with bases to form chlorides and water.

(7) The essential reaction when aqueous solutions of acids and alkalis are mixed is between hydrogen ions and hydroxide ions:

$$H^+_{(aq)} + OH^-_{(aq)} \rightarrow H_2O_{(l)}$$

(8) The test for chloride ions in aqueous solution is to add dilute nitric acid followed by aqueous silver nitrate. A white precipitate of silver chloride is formed.

(9) Some insoluble compounds can be made by mixing aqueous solutions which together contain the component ions of the compound. This is called ionic precipitation.

(10) The rules for constructing ionic equations are summarized on p. 106

Section 12
Chlorine–bromine–iodine

These three elements form part of group VII of the Periodic Table (p. 288); this is a group of non-metallic elements called the *halogens*. The other member of the group, fluorine, will not be studied in this course.

Chlorine is a heavy, green gas; bromine is a heavy, dark, orange-coloured liquid; iodine is a dark, shiny, crystalline solid. Bromine and iodine readily change into vapour. All are poisonous and must be handled with care.

Their sources and uses

Chlorine occurs mainly in combination with sodium in sodium chloride. The element itself is used for killing bacteria particularly in drinking water and swimming baths. Its useful compounds include sodium chloride, polyvinyl chloride (the plastic PVC), chloroform ($CHCl_3$), DDT, and bleaching agents.

Bromine occurs in the combined state; it is found as bromide ions, in the salts in sea water. Its useful compounds include silver bromide which is used in photography, and dibromoethane which is used in the petroleum industry.

Iodine occurs, combined with sodium, either as sodium iodate or sodium iodide. Its compounds find uses in photography and medicine.

Halide ions

The halogen elements occur chiefly in compounds with metals: chlorides, bromides, and iodides. These compounds are given the general name *halides*. The elements are in the form of negative ions—fluoride ions (F^-), chloride ions (Cl^-), bromide ions (Br^-), and iodide ions (I^-)—which are called the halide ions. In common with the ions of other non-metallic elements they carry a negative charge and the halogens, therefore, are electronegative elements.

The preparation of chlorine

We have already observed that chlorine can be made by the electrolysis of concentrated hydrochloric acid. The chlorine was formed at the anode by the discharge of chloride ions into chlorine atoms which then form chlorine molecules:

$$Cl^- \rightarrow Cl + e^-$$
$$2Cl \rightarrow Cl_2$$

It can also be made by the electrolysis of the concentrated aqueous solution of a chloride of a metal. Industrially it is made during the electrolysis of sodium chloride, either in the form of molten sodium chloride or in the form of brine (p. 275).

Experiment 12.1

To investigate the action of oxidizing agents on hydro-chloric acid (C)

You will require four small test tubes. Put one small measure of an oxidizing agent into each:

(1) potassium dichromate ($K_2Cr_2O_7$)
(2) lead dioxide (PbO_2)
(3) manganese dioxide (MnO_2)
(4) potassium permanganate ($KMnO_4$)

Into the first tube put two drops of concentrated hydrochloric acid and then insert a folded piece of moist litmus paper (blue or red) into the mouth of the tube. The laboratory should be well ventilated when chlorine or bromine are present and the elements should not be smelled directly. Repeat the experiment for each oxidizing agent.

Can you arrange the four oxidizing agents in the order of the speed with which they oxidize hydrochloric acid to chlorine?

The collection of chlorine

(a) If larger quantities of chlorine are needed for investigating its properties, it can be collected in gas jars using the apparatus shown in *figure 55*.

Chlorine is collected over brine rather than over water, because it is much less soluble in brine.

(b) Chlorine can also be collected in a dry gas jar by the method of downward delivery (chlorine is heavier than air) in a fume cupboard (*figure 56*). The small amounts of hydrogen chloride and water vapour in the chlorine do not usually interfere with the reactions of chlorine.

(c) For most of the reactions of chlorine which will be studied in this course, its aqueous solution (chlorine water) is the most convenient. This can be made by the usual method for gas absorption (p. 101)

Oxidation

So far we have considered oxidation to be the giving of oxygen to a substance; thus, if carbon is changed to carbon dioxide it has been oxidized. Substances which can cause oxidation, such as the four used in Experiment 12.1, are called oxidizing agents. The idea of oxidation, however, can be extended. Each of the four reactions in Experiment 12.1 has one chemical change in common; the chloride ions in the hydrochloric acid have been changed first into chlorine atoms and then into chlorine molecules:

$$Cl^- \rightarrow \tfrac{1}{2}Cl_2 + e^-$$

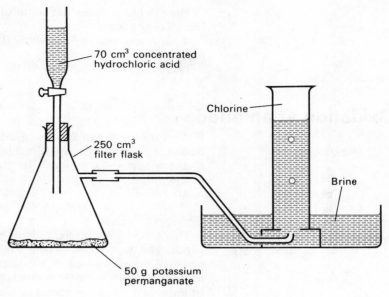

70 cm³ concentrated hydrochloric acid

Chlorine

250 cm³ filter flask

Brine

50 g potassium permanganate

Figure 55

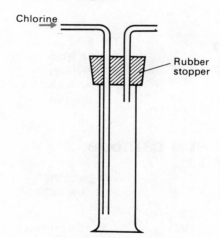

Chlorine

Rubber stopper

Figure 56

The essential part of this change is the removal of an electron from each chloride ion; and this, presumably, is brought about by the oxidizing agent.

Oxygen itself brings about the same removal of electrons when it combines with other elements; for example, when calcium is oxidized by burning it in oxygen, each oxygen atom removes two electrons from each calcium atom:

$$Ca \rightarrow Ca^{2+} + 2e^-$$

$$\left.\begin{array}{l} \\ \tfrac{1}{2}O_2 + 2e^- \rightarrow O^{2-} \end{array}\right\} Ca + \tfrac{1}{2}O_2 \rightarrow Ca^{2+}O^{2-}$$

The extension of the definition of oxidation can therefore be put in the following form:

A particle is said to be oxidized if one or more electrons are removed from it.

There are more examples of this idea of oxidation on p. 113 and p. 114

Oxidation at an anode

If you turn to the explanation of the formation of chlorine at an anode during the electrolysis of hydrochloric acid or an aqueous solution of a chloride (p. 102), you will see that the process at the anode is an oxidation.

An anode has the power to remove electrons from particles of the electrolyte; in this example $Cl^- \rightarrow \frac{1}{2}Cl_2 + e^-$; and chloride ions are therefore oxidized.

This oxidation is brought about by a purely electrical process at the anode, and it is called *anodic oxidation*. Anodic oxidation is a particularly useful method of oxidizing because the anode itself is not changed, so there are no unwanted by-products. Furthermore, the power of the oxidation can be varied by varying the voltage between the anode and the cathode.

Reduction

On p. 62 we learned that reduction is the opposite to oxidation. So far we have considered reduction to be the removal of oxygen from a substance, but we can extend the definition of reduction in the same way as we have extended the definition of oxidation:

A particle is said to be reduced if one or more electrons are given to it.

Reduction at a cathode

Just as an anode can remove electrons from a particle, so a cathode can give electrons to a particle; for example, the discharge of hydrogen ions at a cathode:

$$H^+ + e^- \rightarrow \frac{1}{2}H_2$$

In this process hydrogen ions have gained one electron each and have thus been reduced to hydrogen atoms. Since this is brought about by a purely electrical process at the cathode, it is called *cathodic reduction*.

Chlorine, bromine and iodine as oxidizing agents

Chlorine and bromine are most conveniently used in the form of their saturated solutions in water.* Iodine is only slightly soluble in water, but it dissolves readily if a crystal of potassium iodide is added to the water and this solution is used as the reagent.

* Some of the chlorine and bromine in their aqueous solutions will have reacted with the water. The details of these reactions will not be discussed here and, for simplicity, it will be assumed that all the chlorine and bromine is in the normal molecular form.

Experiment 12.2

To investigate the oxidation of aqueous iron (II) salts **(C)**

Put two drops of an aqueous solution of iron (II) sulphate into a small tube. Add three drops of ammonium hydroxide. The green precipitate is iron (II) hydroxide and this reaction is a convenient test for iron (II) ions in solution:

$$Fe^{2+}_{(aq)} + 2OH^-_{(aq)} \rightarrow Fe(OH)_{2(s)}$$

(Notice that on standing for a minute or two that part of the precipitate which is in contact with the air turns to a rust colour. This is due to oxidation by the air of iron (II) hydroxide to iron (III) hydroxide.)

Into each of three tubes put two drops of aqueous iron (II) sulphate. To the first add six drops of chlorine water; to the second add four drops of bromine water; and to the third add two drops of iodine solution (the different quantities are required simply because of the different concentrations of the three solutions).

Shake the tubes to mix the solutions and then add three drops of ammonium hydroxide to each. A rust-coloured precipitate indicates that iron (III) hydroxide has been formed:

$$Fe^{3+}_{(aq)} + 3OH^-_{(aq)} \rightarrow Fe(OH)_{3(s)}$$

The last reaction is a test for the presence of iron (III) ions in solution.

Experiment 12.2 indicates that chlorine and bromine oxidize iron (II) ions to iron (III) ions, each iron (II) ion having one electron removed from it:

$$\underset{\text{(oxidized)}}{Fe^{2+} \rightarrow Fe^{3+} + e^-}$$

The chlorine and bromine appear to accept electrons from the iron (II) ions; therefore, they are reduced to their respective ions:

$$\underset{\text{(reduced)}}{\tfrac{1}{2}Cl_2 + e^- \rightarrow Cl^-}$$

$$\underset{\text{(reduced)}}{\tfrac{1}{2}Br_2 + e^- \rightarrow Br^-}$$

Combining these half equations:

$$\underset{\text{(oxidized)}}{Fe^{2+}} + \underset{\text{(reduced)}}{\tfrac{1}{2}Cl_2} \rightarrow Fe^{3+} + Cl^-$$

$$\underset{\text{(oxidized)}}{Fe^{2+}} + \underset{\text{(reduced)}}{\tfrac{1}{2}Br_2} \rightarrow Fe^{3+} + Br^-$$

The chlorine and bromine have acted as oxidizing agents; the iron (II) ions have acted as reducing agents.

You will have noticed that iodine has no apparent action on iron (II) sulphate solution. Iodine is a less powerful oxidizing agent than chlorine or bromine.

Experiment 12.3

To investigate the action of chlorine and bromine on aqueous iodides **(C)**

Put two drops of 5% aqueous potassium iodide into each of two small tubes. To the first tube add four drops of chlorine water and to the second add four drops of bromine water.

Notice the formation of a brown solution of iodine. If you add one or two drops of a solution of starch to the iodine solution, a deep blue colour will be formed; this is a sensitive test for iodine.

Repeat the experiment with solutions of other iodides, for example sodium iodide.

These iodides are ionized and the iodide ion is common to them all. The reaction in Experiment 12.3 therefore consists of changing iodide ions into iodine by removing an electron from each of them, i.e. oxidizing them:

$$I^- \rightarrow \tfrac{1}{2}I_2 + e^-$$
(oxidized)

The chlorine and bromine must receive these electrons and be reduced to chloride and bromide ions:

$$\tfrac{1}{2}Cl_2 + e^- \rightarrow Cl^-$$
(reduced)

$$\tfrac{1}{2}Br_2 + e^- \rightarrow Br^-$$
(reduced)

Combining these half equations:

$$I^- + \tfrac{1}{2}Cl_2 \rightarrow \tfrac{1}{2}I_2 + Cl^-$$
(oxidized)   (reduced)

$$I^- + \tfrac{1}{2}Br_2 \rightarrow \tfrac{1}{2}I_2 + Br^-$$
(oxidized)   (reduced)

Chlorine and bromine have acted as oxidizing agents; the iodide ions have acted as reducing agents.

Potassium iodide can be used as a test for many other oxidizing agents. A common method is to use a paper which has been soaked in starch and potassium iodide solutions and then dried. Oxidizing agents liberate iodine on the paper, which then turns blue because of the presence of the starch (see Problem 1, p. 117).

Experiment 12.4
To investigate the relative oxidizing powers of chlorine and bromine **(C)**

To two drops of potassium chloride solution add two drops of bromine water.

To two drops of potassium bromide solution add four drops of chlorine water. Notice the yellow colour of the bromine which is formed.

Experiment 12.4 shows that chlorine has the power to oxidize bromide ions:

$$Br^- + \tfrac{1}{2}Cl_2 \rightarrow \tfrac{1}{2}Br_2 + Cl^-$$
(oxidized)   (reduced)

but bromine has not the power to oxidize chloride ions. It appears therefore that chlorine is the stronger oxidizing agent. It accepts electrons to form chloride ions very readily. Furthermore, these chloride ions do not readily give up their electrons.

The reaction of chlorine with metals

Experiment 12.5
The preparation of iron (III) chloride **(D)**

Set up the apparatus shown in *figure 57*; the boiling tube and the delivery tube must be dry. Run the concentrated hydrochloric acid on to the potassium permanganate at the rate of about one drop every two seconds; allow two minutes for the air to be swept from the apparatus. Heat the iron wire with a small bunsen flame. Remove the flame as soon as the iron glows red hot.

Note that the iron glows more brightly if the flow of chlorine is

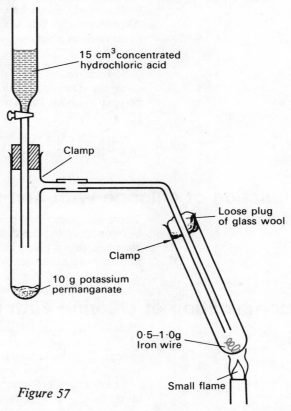

15 cm³ concentrated hydrochloric acid

Clamp

Loose plug of glass wool

Clamp

10 g potassium permanganate

0·5–1·0g Iron wire

Small flame

Figure 57

increased, showing that the reaction between iron and chlorine is exothermic.

After passing chlorine for 2 or 3 minutes, remove the tube containing the product, put a loose plug of glass wool into the open end, and heat it at the closed end holding the tube horizontally (*figure 58*). The product easily vaporizes and it collects as a dark crystalline solid

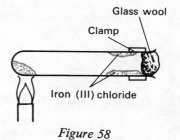

Glass wool

Clamp

Iron (III) chloride

Figure 58

on the cooler parts of the tube, from where it can be scraped with a spatula.

The compound formed is iron (III) chloride:

$$2Fe + 3Cl_2 \rightarrow 2FeCl_3$$

This method can be used for making the chlorides of other metals. Aluminium chloride can be made in this way from aluminium foil; it condenses as a yellow powder in the top part of the tube:

$$2Al + 3Cl_2 \rightarrow 2AlCl_3$$

Sodium reacts violently with chlorine. This can be demonstrated using the same apparatus as in *figure 57*, but the piece of sodium should be small—about the size of a match head—and the tube must be dry:

$$2Na + Cl_2 \rightarrow 2NaCl$$

Since chlorine is removing electrons from sodium in this reaction $(Na + \frac{1}{2}Cl_2 \rightarrow Na^+ + Cl^-)$ it is acting as an oxidizing agent.

The reaction of chlorine with non-metallic elements

There are many compounds of chlorine with non-metallic elements, but generally the direct combination of chlorine with the non-metallic elements takes place less readily than with metallic elements. Phosphorus is an exception to this.

The combination of chlorine with phosphorus

Phosphorus exists in two allotropic forms: red phosphorus and yellow phosphorus. Yellow phosphorus is the more reactive, it burns spontaneously in air when it is dry and for this reason it is stored under water; *it is dangerous and must be treated with caution.*

The reaction between yellow phosphorus and chlorine can be demonstrated with the apparatus used in Experiment 12.5. The piece of phosphorus should be no bigger than a match head and it should be put into the tube, using tongs, while it is still wet.

The phosphorus should not be heated. Within a minute or two it melts and then bursts into flame and forms a pale yellow solid, phosphorus pentachloride:

$$2P + 5Cl_2 \rightarrow 2PCl_5$$

Phosphorus can exert a combining capacity of three as well as five; hence small quantities of phosphorus trichloride, which is a liquid, may also be formed:

$$2P + 3Cl_3 \rightarrow 2PCl_3$$

The combination of chlorine, bromine and iodine with hydrogen

All three elements combine with hydrogen to form hydrogen chloride, hydrogen bromide, and hydrogen iodide respectively. These three compounds are called, collectively, *hydrogen halides.*

The reaction with chlorine is the most vigorous and the reaction with iodine is the least vigorous. Chlorine is said to have the strongest *affinity* for hydrogen.

Some reactions take place more readily if they are irradiated with light rich in ultra-violet rays. The reaction between hydrogen and chlorine, for example, can be explosive in the presence of direct sunlight.

$$H_2 + Cl_2 \rightarrow 2HCl$$
$$H_2 + Br_2 \rightarrow 2HBr$$
$$H_2 + I_2 \rightarrow 2HI$$

The stability of the hydrogen halides

A *stable* substance is one which is difficult to decompose. An *unstable* substance is easy to decompose. At 1000°C, only a trace of hydrogen chloride is decomposed, as opposed to 0·5% of hydrogen bromide, and 33% of hydrogen iodide. Thus hydrogen chloride is the most stable of these three compounds and hydrogen iodide the least stable.

Because of the instability of hydrogen iodide, the reaction between hydrogen and iodine is usually represented as reversible:

$$H_2 + I_2 \rightleftharpoons 2HI$$

Words such as easy, vigorous, stable and unstable, are very loose ways of describing chemical reactions and substances. More precise descriptions must refer to the exchanges of energy which take place during a reaction. (See Section 20.)

The position of the halogens in the periodic table

Having observed the similarities of their properties, you will be reminded that chlorine, bromine, and iodine are in the same group of the Periodic Table. Together with fluorine, they form group VII of the Table.

You should notice that, although the elements within the group are similar, they differ from each other in a regular way. For example, the tendency to form negative ions decreases from chlorine to bromine to iodine, therefore their power as oxidizing agents decreases from chlorine to bromine to iodine. Other examples are to be found in the affinity of the elements for hydrogen and in the stability of their compounds with hydrogen.

In general the reactivity of the elements in Group VII decreases from fluorine to iodine.

Problems

(1) Investigate the oxidizing action of solutions of (a) iron (III) salts and (b) copper (II) salts on potassium iodide (starch-potassium iodide paper can be used).

Hence construct equations for the action between (a) iron (III) ions and iodide ions and (b) copper (II) ions and iodide ions.

(2) To a quarter of a small test tube of bromine water add two small measures of the powdered metal A. Shake the tube until the colour of the bromine disappears. Filter off the excess metal and add ammonium

hydroxide to the solution. Identify A and explain the reactions which have taken place.

(3) To one measure each of the substance X, Y, and Z, add four drops of concentrated sulphuric acid. What do your observations tell you about the nature of the three substances?

(4) 13·85 g of a compound of potassium, chlorine, and oxygen were heated. Oxygen was given off and 7·45 g of potassium chloride remained. Calculate (a) the fraction of a g-formula which 7·45 g of potassium chloride represents (b) the fraction of a g-formula of oxygen (O_2) which is given off (c) the formula of the original compound and the equation for its decomposition.

(5) Report on the use of fluoride in drinking water.

Summary

(1) Fluorine, chlorine, bromine, and iodine are called the halogen elements.

(2) In combination with metals, they occur as halide ions—fluoride (F^-), chloride (Cl^-), bromide (Br^-), iodide (I^-). They are electronegative elements.

(3) Chloride ions, in hydrochloric acid for example, can be changed to chlorine atoms by oxidation, either by chemical oxidizing agents or by the action at an anode (anodic oxidation): $Cl^- \rightarrow Cl + e^-$.

(4) The removal of electrons from a particle is oxidation.

(5) The giving of electrons to a particle is reduction.

(6) Chlorine, bromine, and iodine are oxidizing agents because they can remove electrons from other particles. In this process they themselves are reduced to halide ions.

(7) Chlorine is a more powerful oxidizing agent than bromine, and bromine is a more powerful oxidizing agent than iodine.

(8) Chlorine, bromine, and iodine react readily with metals and with phosphorus.

(9) Chlorine, bromine, and iodine react with hydrogen to form hydrogen halides. The reaction is most vigorous with chlorine and least vigorous with iodine.

(10) The order of stability of the hydrogen halides is (i) hydrogen chloride (most stable) (ii) hydrogen bromide (iii) hydrogen iodide.

Section 13
Sulphur and sulphur dioxide

Occurrence and uses of sulphur

Sulphur occurs as the free element, chiefly in Texas and Louisiana where it is dispersed in limestone. It is extracted by pumping super-heated water into the limestone to melt the sulphur, and then pumping up the molten sulphur by means of compressed air. Sulphur also occurs in the combined state, chiefly as hydrogen sulphide (H_2S) in natural gas and as metal sulphides and sulphates.

Nearly 80 % of all the sulphur is used to make sulphur dioxide which, in turn, is largely used to make sulphuric acid. Some sulphur is mixed with natural rubber to make the rubber more suitable for use in tyres. Smaller quantities are used as a fungicide, in gunpowder, and in many useful compounds such as carbon disulphide (CS_2) and sodium thio-sulphate ($Na_2S_2O_3$).

The allotropes of sulphur

Sulphur at laboratory temperature is a yellow solid. It resembles carbon in that it can exist in two different crystalline forms.

Experiment 13.1

To prepare crystals of sulphur (D)

Put 100 cm³ of xylene into a dry 400 cm³ beaker. Add 30 g of sulphur and heat the beaker on an electric hot plate, stirring occasionally with a 360°C thermometer. When the temperature reaches 135°C remove the beaker from the hot plate, allow it to cool undisturbed, and observe the formation of crystals.

When the temperature falls to 80°C decant the solution into a beaker which has been previously warmed on the hot plate. Decant the solution into a third beaker when the temperature falls to 50°C. Allow to evaporate at room temperature.

Compare the shape of the crystals formed above 80°C with those formed below 50°C; to see the shape of the latter you may have to use a magnifying glass or a low-powered microscope.

Prismatic sulphur
The long, needle-like crystals formed at the higher temperature are

E

crystals of prismatic sulphur, which is also called monoclinic or β sulphur. *Figure 59* is a simplified sketch of their shape.

Rhombic sulphur
The crystals formed at the lower temperature are crystals of rhombic sulphur (*figure 60*), which is also called octahedral or α sulphur.

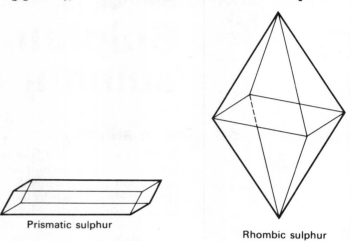

Prismatic sulphur

Rhombic sulphur

Figures 59   *Figure 60*

Transition temperature
If the temperature of rhombic sulphur is raised above 95·5°C it changes into prismatic sulphur, and if prismatic sulphur is kept below 95·5°C it changes into rhombic sulphur. 95·5°C is called the *transition temperature* or *transition point*. An explanation of the existence of different crystalline forms of the same element is to be found on p. 205.

Experiment 13.2
To investigate the action of heat on sulphur **(C)**

Half fill a dry, small test tube with powdered sulphur. Holding the tube with a test tube holder, heat the sulphur very gently. The bunsen flame should be no more than 5 cm high and with just sufficient air to remove the yellow colour from it. You will find that at one point the sulphur becomes very dark and viscous (thick and difficult to pour). Heat it a little longer and you will find that it becomes more mobile (easy to pour). At this point, pour as much of the liquid sulphur as possible into a small beaker half full of cold water. Pick out the pieces of sulphur and examine them.

Plastic sulphur
The rubbery solid obtained by pouring molten sulphur into water is called plastic sulphur. It is non-crystalline.

Sulphur molecules
The smallest individual particles of sulphur which exist normally in the free state consist of groups of eight atoms (S_8). This is the basic unit of which monoclinic, rhombic, and gaseous sulphur are composed. It is conventional in chemical equations, however, to represent sulphur as if it were monatomic (S).

The properties of sulphur

(1) It is insoluble in water. It is a poor conductor of heat and electricity.

(2) It burns to form sulphur dioxide:

$$S + O_2 \rightarrow SO_2$$

(3) It combines with many metals to form sulphides:

$$Fe + S \rightarrow FeS$$

The combining capacity (valency) of sulphur

When it combines with metals, sulphur usually shows a valency of two, and the resulting compounds are called sulphides; e.g. zinc sulphide (ZnS) and aluminium sulphide (Al_2S_3).

If the metal is in group I or II of the Periodic Table the compound which it forms with sulphur is ionic and resembles an oxide (p. 96):

$$\left.\begin{array}{l} Ca \rightarrow Ca^{2+} + 2e^- \\[2em] S + 2e^- \rightarrow S^{2-} \end{array}\right\} Ca + S \rightarrow Ca^{2+}S^{2-}$$

Each sulphur atom receives two electrons and becomes a sulphide ion. In this sort of reaction sulphur and the sulphide ion closely resemble oxygen and the oxide ion.

When sulphur combines with non-metallic elements it exerts valencies of four or six. Thus, when it burns, one atom of sulphur combines with two atoms of oxygen (SO_2); since oxygen has a valency of two, sulphur must be exerting a valency of four. The compound sulphur trioxide (SO_3) can be prepared by the combination of sulphur dioxide with oxygen. In this compound sulphur is exerting a valency of six. Most compounds of sulphur with non-metallic elements are non-ionic.

Sulphur dioxide

Manufacture and uses of sulphur dioxide

Sulphur dioxide occurs in the waste gases from the burning of oil, coal, or the products of oil and coal. Most of it, however, is manufactured by burning sulphur or ores containing sulphur such as iron pyrites (FeS_2). It is used mainly for the manufacture of sulphuric acid (p. 274).

At room temperature and pressure, sulphur dioxide is a gas, but in the laboratory the most convenient source is cylinders of liquid sulphur dioxide. In these cylinders sulphur dioxide is kept under pressure, and the gas can be obtained by carefully opening the valve.

Action of sulphur dioxide on water

In many respects, particularly in its action on water and alkalis, sulphur dioxide resembles carbon dioxide. You should revise the properties of carbon dioxide (Section 7) before going further with this section.

We have already seen in Experiment 5.3 (p. 45) that sulphur dioxide reacts with water to form an acidic solution. The acid which it forms with water is sulphurous acid (H_2SO_3):

$$H_2O + SO_2 \rightarrow H_2SO_3$$

Carbon dioxide behaves in a similar manner except that it is less soluble than sulphur dioxide:

$$H_2O + CO_2 \rightarrow H_2CO_3 \text{ (carbonic acid)}$$

Both sulphurous and carbonic acids are unstable, decomposing readily to water and sulphur dioxide and carbon dioxide respectively:

$$H_2SO_3 \rightarrow H_2O + SO_2$$
$$H_2CO_3 \rightarrow H_2O + CO_2$$

The reactions are, therefore, reversible.

The action of sulphur dioxide and carbon dioxide on water to form acidic solutions is typical of the many oxides of non-metallic elements. These oxides are called *acid anhydrides* (acids without water). Thus sulphur dioxide is the anhydride of sulphurous acid and carbon dioxide is the anhydride of carbonic acid.

Action of sulphur dioxide of alkalis

We learned in Section 7 that carbon dioxide reacts with solutions of alkalis to form two salts of carbonic acid, carbonates and hydrogen carbonates (bicarbonates).

Sulphur dioxide reacts in a similar way to form two salts of sulphurous acid, sulphites and hydrogen sulphites. The apparatus for absorbing the gas is the same as that shown in *figure 36* (p. 60).

Acid and normal salts

The explanation of the formation of two salts by both carbonic and sulphurous acids lies in their ability to give one or two hydrogen ions from each molecule of acid:

$$H_2CO_3 \rightarrow HCO_3^- + H^+$$
hydrogen carbonate ion

$$H_2CO_3 \rightarrow CO_3^{2-} + 2H^+$$
carbonate ion

$$H_2SO_3 \rightarrow HSO_3^- + H^+$$
hydrogen sulphite ion

$$H_2SO_3 \rightarrow SO_3^{2-} + 2H^+$$
sulphite ion

The salts containing HSO_3^- (hydrogen sulphites) or HCO_3^- (hydrogen carbonates) are sometimes called *acid salts* because they contain hydrogen which can form hydrogen ions. Solutions of these salts often —but not always—have an acid reaction to litmus.

The salts containing SO_3^{2-} (sulphites) and CO_3^{2-} (carbonates) are usually called *normal salts* because they do not contain acidic hydrogen.

The nature of the salt which is formed depends on the relative quantities of acid and alkali which are mixed. This can best be seen from the equations:

(a) formation of sodium hydrogen sulphite:

$$NaOH + SO_2 \rightarrow NaHSO_3$$

(b) formation of normal sodium sulphite:

$$2NaOH + SO_2 \rightarrow Na_2SO_3 + H_2O$$

To form the acid salt, the ratio of acidic oxide to alkali (by formulae) is 1:1; to form the normal salt, the ratio of acidic oxide to alkali is 1:2. Starting from a fixed weight of alkali, twice as much acid is required to make the acid salt as is required to make the normal salt.

The same reasoning and equations can be applied to the formation of carbonates and hydrogen carbonates:
sodium hydrogen carbonate:

$$NaOH + CO_2 \rightarrow NaHCO_3$$

sodium carbonate:

$$2NaOH + CO_2 \rightarrow Na_2CO_3 + H_2O$$

Basicity of acids

The basicity of an acid is the number of hydrogen ions which one molecule of an acid can give.

Acids such as sulphurous and carbonic acids are *dibasic* because they can give two hydrogen ions from each molecule. Dibasic acids can form two series of salts—acid salts and normal salts.

Hydrochloric acid is monobasic because it can give only one hydrogen atom from each molecule. Monobasic acids cannot form acid salts.

The properties of sulphites

Experiment 13.3

The action of acids on sulphites (C)

Put one small measure of anhydrous sodium sulphite into a small test tube and half fill the tube with dilute hydrochloric acid. Shake the tube to mix the contents. Do not smell the resulting gas directly.

For these experiments a convenient method of detecting sulphur dioxide is to hold a strip of filter paper, which has been soaked in potassium permanganate solution, in the mouth of the test tube. The purple potassium permanganate turns colourless in the presence of sulphur dioxide.

If you repeat the experiment with calcium sulphite and with dilute nitric and sulphuric acids, you will find that sulphur dioxide is formed in each case.

The formation of sulphur dioxide by the action of any of the three strong acids on sulphites resembles the action of the acids on carbonates. The strong acids displace the weaker acids, carbonic and sulphurous acids. These weaker acids then decompose into water and their acid anhydrides. The essential reactants appear to be carbonate or sulphite ions on the one hand, and hydrogen ions from the acid on the other:

$$2H^+_{(aq)} + CO_3^{2-}_{(aq)} \rightarrow H_2CO_{3(aq)} \rightarrow H_2O_{(aq)} + CO_{2(g)}$$
$$2H^+_{(aq)} + SO_3^{2-}_{(aq)} \rightarrow H_2SO_{3(aq)} \rightarrow H_2O_{(aq)} + SO_{2(g)}$$

Examples of the full formal equations are:

$$Na_2CO_3 + 2HCl \rightarrow 2NaCl + H_2O + CO_2$$
$$Na_2SO_3 + 2HCl \rightarrow 2NaCl + H_2O + SO_2$$

Test for sulphites

The formation of sulphur dioxide by the action of hydrochloric acid is a convenient test for a sulphite. (Sodium hydrogen sulphite is the only common hydrogen sulphite which exists in the solid state).

Sulphites and sulphurous acid as reducing agents

Remember that reducing agents give electrons to the substance which is being reduced.

Before investigating the reducing action of sulphurous acids and sulphites, you will need to know the test for sulphate ions (SO_4^{2-}) in aqueous solution: add dilute hydrochloric acid followed by aqueous barium chloride to a solution of the suspected sulphate. If sulphate ions are present they form a white precipitate of barium sulphate:

$$Ba^{2+}_{(aq)} + SO_4^{2-}_{(aq)} \rightarrow BaSO_{4(s)}$$

Experiment 13.4

To investigate the action of (a) sodium sulphite and (b) sulphurous acid on bromine and iodine (C)

(a) To a quarter of a small test tube of sodium sulphite solution add 3 drops of dilute hydrochloric acid followed by 3 drops of barium chloride solution. You will probably see a slight precipitate of barium sulphate since, unless it is freshly prepared, a solution of sodium sulphite will be partly oxidized to sodium sulphate by the atmosphere. Retain this tube for comparison with later tests.

Fill a small tube one-quarter full with bromine water and another tube one-quarter full with a solution of iodine. To each tube add aqueous sodium sulphite drop by drop until there is a permanent colour change. Test both solutions for sulphate ions. Compare the precipitate of barium sulphate with that obtained in the control experiment.

(b) Repeat the experiment using sulphurous acid solution instead of sodium sulphite.

The heavy precipitate of barium sulphate obtained in Experiment 13.4 indicates that sulphite ions (SO_3^{2-}) have been oxidized to sulphate ions (SO_4^{2-}). This oxidation has been brought about by bromine or iodine and can be represented by the following ionic equations:

$$Br_{2(aq)} + SO_3^{2-}_{(aq)} + H_2O \rightarrow SO_4^{2-}_{(aq)} + 2H^+_{(aq)} + 2Br^-_{(aq)}$$
$$I_{2(aq)} + SO_3^{2-}_{(aq)} + H_2O \rightarrow SO_4^{2-}_{(aq)} + 2H^+_{(aq)} + 2I^-_{(aq)}$$

The sulphite ions have acted as a reducing agent. The bromine has been reduced to bromide ions:

$$Br_2 + 2e^- \rightarrow 2Br^-$$

and the iodine to iodide ions:

$$I_2 + 2e^- \rightarrow 2I^-$$

Problems

(1) Investigate the action of dilute solutions of sulphuric, hydrochloric and nitric acids separately on sodium hydrogen sulphite. Write formal and ionic equations for the reactions which have taken place.

(2) A substance contains 29·1% sodium, 40·5% sulphur, and 30·4% oxygen by weight. 1 g-formula of the substance reacts with 2 g-formulae of hydrogen chloride (hydrochloric acid) to form 2 g-formulae of sodium chloride, 1 g-atom of sulphur, 1 g-formula of sulphur dioxide, and 1 g-formula of water. Calculate the formula of the substance and the equation for the reaction.

(3) Report on the uses of sulphur dioxide and sulphites in industry.

Summary

(1) Sulphur has two crystalline forms:
    (a) Rhombic (octahedral or α) sulphur, which is stable below 95·5°C.
    (b) Prismatic (monoclinic or β) sulphur, which is stable above 95·5°C.
    95·5°C is called the transition temperature.

(2) Sulphur burns to form sulphur dioxide.

(3) Sulphur combines with many metals to form sulphides. The sulphides of metals in groups I and II of the Periodic Table are ionic. The sulphide ion (S^{2-}) resembles the oxide ion (O^{2-}).

(4) In combination with metals, sulphur shows a combining capacity of 2; in combination with oxygen, it shows combining capacities of 4 and 6.

(5) Sulphur dioxide is made by burning sulphur or compounds which contain sulphur.

(6) Sulphur dioxide reacts with water to form sulphurous acid (H_2SO_3).

(7) Sulphurous acid is dibasic; it can give two hydrogen ions from each molecule. It forms two series of salts: acid salts (hydrogen sulphites) and normal salts (sulphites).

(8) Sulphurous acid is a weak acid; it can be displaced from its salts by the action of a stronger acid. It is also unstable, decomposing into water and sulphur dioxide.

(9) The formation of sulphur dioxide by the action of hydrochloric acid on a sulphite serves as a test for sulphites. The sulphur dioxide can be detected by its decolorizing action on potassium permanganate.

(10) The test for sulphates in aqueous solution is to add hydrochloric acid followed by barium chloride solution. A white precipitate indicates the presence of sulphate ions in the solution.

(11) Sulphites and sulphurous acid reduce bromine and iodine to bromide and iodide ions respectively.

Section 14
Sulphuric acid– sulphates and sulphides

Manufacture and uses

Sulphur dioxide is oxidized to sulphur trioxide and this reacts with water to form sulphuric acid:

$$2SO_2 + O_2 \rightarrow 2SO_3$$
$$SO_3 + H_2O \rightarrow H_2SO_4$$

(for details of this process and a laboratory preparation see p. 274)

Sulphuric acid is used in industry in large quantities for many purposes. Three of the heaviest users of sulphuric acid are the fertilizer, general chemical, and petro-chemical (chemicals from petroleum) industries.

General properties of the pure acid

Sulphuric acid is a colourless, oily liquid; it has a higher specific gravity (1·83) and a higher boiling point (356°C) than most other common acids.

The concentrated acid, used in the laboratory, contains at least 2% water and it is completely miscible (mixes in all proportions) with water. Sulphur trioxide dissolves readily in concentrated sulphuric acid, forming a fuming liquid called oleum.

Pure sulphuric acid does not appear to be ionic because it does not conduct electricity readily. It is very corrosive and must be handled with caution, particularly in the presence of water. When diluting it, *always add acid to water*; the addition of water to acid frequently causes a sudden and dangerous eruption of the acid.

Its heat of reaction with water

Experiment 14.1

To measure the approximate heat of reaction between acid and water **(D)**

Stand 700 cm³ of water in a litre beaker until it reaches room temperature. Measure this temperature and pour 1 g-formula (54 cm³ or 98 g) of concentrated sulphuric acid from a measuring cylinder in one slow, continuous movement into the water. Stir with a thermometer during this operation and note the rise in temperature.

SULPHURIC ACID AND SULPHATES

Results

Weight of solution $= (700+98)$ g $= 0.8$ kilogramme

Suppose the temperature rise $= x°C$

Specific heat capacity of solution $=$ that of water

$\qquad = 4.2$ kilojoule per kg per °C (1 kcal per kg per °C)

$\therefore$ Heat evolved $= 4.2 \times 0.8x$ kJ or $0.8x$ kcal

More accurate measurements show that when 1 g-formula of sulphuric acid is added to a large volume of water 71 kJ (17 kcal) are evolved, the change can be represented:

$$H_2SO_{4(l)} + (aq) \rightarrow H_2SO_{4(aq)}$$

N.B. the S.I. unit for energy is the kilojoule not the kilocalorie. The temperature interval in S.I. units is the kelvin; it is identical to the °C and the latter is likely to be retained in elementary work for some time.

The ionization of sulphuric acid

We have already observed (p. 52) that an aqueous solution of sulphuric acid is a good conductor of electricity and therefore contains ions. Since neither pure sulphuric acid nor water is ionic, these ions must be formed by a reaction between the two. If you turn to p. 103 you will see how the reaction between hydrogen chloride and water is explained, and it is likely that the reaction of sulphuric acid with water is similar:

$$H_2SO_4 + H_2O \rightarrow \underset{\substack{\text{hydronium} \\ \text{ion}}}{H_3O^+} + \underset{\substack{\text{hydrogen sulphate} \\ \text{ion}}}{HSO_4^-}$$

1 molecule of sulphuric acid has given 1 hydrogen ion to 1 molecule of water:

$$\begin{cases} H_2SO_4 \rightarrow H^+ + HSO_4^- \\ H_2O + H^+ \rightarrow H_3O^+ \end{cases}$$

Sulphuric acid, however, is dibasic. It can form two series of salts—sulphates and hydrogen sulphates. Like sulphurous acid, therefore, it appears that one molecule of sulphuric acid can give two hydrogen ions. The first is given and the hydrogen sulphate ion remains:

$$H_2SO_4 \rightarrow H^+ + HSO_4^-$$

the second is given and the sulphate ion remains:

$$HSO_4^- \rightarrow H^+ + SO_4^{2-}$$

(Remember that in each case the hydrogen ion reacts with a molecule of water.)

Its action on compounds containing the elements of water

Experiment 14.2

The action of concentrated sulphuric acid on (a) filter paper (b) sugar **(D)**

(a) Put two drops of concentrated sulphuric acid on to a filter paper and hold the paper vertically so that the drops run down. Notice the charring effect.

(b) Put about 20 g of sugar into a glass evaporating dish and add 10 cm³ of concentrated sulphuric acid. Note the formation of sugar carbon.

Filter paper consists of cellulose $C_6H_{10}O_5$.* Cane sugar has the formula $C_{12}H_{22}O_{11}$. Neither of these substances contains water but they do contain the elements of water—hydrogen and oxygen—in the ratio 2:1 by atoms.

Sulphuric acid appears to react with the elements of water leaving carbon as a residue:

$$C_6H_{10}O_5 \xrightarrow[\text{acid}]{\text{conc. sulphuric}} 6C + 5H_2O$$

$$C_{12}H_{22}O_{11} \xrightarrow[\text{acid}]{\text{conc. sulphuric}} 12C + 11H_2O$$

Its action on salts of other acids

We have already seen (p. 100) that concentrated sulphuric acid will displace hydrogen chloride and that this is because sulphuric acid is less volatile than hydrogen chloride. This is a common feature of the action of concentrated sulphuric acid on salts; for example, it will displace nitric acid from nitrates:

$$NaNO_3 + H_2SO_4 \rightarrow NaHSO_4 + HNO_3$$

Its action as an oxidizing agent

Concentrated sulphuric acid will oxidize carbon to carbon dioxide and sulphur to sulphur dioxide, when it is heated with these elements. The acid itself is reduced by this action to sulphur dioxide and water:

$$H_2SO_4 - (O) \rightarrow H_2SO_3 \rightarrow H_2O + SO_2$$

Work out formal equations for these two reactions.

Aqueous (dilute) sulphuric acid

Sulphuric acid, in common with other strong acids, is largely ionized in dilute aqueous solution and these solutions contain a high concentration of hydrated hydrogen ions (H_3O^+). Most of the reactions of aqueous acids are reactions of these ions; therefore ionic, as well as formal, equations can be used to represent them.

Those reactions of pure sulphuric acid which are brought about by it affinity for water or by its non-volatile nature will not be shown by its aqueous solution. Here is a summary of the reactions of aqueous sulphuric acid:

(1) *With metals*
Some metals react with aqueous sulphuric acid to form hydrogen plus a sulphate:

$$Mg + H_2SO_4 \rightarrow MgSO_4 + H_2$$
$$\text{or}$$
$$Mg_{(s)} + 2H^+_{(aq)} \rightarrow Mg^{2+}_{(aq)} + H_{2(g)}$$

* The actual molecules of cellulose are much larger than this formula indicates; they are made up of many of these formula units, so that a molecule is more accurately represented by $(C_6H_{10}O_5)n$ where n is a variable number of several hundreds.

Less reactive metals such as copper do not react with dilute sulphuric acid.

Note that in this reaction magnesium atoms are being oxidized, $Mg \rightarrow Mg^{2+} + 2e^-$, and hydrogen ions are being reduced, $2H^+ + 2e^- \rightarrow H_2$.

(2) *With oxides or hydroxides of metals*

Oxides and hydroxides of metals are usually basic and they react with aqueous sulphuric acid to form sulphates plus water:

$$CuO + H_2SO_4 \rightarrow CuSO_4 + H_2O$$
$$Zn(OH)_2 + H_2SO_4 \rightarrow ZnSO_4 + 2H_2O$$

(3) *With solutions of alkalis*

Either the normal or the acid salt is formed, depending on the relative quantities of the alkali and acid:

acid salt:
$$\underset{\text{1 g-formula}}{NaOH} + \underset{\text{1 g-formula}}{H_2SO_4} \rightarrow \underset{\substack{\text{sodium hydrogen} \\ \text{sulphate}}}{NaHSO_4} + H_2O$$

normal salt:
$$\underset{\text{2 g-formula}}{2NaOH} + \underset{\text{1 g-formula}}{H_2SO_4} \rightarrow \underset{\text{sodium sulphate}}{Na_2SO_4} + 2H_2O$$

To make the acid salt the ratio of acid:alkali must be twice that required to make the normal salt. Ionically, like all reactions between acids and alkalis (p. 138), the reaction can be represented by the equation:

$$OH^-_{(aq)} + H^+_{(aq)} \rightarrow H_2O_{(l)}$$

In the reaction to form the acid salt, the acid appears to be ionized only to the first stage ($H_2SO_4 \rightarrow H^+ + HSO_4^-$). In the reaction to form the normal salt, it appears to be ionized to the second stage ($H_2SO_4 \rightarrow 2H^+ + SO_4^{2-}$).

(4) *With carbonates*

As carbonates are salts of the weak carbonic acid, aqueous sulphuric acid displaces carbon dioxide from them and forms the sulphate:

$$Na_2CO_3 + H_2SO_4 \rightarrow Na_2SO_4 + H_2O + CO_2$$
$$\text{or}$$
$$CO_3^{2-}_{(aq)} + 2H^+_{(aq)} \rightarrow H_2CO_{3(aq)} \rightarrow H_2O_{(l)} + CO_{2(g)}$$

(5) *With salts of other weak acids*

Aqueous sulphuric acid will undergo other reactions similar to 4. For example, it will displace hydrogen sulphide from sulphides, acetic acid from acetates, and sulphurous acid (sulphur dioxide + water) from sulphites.

Sulphates

Insoluble sulphates

The most familiar insoluble sulphates are those of lead, calcium, barium, and strontium. Notice that the last three elements are all in group II of the Periodic Table.

The most convenient method of making these sulphates is to mix a solution containing ions of the metal with a solution containing sulphate ions; the sulphate of the metal is precipitated and then washed and dried. For example, calcium sulphate can be precipitated by mixing solutions of calcium chloride and sulphuric acid:

$$CaCl_{2(aq)} + H_2SO_{4(aq)} \rightarrow CaSO_{4(s)} + 2HCl_{(aq)}$$

An ionic equation is better, because it serves for all reactions in solution between soluble calcium salts and soluble sulphates:

$$Ca^{2+}_{(aq)} + SO_4^{2-}_{(aq)} \rightarrow CaSO_{4(s)}$$

Soluble sulphates

These can be made in solution by the action of aqueous sulphuric acid on the metal or on its oxide, hydroxide, or carbonate. The resulting solution can then be partially evaporated to form crystals, which can be separated from the liquid by decantation and then dried.

Acid sulphates

These contain the hydrogen sulphate ion (HSO_4^-).

Like most acid salts, hydrogen sulphates are more soluble in water than the corresponding normal sulphates.

Experiment 14.3

Some properties of sodium hydrogen sulphate (C)

(a) Make a solution of sodium hydrogen sulphate—the concentration is not important—and investigate its action on (i) litmus (ii) sodium carbonate (iii) magnesium (iv) hydrochloric acid plus aqueous barium chloride.

(b) Heat a very small quantity of solid sodium hydrogen sulphate in a dry test tube. Observe the white smoke which is formed (do not smell it) and test it with moist blue litmus paper. Interpret your observations and write equations for the reactions.

The test for sulphates in solution

Add dilute hydrochloric acid (to prevent the precipitation of carbonates, etc.) followed by barium chloride solution. A white precipitate of barium sulphate indicates the presence of sulphate ions:

$$Ba^{2+}_{(aq)} + SO_4^{2-}_{(aq)} \rightarrow BaSO_{4(s)}$$

Weak acids and strong acids

So far we have distinguished weak acids from strong acids by either (a) the action of universal indicator on their aqueous solutions (p. 48) or (b) the ability of a strong acid to displace a weak acid from salts of the latter. Neither of these tests is very conclusive and we now know that the displacement of one acid by another can depend on the difference in volatility of the acids rather than the difference in their strength. The time has come to seek a better method of distinguishing strong acids from weak acids.

Experiment 14.4

The electrical conductance
of various aqueous acids
(C or D)

The apparatus consists of the standard U-tube and platinum electrodes used in previous experiments on electrolysis (p. 51, *figure 30*). Using a constant source of 20 volts d.c., measure the current which flows through aqueous solutions of sulphuric acid, acetic acid, and sulphurous acid.

Experiment 14.4 indicates that aqueous sulphuric acid is a much better conductor than aqueous acetic or sulphurous acids. This, in turn, indicates that aqueous sulphuric acid is largely ionized whereas the other two are only slightly so.

In other words, aqueous solutions of strong acids are ionized to a greater degree than aqueous solutions of weak acids. This reflects a greater ability on the part of strong acids to give hydrogen ions.

In a dilute aqueous solution of sulphuric acid the ionization is complete:

$$H_2SO_{4(l)} + H_2O_{(aq)} \rightarrow H_3O^+_{(aq)} + HSO_4^-_{(aq)}$$

Whereas, in aqueous solutions of weak acids both ions and molecules are present:

$$H_2SO_{3(aq)} \rightleftharpoons H^+_{(aq)} + HSO_3^-_{(aq)}$$
$$CH_3COOH_{(aq)} \rightleftharpoons H^+_{(aq)} + CH_3COO^-_{(aq)}$$

In solutions of weak acids the concentration of molecules far exceeds the concentration of ions and this can be indicated by using a bigger arrow pointing towards the molecules ($\rightleftharpoons$).

The action of strong acids on the salts of weak acids

Our new theory of the relative strength of acids can be used to explain the displacement of weak acids by strong acids.

Example 1   The action of hydrochloric acid on sodium carbonate:
Hydrochloric acid is fully ionized in aqueous solution ($H^+ + Cl^-$).

Sodium carbonate is a salt and, like most salts, it is also fully ionized in aqueous solution ($2Na^+ + CO_3^{2-}$).

Therefore, when we mix these two substances we are really mixing four different ions ($H^+ + Cl^-$ and $Na^+ + CO_3^{2-}$). Of these four ions, two of them (H^+ and CO_3^{2-}) can react to form molecules:

$$2H^+_{(aq)} + CO_3^{2-}_{(aq)} \rightarrow H_2CO_{3(aq)}$$

The carbonic acid then decomposes into water + carbon dioxide:

$$H_2CO_{3(aq)} \rightarrow H_2O_{(l)} + CO_{2(g)}$$

Since hydrogen ions are common to all strong acids and carbonate ions to all carbonates, the ionic equation given above will serve for the action between any carbonate and any strong acid.

Example 2   The action of strong acids on sulphites:
Hydrogen ions from the acid combine with sulphite ions from the sulphite to form sulphurous acid. The sulphurous acid then decomposes into sulphur dioxide and water. Write equations.

Example 3 The action of strong acids on acetates:

Hydrogen ions from the acid combine with acetate ions from the acetate to form acetic acid. Acetic acid is a stable liquid, soluble in water; it can be detected by its vinegary smell. Write an equation.

Sulphides
Experiment 14.5

The action of acids on iron (II) sulphide **(C)**

Put one small piece of iron (II) sulphide into a small tube and add half a tube of dilute hydrochloric, sulphuric, or acetic acids. Test the resulting gas with a paper soaked in a lead acetate solution. Do not smell the gas directly and as soon as you have made the test pour off the acid and fill the tube with water. You may have to warm the tube slightly if you use acetic acid.

The acids used in Experiment 14.5 all displace hydrogen sulphide gas from the sulphides of metals and this reaction can be used as a test for sulphides. This leads us to suppose that sulphides are the salts of hydrogen sulphide which is a weaker acid than hydrochloric, sulphuric, and acetic acids.

$$FeS + 2HCl \rightarrow FeCl_2 + H_2S$$

Gaseous hydrogen sulphide is usually prepared for laboratory use in a generator called Kipp's apparatus.

Properties of hydrogen sulphide

You will have observed that the solution of hydrogen sulphide which was used in earlier experiments rapidly becomes milky in appearance; the hydrogen sulphide is being oxidized to sulphur by oxygen in the air. If a substance is easily oxidized, it is likely to be a good reducing agent.

Experiment 14.6

The action of hydrogen sulphide on the solutions of some salts **(C)**

Put four drops of each of the following aqueous solutions into separate small tubes: copper sulphate, lead nitrate, and zinc sulphate. Add four drops of freshly prepared, saturated hydrogen sulphide solution to each. The reaction with copper sulphate is:

$$Cu^{2+}_{(aq)} + S^{2-}_{(aq)} \rightarrow CuS_{(s)}$$

Write equations for the other reactions.

How does hydrogen sulphide form precipitates of other sulphides?

Hydrogen sulphide is a very weak acid; its aqueous solution is very slightly ionized, therefore the concentration of sulphide ions is low. Why, then, do small quantities of hydrogen sulphide solution produce such substantial precipitates?

The molecules and ions are in equilibrium:

$$H_2S_{(aq)} \rightleftharpoons 2H^+_{(aq)} + S^{2-}_{(aq)}$$

If the sulphide ions are removed from solution by precipitation, the equilibrium is disturbed and more hydrogen sulphide molecules ionize to replace those ions which have been removed. Thus, if sufficient metals ions are present, most of the hydrogen sulphide will ionize.

The two processes, ionization and precipitation, go on at the same time and can be represented by a double equation:

$$H_2S_{(aq)} \rightleftharpoons 2H^+_{(aq)} + S^{2-}_{(aq)}$$
$$+$$
$$Cu^{2+}_{(aq)}$$
$$\downarrow$$
$$CuS_{(s)}$$

This disturbance of a position of equilibrium, by the removal of the whole or part of one side of it, is important; you will meet many similar situations both in chemistry and in the environment at large.

Hydrogen sulphide as a reducing agent

You will have observed that the solution of hydrogen sulphide which was used in earlier experiments rapidly becomes milky in appearance; the hydrogen sulphide is being oxidized to sulphur by oxygen in the air. If a substance is easily oxidized, it is likely to be a good reducing agent.

Experiment 14.7

The action of hydrogen sulphide on iron (III) salts
(C)

Put six drops of freshly prepared hydrogen sulphide solution into a small tube and add a solution of iron (III) chloride to it dropwise:

$$2Fe^{3+}_{(aq)} + S^{2-}_{(aq)} \rightarrow 2Fe^{2+}_{(aq)} + S_{(s)}$$

What has been oxidized and what has been reduced? Write ionic half equations for this reaction and indicate how oxidation and reduction have taken place.

Problems

(1) You are given a solution of the salt A. To two drops of A add hydrochloric acid followed by barium chloride solution to form the precipitate B. To two more drops of A add ammonium hydroxide to form the precipitate C. To two more drops of A add four drops of bromine water to form the solution D. To D add ammonium hydroxide to form the precipitate E.

Identify A, B, C, D, and E, and write ionic equations for all the reactions which have taken place.

(2) You are given an aqueous solution of X. Investigate the action of the solution on (a) magnesium (b) copper oxide (heat the mixture) (c) copper carbonate (d) hydrochloric acid and aqueous barium chloride. Evaporate one or two drops of the solution of X to dryness.

Give an account of your observations and explain, as far as you can, the nature of X and the reactions which have taken place.

(3) P is the soluble salt of the acid Q. Q is a weak acid, soluble in hot water but not in cold water.

Make 20 cm³ of approx. 10% solution of P and from this precipitate

Q. Dissolve *Q* in hot water and allow it to crystallize. Prepare a dry specimen of *Q* and determine its melting point.

(4) You are given 150 cm³ of M NaOH solution and 100 cm³ of M H_2SO_4 solution. Calculate the fraction of a g-formula of each substance present in the solutions.

Use the two solutions to make solutions of (a) normal sodium sulphate (b) sodium hydrogen sulphate (use a measuring cylinder to deliver the volumes of solution needed). Partially evaporate the solutions and prepare crystals of the two salts.

(5) Make up 200 cm³ of universal indicator solution. Divide the solution into two equal parts, retain one part as a control and pour the other into the apparatus for dissolving gases. Pass washed hydrogen sulphide gas into the solution until the colour of the indicator is yellow. Disconnect the solution from the hydrogen sulphide generator and add 10 drops of iodine solution. Add 10 drops of iodine solution to the control solution.

Explain the colour changes which take place.

Summary

(1) Concentrated sulphuric acid reacts exothermically with water. It will displace more volatile acids (hydrogen chloride and nitric acid) from their salts.

(2) Sulphuric acid ionizes in water to form hydrogen ions (hydrated), hydrogen sulphate ions (HSO_4^-), and sulphate ions (SO_4^{2-}).

(3) Sulphuric acid is dibasic. It forms acid salts (hydrogen sulphates) and normal salts (sulphates).

(4) Aqueous sulphuric acid has the typical reactions of a strong acid: it reacts with some metals to form sulphates plus hydrogen, with oxides and hydroxides of metals to form sulphates plus water, and with carbonates to form sulphates plus water and carbon dioxide.

(5) Soluble sulphates can be made by the action of aqueous sulphuric acid on a metal, an oxide, a hydroxide, or a carbonate. Insoluble sulphates—those of lead, calcium, barium, and strontium—are made by precipitation.

(6) Hydrogen sulphates give rise to hydrogen ions in aqueous solution, and therefore react in many ways like sulphuric acid. They decompose into the normal sulphate, water, and sulphur trioxide when heated.

(7) The relative strengths of acids can be measured by the degree to which their aqueous solutions are ionized.

(8) A weak acid can be displaced from its salts by a stronger acid. The hydrogen ions from the stronger acid combine with the negative ions from the salt to form molecules of the weak acid.

(9) Hydrogen sulphide is a very weak acid. It is dibasic, forming hydrogen sulphides and normal sulphides, and it is readily displaced from both of these by other acids.

(10) Insoluble sulphides of metals can be precipitated by adding hydro-

gen sulphide or any other aqueous sulphide to a solution containing the ions of the metal.

(11) The position of a chemical equilibrium can be altered by removing the whole or part of one of the components. Thus, hydrogen sulphide continues to ionize if sulphide ions are continuously removed by precipitation:

$$H_2S_{(aq)} \rightleftharpoons 2H^+_{(aq)} + S^{2-}_{(aq)}$$
$$+ M^{2+}_{(aq)}$$
$$\downarrow$$
$$MS_{(s)}$$
$$(M^{2+} = \text{a metallic ion})$$

(12) Hydrogen sulphide is a reducing agent. Sulphur is frequently formed as a result of a reaction in which hydrogen sulphide has been oxidized. (Remember that in a reaction of this sort, if one substance is reduced, the other is oxidized.)

Section 15
Rates of reactions

In the reactions studied so far we have mainly discussed *what* is formed, i.e. the *products*. But equally important is a study of *how fast* they are formed, i.e. the *rate* of the reactions. A manufacturer of chemicals has to consider how much his products will cost, and something which is formed slowly is usually more expensive than something which is formed quickly. Time and cost can be equated.

To take examples from Sections 13 and 14, the precipitation of barium sulphate is quicker than the action of dilute sulphuric acid on zinc, and both are quicker than the atmospheric oxidation of aqueous hydrogen sulphide.

In this Section we shall study rates of reaction more exactly and determine those factors which can change the rate of reactions.

Experiment 15.1

To investigate the rate of reaction between calcium carbonate and hydrochloric acid **(C)**

You will require three test tubes. Into test tubes 1 and 2 put two medium sized marble chips of approximately equal size (about 1 g each). Into test tube 3 put about 1 g of powdered marble chip. Into a measuring cylinder put 5 cm³ of 2 M hydrochloric acid and make it up to 20 cm³ with water; swirl the cylinder to mix the solution. What is the molarity of the resulting hydrochloric acid?

To test tube 1 add 2·5 cm³ of 2 M hydrochloric acid. To test tube 2 add 10 cm³ of the diluted acid. To test tube 3 add 10 cm³ of the diluted acid.

  (i) In which test tube is the reaction quickest at the start? In which is it slowest?

 (ii) What factors are approximately equal in all three test tubes at the start of the reaction?

(iii) What factors are common to test tubes 1 and 2 but not to test tube 3?

(iv) What factors are common to test tubes 2 and 3 but not to test tube 1?

 (v) Which two factors seem to affect the rate of the reaction and in what way?

Experiment 15.2

To investigate the effect of concentration change on rate of reaction **(C)**

Measure 50 cm³ of 0·2 M sodium thiosulphate solution into a conical flask. Have ready 5 cm³ of 2 M hydrochloric acid in another small measuring cylinder. Place the conical flask onto a filter paper on which has been marked a cross. Add the 5 cm³ of hydrochloric acid, start a stop-clock immediately, swirl the contents of the flask, then allow the flask to remain still on the filter paper.

Look vertically down through the solution at the cross on the filter paper and stop the stop-clock when the cross just disappears. Rinse the flask immediately.

Put 40 cm³ of the 0·2 M sodium thiosulphate solution into a measuring cylinder and make it up to 50 cm³ with water. Repeat the experiment using the 50 cm³ of diluted sodium thiosulphate.

Repeat the experiment four more times using 30, 20, 15, and 10 cm³ of sodium thiosulphate solution, making it up to 50 cm³ with water each time.

Plot a graph of molarity of the sodium thiosulphate solution (after dilution) against time taken for the cross to disappear. Plot another graph of molarity of sodium thiosulphate solution against the reciprocal of the time $\left(\dfrac{1}{T}\right)$.

Sodium thiosulphate crystals have the formula, $Na_2S_2O_3.5H_2O$, and a 0·2 M solution contains approximately 50 g/litre. Its reaction with hydrochloric acid can be represented:

$$S_2O_3^{2-}{}_{(aq)} + 2H^+{}_{(aq)} \rightarrow H_2O + SO_{2(g)} + S_{(s)}$$

(i) What causes the cross to disappear?

(ii) What factors are constant at the beginning of each experiment?

(iii) How does the rate of reaction change with concentration? Suggest an explanation.

(iv) Why should the flask be rinsed immediately after each experiment? If you cannot think of a reason, repeat one of the experiments without rinsing the flask immediately.

Experiment 15.3

To investigate the effect of temperature change on rate of reaction (C)

Measure 50 cm³ of 0·04 M sodium thiosulphate solution in a measuring cylinder and pour it into a conical flask. Have ready 5 cm³ of 2 M hydrochloric acid in another small measuring cylinder. Warm the sodium thiosulphate solution gently on a tripod and gauze until its temperature is one or two degrees above 20°C. Place the conical flask onto a filter paper on which has been marked a cross. Add the 5 cm³ of hydrochloric acid; start a stop-clock immediately; quickly swirl the contents of the flask; take the temperature and allow the flask to remain still on the filter paper.

Look vertically down through the solution at the cross on the filter paper and stop the stop-clock when the cross just disappears. Rinse the flask immediately. Repeat the experiment, using fresh 50 cm³ portions of sodium thiosulphate solution each time, at temperatures of approximately 30, 40, 50, and 60°C.

Plot a graph of the time taken for the cross to disappear against temperature. Plot another graph of the reciprocal of the time against temperature. The products of the reaction are given in Experiment 15.2.

(i) What factors are constant at the beginning of each experiment?

(ii) How does the rate of reaction change with temperature. Suggest an an explanation.

Experiment 15.4

To investigate the effect of manganese dioxide on the rate of decomposition of hydrogen peroxide (C)

You will remember that in Experiment 2.6 manganese dioxide was used as a catalyst to hasten the production of oxygen from hydrogen peroxide:

$$2H_2O_2 \rightarrow 2H_2O + O_2$$

In the present experiment the same reaction will be investigated quantitatively. The apparatus is shown in *figure 61*.

The burette is filled with water and inverted and clamped in the position shown. Allow air slowly in through the tap until the level of the water is on the burette scale. Take the reading. Measure 5 cm³ of hydrogen peroxide (20 volume) in a measuring cylinder and make up to 50 cm³ with water. Pour this diluted hydrogen peroxide into the conical flask, add a small measure of manganese dioxide and insert the bung tightly. Place the burette over the end of the delivery tube and start the stop-clock immediately.

Read the level of the water in the burette every minute for 20 minutes and then every 5 minutes for as long as possible. It is not easy to read the burette when it is upside down and you may have to tap the burette to break any bubbles which do not break on their own when they arrive at the surface.

Calculate the volume of oxygen which has been formed at each time reading and then plot a graph of volume of oxygen against time.

  (i) State in general terms the change in the rate of reaction during the experiment.

 (ii) What factor is most likely to cause the change in rate which takes place as the reaction proceeds?

(iii) Suggest another method by which the amount of oxygen formed could be measured.

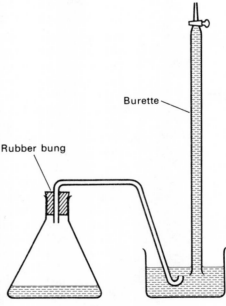

Burette

Rubber bung

Figure 61

If the graph had been a straight line the rate of formation of oxygen would have been constant and could be measured in cm³ of oxygen formed per minute by measuring the slope of the line, i.e. volume ÷ time, as in *figure 62*.

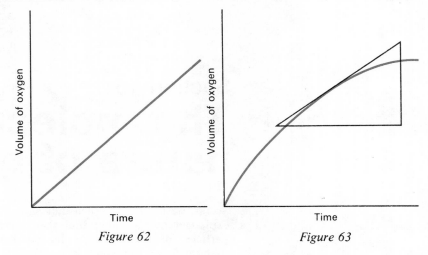

Figure 62   *Figure 63*

But if the graph was not a straight line as in *figure 63*, the slope of the graph changes all the time.

To determine the rate of reaction at any particular time, you should draw a tangent to the curve and measure the slope of the tangent (volume ÷ time).

A similar graph could be obtained if you had measured the amount of hydrogen peroxide used up at intervals of time, instead of the amount of oxygen formed.

Problems

(1) Adapt Experiment 15.4 to investigate the effect on the rate of reaction of:

(a) a different initial concentration of hydrogen peroxide,
(b) a different amount of manganese dioxide,
(c) A different temperature throughout the experiment.
(2) Find out why the rate of production of a chemical is so important to the economics of the chemical industry.

Summary

The factors which affect the rate of a reaction include:
(1) The state of division of the solid reactants—the finer the quicker.
(2) The concentration of reacting solutions—the more concentrated the quicker.
(3) The temperature—the hotter the quicker.
(4) The use of a catalyst.

Section 16
The molecular nature of gases

So far, we have established that part of the behaviour of gases can be explained by assuming that they consist of small, quickly moving particles (molecules) whose distance from each other is much greater than their size. In this section we shall discuss the weight and volume of gases, the volume occupied by 1 g-formula of a gas, and the molecular formulae for gases.

Before going further, however, it will be necessary to examine the effect of changes in pressure and temperature on the volume of a gas.

The effect of a change in pressure on the volume of a gas

The pressure of a gas is usually given in centimetres or millimetres of mercury (the units of a barometer tube) or in atmospheres (1 atmosphere = 760 mm of mercury).

If the effect on the volume of gas of a change in pressure is to be measured, then all other factors likely to change the volume (temperature, for example) must be kept constant. Furthermore, the weight of gas must be kept constant.

If a balloon with expandable walls is filled with gas and then allowed to rise in the atmosphere, the pressure of the air on the outside of the balloon decreases, the balloon expands, and its volume increases. If the same balloon were sent down a coal mine, the pressure on the outside would increase and the balloon would contract and its volume decrease. Note that the amount of gas inside the balloon, in terms of weight and therefore of numbers of molecules, does not change. It is the volume of the balloon and therefore the distance between each molecule which changes.

This simple illustration indicates that if the pressure on a fixed mass of gas increases then its volume will decrease, and vice versa.

Experiments, the details of which will not be given here, can be devised to show more accurately the effect of a change in pressure on a gas. Table 7 gives some typical results in a simplified form. It indicates that if the pressure is doubled, the volume is halved. In this sort of relationship the two things, pressure and volume, are said to be inversely proportional to each other.

If P represents the pressure and V represents the volume, $P \propto \dfrac{1}{V}$.

Table 7

Volume	Pressure
16 cm³	1 atm
8 cm³	2 atm
4 cm³	4 atm
2 cm³	8 atm
1 cm³	16 atm

(Temperature and mass of the gas constant)

Table 7 also indicates that if the pressure is multiplied by the volume the answer is always the same. In other words, the product of the pressure and volume is constant:

$$P \times V = \text{constant} \ (k)$$
$$\text{or}$$
$$P_1 \times V_1 = P_2 \times V_2$$

P_1 and V_1 are the initial pressure and volume of the gas, and P_2 and V_2 are the final pressure and volume of the gas.

This relationship was first determined experimentally by Boyle (1627–91) and it is dignified by the title *Boyle's Law: The volume of a fixed mass of gas is inversely proportional to its pressure at constant temperature.*

The mathematical way of expressing Boyle's Law is given above and a knowledge of this enables the change in volume brought about by a known change in the pressure of the gas to be predicted.

Example 1 The volume of a fixed mass of gas is 550 cm³ at a pressure of 810 mm. Calculate its volume at 750 mm (temperature constant).

$$P_1 V_1 = P_2 V_2$$
$$\therefore \ 810 \times 550 = 750 \times V_2$$
$$\therefore \ V_2 = \frac{810}{750} \times 550 \text{ cm}^3$$
$$= \underline{594 \text{ cm}^3}$$

The effect of a change in temperature on the volume of a gas

Absolute temperature: The lowest temperature which can be attained is $-273°C$. This is called absolute zero, 0K (K stands for the kelvin).

To calculate the absolute temperature add 273 to the centigrade temperature. Thus, $0°C = 273K$, $10°C = 283K$, $-10°C = 263K$.

Charles' law

Absolute zero is the temperature at which all molecules cease to move and an increase in temperature indicates an increase in the kinetic energy of the molecules. Thus, if the absolute temperature of a gas is doubled, the kinetic energy of the molecules will be doubled, this can show itself in one of two ways:

(a) If the volume of the container is constant, then the pressure of the gas will increase.

(b) If the container can expand at constant pressure, then the volume of the gas will increase.

The effect of temperature on the volume of a gas is summarized in *Charles' Law: The volume of a fixed mass of gas is proportional to its absolute temperature at constant pressure.* Table 8 gives some typical results in a simplified form:

Table 8

Volume	Temperature
1 cm³	50K
2 cm³	100K
4 cm³	200K
8 cm³	400K

(Pressure and mass of the gas constant)

If the absolute temperature is doubled ,the volume of the gas doubles Mathematically this is expressed: $V \propto T$,

or
$$\frac{V}{T} = \text{constant}$$

or
$$\frac{V_1}{T_1} = \frac{V_2}{T_2}$$

where V_1 and T_1 are the initial volume and temperature of the gas, and V_2 and T_2 are the final volume and temperature of the gas.

The mathematical form of Charles' Law enables us to calculate the change in volume caused by a known change in temperature.

Example 2   The initial volume of a fixed mass of gas is 224 cm³ at 15°C. Calculate its volume at 87°C (pressure constant).

$$15°C = (273 + 15)K = 288K$$
$$87°C = (273 + 87)K = 360K$$
$$\frac{V_1}{T_1} = \frac{V_2}{T_2}$$
$$\therefore \frac{224}{288} = \frac{V_2}{360}$$
$$\therefore V_2 = 224 \times \frac{360}{288} \text{ cm}^3$$
$$= \underline{280 \text{ cm}^3}$$

The effect of a change in both temperature and pressure on the volume of a gas

If both the pressure and the temperature of a fixed mass of gas are changed, both Boyle's and Charles' Laws must be applied in order to calculate the final volume of the gas:

If $P \times V$ does not change and $\dfrac{V}{T}$ does not change, then $\dfrac{P \times V}{T}$ does not change.

$$\frac{P_1 \times V_1}{T_1} = \frac{P_2 \times V_2}{T_2}$$

(P_1, P_2, etc. have the same meaning as that given above)

The expression $\dfrac{PV}{T}$ = constant is called the Gas Equation.

Example 3 A fixed mass of gas has a volume of 750 cm³ at $-23°C$ and 800 mm pressure. Calculate the pressure at which it will have a volume of 720 cm³ at $-3°C$.

$$-23°C = 250K \qquad -3°C = 270K$$

$$\frac{P_1 V_1}{T_1} = \frac{P_2 V_2}{T_2}$$

$$P_1 = 800 \text{ cm}^3 \qquad V_1 = 750 \text{ cm}^3 \qquad T_1 = 250K$$
$$P_2 = \quad ? \qquad V_2 = 720 \text{ cm}^3 \qquad T_2 = 270K$$

$$\therefore \frac{800 \times 750}{250} = \frac{P_2 \times 720}{270}$$

$$\therefore P_2 = 800 \times \frac{750}{720} \times \frac{270}{250} \text{ mm}$$

$$= \underline{900 \text{ mm}}$$

If the fixed mass of gas is 1 g-molecule (p. 146), the constant in the gas equation is given the special symbol R $\left(\dfrac{PV}{T} = R\right)$. R is called the Gas Constant.

Standard temperature and pressure
The weight of a gas does not vary with temperature and pressure so that, when comparing the combining weight of two gases, no account need be taken of the temperature or pressure. But if it is necessary to compare the volumes of the gases, it must be done under the same conditions of temperature and pressure. For this reason, certain standard conditions of temperature and pressure have been chosen at which volumes of different gases can be compared.

These conditions are 0°C (273K) and 760 mm (1 atmosphere). They are called standard temperature and pressure (s.t.p.).

It is not always convenient or necessary to measure the volume of a gas under these conditions. Fortunately the volume can be measured under the conditions of the experiment and then the Gas Equation can be used to convert this volume to the volume it would occupy at s.t.p.

Example 4 A fixed mass of gas has a volume of 440 cm³ at 13°C and 836 mm pressure. Calculate its volume at s.t.p.

$$13°C = 286K \qquad 0°C = 273K$$

$$\frac{P_I V_I}{T_I} = \frac{P_2 V_2}{T_2}$$

$$P_I = 836 \text{ mm} \qquad V_I = 440 \text{ cm}^3 \qquad T_I = 286K$$
$$P_2 = 760 \text{ mm} \qquad V_2 = \quad ? \qquad T_2 = 273K$$

$$\therefore \frac{836 \times 440}{286} = \frac{760 \times V_2}{273}$$

$$\therefore V_2 = 440 \times \frac{836}{760} \times \frac{273}{286} \text{ cm}^3$$

N.B. When you reach this stage, check

(a) that the change in volume is what you would expect; e.g. a decrease in pressure should result in an increase in volume, thus 836/760, NOT 760/836, and a decrease in temperature should result in a decrease in volume, thus 273/286, NOT 286/273;

(b) in a calculation involving s.t.p., that 760 and 273 are on opposite sides of the dividing line.

$$V_2 = \underline{462 \text{ cm}^3}$$

The relationship between the weight of a gas and its volume

Having established a method of converting the volume of a gas to its volume under standard conditions (s.t.p.), we can now investigate how the weights of equal volumes of gases vary from one gas to another.

One method of doing this is to weigh a container full of one gas, then fill it with another gas and weigh it again. In order to find the weight of each gas, of course, the weight of the container itself must be known; and this must be its weight without air. If all the air could be pumped

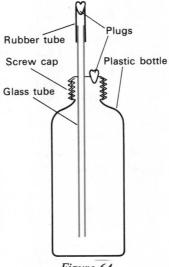

Rubber tube

Plugs

Screw cap

Plastic bottle

Glass tube

Figure 64

out, the container could be weighed when completely empty (evacuated); but facilities for doing this efficiently are not usually available in a school laboratory. The next best thing is to calculate the weight of the air from the knowledge of its volume and its density and then to subtract this from the weight of the container full of air.

Experiment 16.1

To measure the volume of 1 g-formula of various gases (**C** or **D**)

Fit a plastic bottle with a narrow delivery tube as shown in *figure 64*; another small hole in the plastic cap of the bottle acts as a vent when the bottle is being filled with gas. You can use small plastic plugs to block the holes in the bottle and the hole in the tube while weighing the gas. The bottle should have a volume of about 500 cm³ and should be as light as possible (50–70 g).

Weigh the bottle complete with plugs and full of air. Remove the plugs and connect the delivery tube to a sulphur dioxide cylinder, turn on the gas (fume cupboard) for one or two minutes in order to sweep the air from the container and to fill it with sulphur dioxide (see *Notes for Teachers*). Insert the plugs and weigh the bottle again. This can be repeated with carbon dioxide and hydrogen sulphide from Kipp's apparatus, and with oxygen from a cylinder.

Fill the container completely with water. Pour the water into a measuring cylinder and thus determine the volume of the container. Note the temperature and pressure of the air in the laboratory.

Specimen Results

$$\text{Volume of gas} = 550 \text{ cm}^3$$

$$\text{Temperature} = 20°C \ (293K), \qquad \text{Pressure} = 752 \text{ mm}$$

$$\therefore \ \text{Volume of gas at s.t.p.} = 550 \times \frac{273}{293} \times \frac{752}{760}$$

$$= \underline{507 \text{ cm}^3}$$

$$\text{Density of air at s.t.p.} = 1 \cdot 29 \text{ g per litre}$$

$$\therefore \ \text{Weight of 507 cm}^3 \text{ of air at s.t.p.} = 1 \cdot 29 \times \frac{507}{1000} \text{ g}$$

$$= \underline{0 \cdot 65 \text{ g}}$$

$$\text{Weight of bottle} + \text{air} = 59 \cdot 08 \text{ g}$$

$$\therefore \ \text{Weight of empty bottle} = (59 \cdot 08 - 0 \cdot 65) \text{ g}$$

$$= \underline{58 \cdot 43 \text{ g}}$$

Weight of bottle + sulphur dioxide	=	59·89 g
„ „ „ + carbon dioxide	=	59·44 g
„ „ „ + hydrogen sulphide	=	59·18 g
„ „ „ + oxygen	=	59·14 g

∴ Weight of 507 cm³ of sulphur dioxide	=	1·46 g
„ „ „ „ carbon dioxide	=	1·01 g
„ „ „ „ hydrogen sulphide	=	0·75 g
„ „ „ „ oxygen	=	0·71 g

The volume occupied by 1 gram formula of a gas (revise p. 78 before going further)

This can now be calculated from the information obtained in Experiment 16.1:

Sulphur dioxide: formula SO_2, formula weight = 64, g-formula weight = 64 g

1·46 g of sulphur dioxide has a volume of 507 cm³ at s.t.p.

∴ 1 g-formula of sulphur dioxide has a volume of $507 \times \dfrac{64}{1 \cdot 46}$ cm³

$$= 22\ 200\ \text{cm}^3\ (22 \cdot 2\ \text{litres})$$

Carbon dioxide: formula CO_2, formula weight = 44, g-formula weight = 44 g

1·01 g of carbon dioxide has a volume of 507 cm³ at s.t.p.

∴ 1 g-formula of carbon dioxide has a volume of $507 \times \dfrac{44}{1 \cdot 01}$ cm³

$$= 22\ 100\ \text{cm}^3\ (22 \cdot 1\ \text{litres})$$

Hydrogen sulphide: formula H_2S, formula weight = 34, g-formula weight = 34 g

0·75 g of hydrogen sulphide has a volume of 507 cm³ at s.t.p.

∴ 1 g-formula hydrogen sulphide has a volume of $507 \times \dfrac{34}{0 \cdot 75}$ cm³

$$= 23\ 000\ \text{cm}^3\ (23 \cdot 0\ \text{litres})$$

Oxygen will be considered later.

The first thing which is obvious from the figures is that although the actual weight (in grams) of each gas is different, the volume occupied by 1 g-formula of each is approximately the same. This is confirmed by more careful experiments with many more gases. It is then found that 1 g-formula of most gases occupies 22·4 litres at s.t.p. (some gases have a smaller volume than this but 1 g-formula of a gas never has a greater volume than this).

Why is the volume of one gram formula of many gases the same?

If the smallest particle of sulphur dioxide which can exist freely is represented by the formula SO_2, then this formula represents *one molecule* of sulphur dioxide and the formula weight is the same as the

Table 9

Gas	Weight of 1 molecule	Weight of N_A molecules (1 g-molecules)	Volume of N_A molecules (s.t.p.)
sulphur dioxide (SO_2)	64	64 g	22·4 litres
carbon dioxide (CO_2)	44	44 g	22·4 litres
hydrogen sulphide (H_2S)	34	34 g	22·4 litres
ammonia (NH_3)	17	17 g	22·4 litres
methane (CH_4)	16	16 g	22·4 litres
carbon monoxide (CO)	28	28 g	22·4 litres

weight of 1 molecule (*molecular weight*). Avogadro's number (N_A) of SO_2 molecules will weigh 64 g .This weight can be called 1 g-formula or 1 *g-molecule* of sulphur dioxide (*See table 9*).

By a similar argument, 44 g of carbon dioxide is 1 g-molecule and would contain N_A molecules of formula CO_2; 34 g of hydrogen sulphide is 1 g-molecule and would contain N_A molecules of formula H_2S.

Since the volumes of 64 g of sulphur dioxide, 44 g of carbon dioxide, and 34 g of hydrogen sulphide are all the same (22·4 litres at s.t.p.), our argument leads us to suppose that 22·4 litres of each gas contains an equal number (N_A) of molecules. This applies to many other gases.

This occurs so often that it is reasonable to suppose that each molecule of any gas occupies the same volume under the same conditions of temperature and pressure. This is true regardless of the actual size of the molecule, which is generally insignificant compared with the space it occupies.

The volume occupied by N_A molecules of any gas (1 g-molecule) is the same (22·4 litres at s.t.p.) and is called the *molar volume* of a gas.

The fact that 22·4 litres of any gas contain an equal number of molecules leads to the general statement: *Equal volumes of gases (under the same conditions of temperature and pressure) contain an equal number of molecules*. This idea was first put forward by Avogadro as early as 1810 and it is known as *Avogadro's Hypothesis*.

The atomicity of gaseous elements

The smallest part of the element oxygen is one atom and it weighs 16. If oxygen itself consisted of separate single atoms of oxygen, N_A of these atoms would weigh 16 g and we should expect 16 g (1 g-atom) of oxygen to occupy 22·4 litres at s.t.p.

Experiment 16.1 indicates, however, that this is not so; it is in fact 32 g of oxygen which occupy 22·4 litres at s.t.p. If our theory of molar volume is correct, then 22·4 litres of oxygen will contain N_A particles of oxygen each weighing 32; i.e. each particle must consist of two atoms (O_2) of oxygen.

The same argument can be applied to hydrogen, nitrogen, chlorine, bromine, and iodine; 22·4 litres (s.t.p.) of each of these in the gaseous state weigh 2×1 g-atom.

All this does not prove beyond doubt that free particles of these elements, as gases, consist of a pair of atoms, but the evidence is sufficiently strong for us always to represent them as diatomic molecules when they are not combined with any other element: H_2, O_2, N_2, Cl_2, Br_2, I_2.

Reacting volumes of gases

It is generally more convenient to measure the volumes of gases taking part in a chemical action than to measure their weight.

Experiment 16.2

To investigate the action between nitrogen monoxide (NO) and oxygen by measuring their reacting volumes **(D)**

The apparatus is shown in *figure 65*. The two syringes are made of glass and each has a capacity of 100 cm³. They are joined through a three-way stop-cock by two pieces of rubber tube. To keep the volume of gas in the connections as small as possible, the three arms of the stop-cock are made of capillary tube and the connecting tubes are as short as possible.

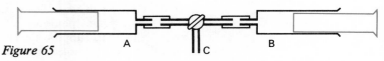

A   C   B

Figure 65

Turn the stop-cock so that syringe B is connected to the outlet tube C. Pass about 20 cm³ of oxygen from a cylinder into syringe B. Expel this oxygen and repeat once more to wash all the air from this part of the apparatus. Finally, pass about 60 cm³ of oxygen into B and push in the plunger until exactly 50 cm³ of oxygen are contained in B. Turn the stop-cock until A is connected to C.

Connect C by a short piece of rubber tube to a supply of pure dry nitrogen monoxide. (This gas can be made by dripping 2 molar sulphuric acid into a gently warmed mixture of molar sodium nitrite and molar iron (II) sulphate solutions. The gas may be dried by passing it through a tube containing glass wool moistened with concentrated sulphuric acid.)

Wash syringe A twice with 20 cm³ of nitrogen monoxide and then fill it with exactly 40 cm³ of the gas in the same way as that used for oxygen. Turn the stop-cock so that A, B, and C are not connected to each other. Remove the nitrogen monoxide generator.

Turn the stop-cock so that the two syringes are connected to each other. By pushing gently on the plunger of B, transfer 5 cm³ of oxygen to A. Immediately turn the stop-cock so that A, B, and C are disconnected. Manipulate the plunger of A gently for about two minutes to equalize the pressure inside the syringe with atmospheric pressure while the reaction takes place. Record the volume of gas in both syringes. Reconnect the two syringes and proceed as before, transferring 5 cm³ portions of oxygen from B to A.

Specimen Results (cm³)

Volume in A	Volume in B	Volume of oxygen transferred to A	Total volume (A+B)
40	50	0	90
36	45	5	81
31	40	10	71
27	35	15	62
20	30	20	50
26	25	25	51
31	20	30	51
36	15	35	51

Draw a graph of total volume (A+B) against volume of oxygen transferred to A.

The reaction between nitrogen monoxide and oxygen appears to cause a decrease in volume, so it is reasonable to suppose that the reaction is complete when the combined volume of the gases stops decreasing. From the graph determine the minimum volume of oxygen which will complete the reaction with 40 cm³ of nitrogen monoxide. Express your findings as a simple ratio:

volume of nitrogen monoxide : volume of reacting oxygen; hence, molecules of NO : molecules of O_2.

Another example

100 cm³ of carbon monoxide react with 50 cm³ of oxygen to form 100 cm³ of carbon dioxide.

These volumes are in simple ratio (2:1:2)

∴ 2 volumes of carbon monoxide react with 1 volume of oxygen to form 2 volumes of carbon dioxide (1 volume, in this example, represents 50 cm³);

or diagrammatically

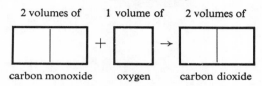

2 volumes of   1 volume of   2 volumes of

carbon monoxide   oxygen   carbon dioxide

Gay Lussac's law

This simple ratio between volumes is common to most reactions between gases. It was first observed by Gay Lussac (1802) who summarized these observations into the generalization which is now called *Gay Lussac's Law: In a reaction the volumes (under the same conditions) of all gaseous reactants and products bear a simple ratio to each other*

We shall now apply Avogadro's Hypothesis to Gay Lussac's Law:

The relationship between reacting volumes and reacting molecules

(the typical results quoted above will be used)

Two volumes of carbon monoxide react with 1 volume of oxygen to form 2 volumes of carbon dioxide.

But equal volumes of gases contain an equal number of molecules. Suppose 1 volume contains x molecules.

∴ $2x$ molecules of carbon monoxide + x molecules of oxygen → $2x$ molecules of carbon dioxide.

∴ 2 molecules of carbon monoxide + 1 molecule of oxygen → 2 molecules of carbon dioxide. If this is multiplied by N_A, $2N_A$ molecules of carbon monoxide + N_A molecules of oxygen → $2N_A$ molecules of carbon dioxide.

∴ 2 g-molecules of carbon monoxide + 1 g-molecule of oxygen → 2 g-molecules of carbon dioxide.

Assuming that the formula of a molecule of each of the substances is known, the application of Avogadro's Hypothesis to the experimental results has enabled us to deduce the chemical equation for the reaction:

$$2CO_{(g)} + O_{2(g)} \rightarrow 2CO_{2(g)}$$

or diagrammatically

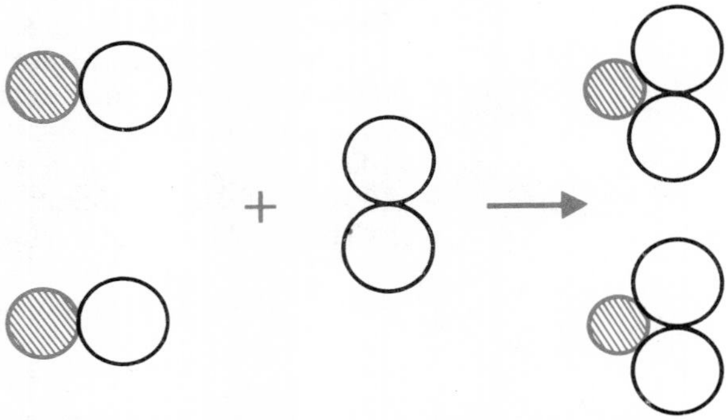

| 2 Molecules of carbon monoxide | + | 1 Molecule oxygen | → | 2 Molecules of carbon dioxide |

Figure 66

In other words, the ratio of the reacting volumes of gases is the same as the ratio of the reacting molecules or g-molecules of gases; for example:

1 volume of A + 3 volumes of B → 2 volumes of C
∴ 1 molecule of A + 3 molecules of B → 2 molecules of C
∴ 1 g-molecule of A + 3 g-molecules of B → 2 g-molecules of C

Some other applications of molar volume

So far, the idea of molar volume and Avogadro's Hypothesis has been used to deduce an equation from a knowledge of the volumes of gases which take part in a reaction. This process can be reversed: some equations are now so firmly established that they can be used to forecast the volumes of gases in a reaction.

Example 1 Calculate the volume of hydrogen sulphide formed at s.t.p. when 22 g of iron (II) sulphide react with excess hydrochloric acid.

$$FeS + 2HCl \rightarrow FeCl_2 + H_2S_{(g)}$$

56 + 32	1 molecule
88 g	1 g-molecule
	occupying 22·4 litres
	at s.t.p.

∴ 88 g of iron (II) sulphide form 22·4 litres of hydrogen sulphide at s.t.p.

∴ 22 g of iron (II) sulphide form $22·4 \times \dfrac{22}{88}$ litres

$= \underline{5·6}$ litres of hydrogen sulphide

Example 2 Calculate the volume of hydrogen measured at s.t.p. which on burning will form 1·8 g of water.

$$2H_{2(g)} + O_{2(g)} \rightarrow 2H_2O_{(l)}$$

2 molecules	36
2 g-molecules	36 g
occupying 2 × 22·4 litres	
at s.t.p.	

$$\therefore \text{ 36 g of water are formed from 44·8 litres of hydrogen}$$

$$\therefore \text{ 1·8 g of water are formed from } 44·8 \times \frac{1·8}{36} \text{ litres}$$

$$= 2·24 \text{ litres of hydrogen}$$

Example 3   A quantity of carbon was burned in an excess of oxygen. If 187 cm³ of carbon dioxide were formed, calculate the volume of oxygen used in the burning, all measurements being made at the same temperature and pressure.

$$C_{(s)} \quad + \quad O_{2(g)} \quad \rightarrow \quad CO_{2(g)}$$
1 atom of+1 molecule of → 1 molecule of
carbon   oxygen   carbon dioxide

As carbon is solid, its volume will be small enough to be neglected.

$$\therefore \text{ 1 vol. of oxygen } \rightarrow \text{ 1 vol. of carbon dioxide}$$
The volume of carbon dioxide = 187 cm³
$$\therefore \text{ The volume of oxygen used} = \underline{187 \text{ cm}^3}$$

Example 4   50 cm³ of carbon monoxide and 30 cm³ of oxygen were allowed to react. Calculate the composition by volume of the resulting gas, volumes being measured at the same temperature and pressure.

$$2CO_{(g)} \quad + \quad O_{2(g)} \quad \rightarrow \quad 2CO_{2(g)}$$
2 molecules of +1 molecule of → 2 molecules of
carbon monoxide   oxygen   carbon dioxide

$\therefore$ 2 vol. of carbon monoxide+1 vol. of oxygen → 2 vol. of carbon dioxide.

The number of cm³ in 1 volume can be calculated from the volume of that gas which reacts completely. Since oxygen can react with twice its volume of carbon monoxide, 30 cm³ of oxygen could react with 60 cm³ of carbon monoxide. There are only 50 cm³ of carbon monoxide, therefore all the carbon monoxide must react.

$$\therefore \text{ 2 vol.} = 50 \text{ cm}^3$$
$$\therefore \text{ 1 vol.} = 25 \text{ cm}^3$$

$\therefore$ 50 cm³ of carbon monoxide+25 cm³ of oxygen → 50 cm³ of carbon dioxide.

$$\therefore \text{ Gas remaining is oxygen } (30-25) \text{ cm}^3 = \underline{5 \text{ cm}^3}$$
$$\text{and carbon dioxide} = \underline{50 \text{ cm}^3}$$

Example 5   50 cm³ of hydrogen were exploded with 80 cm³ of air (80% nitrogen, 20% oxygen). Calculate the composition of the resulting gas, all measurements being made at room temperature and pressure.

At room temperature no steam will be formed and the water will have negligible volume.

$$\text{Volume of oxygen} = 20\% \text{ of 80 cm}^3 = 16 \text{ cm}^3$$
$$2H_{2(g)} \quad + \quad O_{2(g)} \quad \rightarrow \quad 2H_2O_{(l)}$$
2 molecules of+1 molecule of → 2 molecules of
hydrogen   oxygen   water
$\therefore$ 2 vol. of hydrogen react with 1 vol. of oxygen

F

As hydrogen reacts with half its volume of oxygen, 50 cm³ of hydrogen could react with 25 cm³ of oxygen. There are only 16 cm³ of oxygen, therefore all the oxygen must react.

$$\therefore \text{1 vol.} = 16 \text{ cm}^3$$
$$\therefore \text{2 vol.} = 32 \text{ cm}^3$$
$$\therefore \text{32 cm}^3 \text{ of hydrogen react with 16 cm}^3 \text{ of oxygen}$$
$$\therefore \text{Gas remaining is hydrogen } (50-32) \text{ cm}^3 = 18 \text{ cm}^3$$
$$\text{and nitrogen } (80-16) \text{ cm}^3 = \overline{64 \text{ cm}^3}$$

Example 6 The gas, ethane, contains carbon and hydrogen atoms in the ratio 1:3. Its simplest formula is, therefore, CH_3. When 1 litre of ethane is burned, it forms 2 litres of carbon dioxide. Assuming the formula of carbon dioxide to be CO_2, deduce the molecular formula of ethane.

1 volume of ethane forms 2 volumes of carbon dioxide
$\therefore$ 1 molecule of ethane forms 2 molecules of carbon dioxide
$\therefore$ 1 molecule of ethane must contain 2 carbon atoms
$\therefore$ The molecular formula of ethane $= \underline{C_2H_6}$

Problems

(1) 2·56 g of sulphur formed a vapour, at 546°C and 1 atm pressure, which had a volume of 672 cm³. Calculate:

(a) the volume of the vapour at s.t.p.
(b) the weight of 22·4 litres of sulphur vapour at s.t.p.
(c) the weight of 1 g-molecule of sulphur
(d) the weight of 1 molecule of sulphur
(e) the formula of a sulphur molecule.

(2) Phosphorus vapour is said to have a molecular formula of P_4. Assuming this to be true, calculate:

(a) the molecular weight of phosphorus.
(b) the weight of 22·4 litres of phosphorus vapour at s.t.p.
(c) the volume of 1 g-atom of phosphorus vapour at s.t.p.
(d) the volume of 1 g-atom of phosphorus vapour at 273°C and 0·2 atm pressure.

(3) 72 cm³ of hydrogen sulphide were mixed with 16 cm³ of sulphur dioxide and allowed to react a at constant temperature and pressure (the temperature was above 100°C). The gas so formed was found to consist of 40 cm³ of hydrogen sulphide and 32 cm³ of steam. Deduce:

(a) the volume of hydrogen sulphide used in the reaction.
(b) the ratio of the reacting volumes of hydrogen sulphide and sulphur dioxide and the volume of steam which was formed.
(c) the equation for the reaction (assume that the only other product was sulphur).

(4) (i) 4·6 g of the gas X consist of 1·4 g nitrogen and 3·2 g of oxygen. Calculate the formula of the gas.

(ii) At 273°C and 1 atm pressure 4·6 g of X occupy 4·48 litres.

Deduce (a) the weight of X which would occupy 22·4 litres at s.t.p.
(b) the apparent molecular weight of X
(c) the molecular formula of X.

(5) 1·62 g of hydrogen selenide contain 0·04 g of hydrogen and 1·58 g of selenium. Calculate the formula of hydrogen selenide. When 2 litres of hydrogen selenide were decomposed they formed 2 litres of hydrogen. Assuming hydrogen to be diatomic, deduce the molecular formula of hydrogen selenide.

(6) 5·2 g of the gas acetylene contain 4·8 g of carbon and 0·4 g of hydrogen; deduce the simplest formula of acetylene. When 100 cm³ of acetylene are burned they form 200 cm³ of carbon dioxide (measured under the same conditions). Deduce the molecular formula of acetylene.

(7) Propane gas has a molecular formula of C_3H_8. Calculate the volume of carbon dioxide which can be formed by burning 223 cm³ of propane (all volumes measured under the same conditions).

Summary

(1) Boyle's Law: The volume of a fixed mass of gas is inversely proportional to its pressure at constant temperature (PV = constant, $P_1V_1 = P_2V_2$).

(2) Charles' Law: The volume of a fixed mass of gas is proportional to its absolute temperature at constant pressure.

$$\left(\frac{V}{T} = \text{constant}, \frac{V_1}{T_1} = \frac{V_2}{T_2}\right).$$

(3) The Gas Equation: $\frac{PV}{T}$ = constant (for a fixed mass of gas). If this fixed mass of gas is 1 g-molecule, the constant is given the symbol R and is called the Gas Constant.

(4) s.t.p. The standard conditions under which volumes of gases are usually compared (273K and 760 mm).

(5) 1 g-molecule of any gas occupies 22·4 litres at s.t.p. But 1 g-molecule of any gas contains N_A molecules; therefore 22·4 litres of any gas, at s.t.p., contain N_A molecules.

(6) Avogadro's Hypothesis: Equal volumes of gases (under the same conditions of temperature and pressure) contain an equal number of molecules.

(7) The weight of 22·4 litres of some gaseous elements (H_2, O_2, N_2, Cl_2, Br_2, I_2) is that of 2 g-atoms. Therefore 1 g-molecule of each of these gases contains 2 g-atoms. Therefore 1 molecule of each of these gases contains 2 atoms: the gases are diatomic.

(8) Gay-Lussac's Law: In a reaction the volumes (under the same conditions) of all gaseous reactants and products bear a simple ratio to each other.

(9) The ratio of volumes in a gaseous reaction is the same as the ratio of the numbers of molecules and the same as the ratio of the numbers of g-molecules.

Nitrogen–ammonia-ammonium compounds-bases (2)

Nitrogen

Occurrence

Nitrogen is abundant. It makes up 80% by volume of the atmosphere, from which it can be made by liquefying air and then allowing the more volatile nitrogen to evaporate. It is not very reactive, and, unlike some other gaseous elements, there is no simple reaction which can be used to test for it. The reactions of nitrogen with hydrogen and oxygen are described below.

Uses

The element has a limited commercial use as an inert atmosphere when gaseous and a coolant when liquid. Its compounds, however, are essential to life and industry. They are extensively used as plant fertilizers to increase the production of food. Proteins, which form a part of all living things, are themselves compounds of nitrogen. Nitrogen compounds are also used in explosives; nitroglycerine, trinitrotoluene (TNT), and nitrocellulose (guncotton) have been made in large quantities, particularly for destructive purposes.

This twofold potential—construction or destruction—is not confined to the compounds of nitrogen. The same choice faces us in the use of many other products of nature or of mankind's ingenuity: uranium, petroleum and drugs can all be wisely used or foolishly squandered. We cannot alter the natural properties of these things, but we do govern their use.

Ammonia

Ammonia is the name of the principal compound of nitrogen and hydrogen. At room temperature and pressure it is a gas.

Formula

The ratio of nitrogen to hydrogen by weight in ammonia is 14:3, therefore the ratio of nitrogen atoms to hydrogen atoms in ammonia is $1:3$ and its formula is NH_3.

$$\text{The formula weight} = (14+3) = 17$$

It is found that 17 g (1 g-formula) of ammonia occupies 22·4 litres at s.t.p. But N_A molecules (1 g-molecule) of any gas occupies this volume at s.t.p.; therefore, a g-molecule of ammonia is the same as a g-formula and NH_3 correctly represents the composition of one molecule of ammonia.

Occurrence

Free ammonia is not found in nature in large quantities. It does occur in the excretions of some animals and its smell is particularly noticeable if one goes into a stable after the horses have been shut up for some time. Ammonia reacts readily to form ammonium compounds and these are also found in decaying organic material.

Manufacture

Ammonia is made by combining nitrogen and hydrogen in the presence of a catalyst.

The reaction is reversible:

$$N_2 + 3H_2 \rightleftharpoons 2NH_3$$

If the three components are left together, they will reach a dynamic equilibrium in which the reaction left to right goes at the same rate as the reaction right to left; thus, not all the nitrogen and hydrogen will be converted into ammonia.

The conditions for obtaining the best yield of ammonia vary in different processes. A high pressure, over 200 atmospheres, is used, together with a moderate temperature, 475°C to 600°C.

The catalyst, usually iron mixed with small quantities of aluminium oxide and potassium oxide, increases the speed of the reactions, both left to right and right to left, but does not increase the yield of ammonia.

In the laboratory a supply of ammonia is most conveniently made by warming a concentrated aqueous solution of the gas or by warming an ammonium salt with strong alkali.

The action of ammonia on water

Experiment 17.1
The fountain experiment (D)

Construct the apparatus shown in *figure 67*.

The bottom flask is almost filled with water coloured red by adding some litmus solution and a few drops of acid. The straight delivery tube goes from the bottom of this flask to within an inch of the top of the flask. Its top end is constricted to form a jet.

Remove the top flask and fill it with ammonia as shown in *figure 68*. Clamp the flask full of ammonia firmly and quickly into its position shown in *figure 67*. Blow a few drops of water into the top flask and stand back.

The spectacular eruption of the water from the bottom flask to the top flask in Experiment 17.1 is caused by the sudden lowering of pressure when most of the ammonia in the top flask dissolves in the first few cm³ of water which enter it.

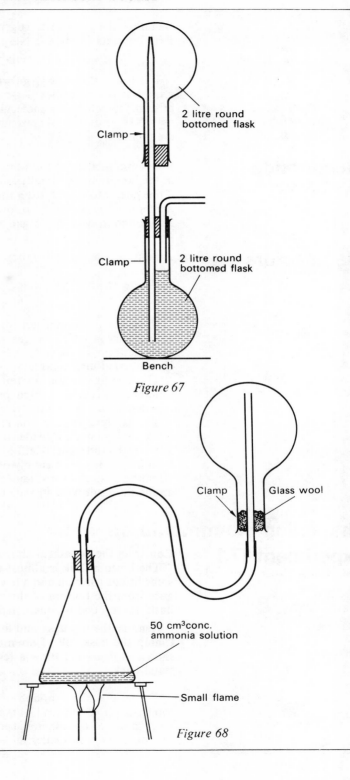

Figure 67

Figure 68

Aqueous solution of ammonia (ammonium hydroxide)

Action on indicators The colour change from red to blue in Experiment 17.1 shows that the solution of ammonia in water is alkaline. Furthermore, it has already been shown by its action on universal indicator (p. 48) that it is a weak alkali compared with aqueous sodium hydroxide.

All the alkaline solutions which we have studied so far have been solutions of hydroxides. It is likely, therefore, that ammonia reacts with water to form a hydroxide (ammonium hydroxide):

$$NH_3 + H_2O \rightarrow NH_4OH$$

The action of heat on ammonium hydroxide

Experiment 17.2

(C)

Put 2 or 3 drops of ammonium hydroxide into a clean dry test tube. Notice the smell of ammonia gas; this increases if the solution is warmed gently. Evaporate the liquid and note that the amount of solid residue is negligible—solid ammonium hydroxide is unknown.

It appears that ammonium hydroxide readily yields ammonia, so that the reaction given above is reversible:

$$NH_3 + H_2O \rightleftharpoons NH_4OH$$

The ionization of ammonium hydroxide

Experiment 17.3

To compare the conductance of aqueous sodium hydroxide and aqueous ammonium hydroxide **(C or D)**

The apparatus and procedure are the same as in other conductance experiments (p. 51). The solutions should be of the same molarity (2 M will do).

Put the electrodes into a U-tube containing ammonium hydroxide and attach them to a 20 volt source of d.c. Note the current which flows. Rinse the U-tube and repeat the experiment with aqueous sodium hydroxide.

Experiment 17.3 shows that aqueous sodium hydroxide is a better conductor than aqueous ammonium hydroxide, and this, in turn, indicates that sodium hydroxide is more completely ionized than ammonium hydroxide in aqueous solution.

Experiment 17.4

To investigate the action of ammonium hydroxide on some solutions of salts **(C)**

Put four drops of iron (II) sulphate solution into a small test tube and add ammonium hydroxide drop by drop. Repeat this with solutions of iron (III) chloride, aluminium sulphate, and chromium (III) sulphate (the chromium ion is Cr^{3+}). Record and explain your observations, and construct ionic equations for the reactions.

The precipitation of insoluble hydroxides of metals in Experiment 17.4 indicates that ammonium hydroxide contains hydroxide ions. But the low conductivity of ammonium hydroxide indicates that this ionization is not complete; in fact ammonium hydroxide is only slightly ionized. The ammonium ions and hydroxide ions appear to be in dynamic equilibrium with unchanged ammonium hydroxide:

$$NH_4OH_{(aq)} \rightleftharpoons NH_4^+{}_{(aq)} + OH^-{}_{(aq)}$$

How does ammonium hydroxide precipitate insoluble hydroxides?

Although the concentration of hydroxide ions in ammonium hydroxide is low, the removal of these ions as a precipitate upsets the equilibrium shown above and the reaction moves from left to right, producing more hydroxide ions and hence more precipitate. Turn to p. 132 and compare this with the precipitation of insoluble sulphides by the action of aqueous hydrogen sulphide.

What does an aqueous solution of ammonia contain?

It seems that in aqueous ammonia there are several things in equilibrium: ammonia, water, ammonium hydroxide, ammonium ions, and hydroxide ions:

$$NH_3 + H_2O \rightleftharpoons NH_4OH \rightleftharpoons NH_4^+ + OH^-$$

If ammonia is removed by warming the solution, the equilibrium is upset and the reaction moves to the left.

If hydroxide ions are removed by precipitation, the equilibrium is upset and the reaction moves to the right.

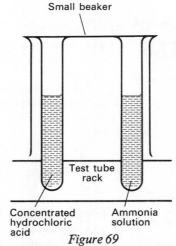

Small beaker

Test tube rack

Concentrated hydrochloric acid

Ammonia solution

Figure 69

It is beyond the scope of this course to determine the relative amounts of ammonia and ammonium hydroxide in an aqueous solution of ammonia.

The formation of ammonium salts (Experiments 17.5 and 17.6 should be done at the same time)

Experiment 17.5

To investigate the reaction between ammonia and hydrogen chloride **(C)**

Half fill a small test tube with concentrated hydrochloric acid and half fill another with aqueous ammonia. Stand them together in a test tube rack, covered with a small beaker (*figure 69*), for about twenty minutes.

Experiment 17.6

To investigate the action between aqueous ammonia and aqueous acids **(C)**

Put one drop of dilute hydrochloric acid on to the centre of a small watch glass. Add two drops of ammonium hydroxide and evaporate to dryness carefully (see p. 9).

When the watch glass has cooled so that it can be held on the hand, add one drop of water to the white solid which has been formed. Can you detect ammonia, either by smell or by holding a piece of damp red litmus paper just above the solution in the watch glass? Add one drop of sodium hydroxide solution to the solution and test for the evolution of ammonia. Repeat the experiment using sulphuric acid.

By this time, some white solid will have been deposited either in the beaker or round the mouths of the test tubes used in Experiment 17.5. Scrape out some of the solid with a spatula, transfer it to a small watch glass, and treat it in the same way as the solid from Experiment 17.6.

The white solids formed in the last two experiments are ammonium salts, ammonium chloride (NH_4Cl) and ammonium sulphate ($(NH_4)_2SO_4$).

For the moment the reactions can be represented by formal equations:

Experiment 17.5 $\quad NH_3 + HCl \rightarrow NH_4Cl$

Experiment 17.6

$$NH_4OH + HCl \rightarrow NH_4Cl + H_2O$$
$$2NH_4OH + H_2SO_4 \rightarrow (NH_4)_2SO_4 + 2H_2O$$

The properties of ammonium salts

(1) Conductance

Using the method which by now should be familiar, aqueous solutions of ammonium salts can be shown to be good conductors of electricity. This indicates that they are ionized and, although this is not easily demonstrated, they are also ionic in the solid state. Therefore, they all contain the ammonium ion, NH_4^+.

(2) The action of strong alkalis

Experiment 17.6 has already shown that ammonium chloride and ammonium sulphate yield ammonia when treated with sodium hydroxide. In fact all ammonium salts when treated with any of the strong alkalis (sodium, potassium, and calcium hydroxides) yield ammonia at room temperature and do so more quickly when heated:

$$NH_4Cl + NaOH \rightarrow NaCl + H_2O + NH_3$$

Since all ammonium salts have the ammonium ion in common, and all alkalis have the hydroxide ion in common, it is more convenient to write one ionic equation to represent all these reactions rather than formal equations for each one:

$$NH_4{}^+{}_{(aq)} + OH^-{}_{(aq)} \rightarrow NH_4OH_{(aq)} \rightarrow NH_{3(g)} + H_2O_{(l)}$$

(3) The action of heat

Experiment 17.7

The action of heat on ammonium chloride (C)

Put two small measures of ammonium chloride into a dry, small test tube. Heat the ammonium chloride, holding the tube horizontally and confining the heat to the end of the tube.

Scrape out some of the solid which has sublimed along the tube and test it for (a) ammonium ions (b) chloride ions (p. 105).

Experiment 17.7 shows that ammonium chloride *sublimes*: it changes from a solid to a gas on heating and back to the same solid on cooling. It it is mixed with a non-volatile impurity, this can be a useful method of purifying an ammonium salt (see Problem 2, p. 165).

It appears that when ammonium chloride is heated it decomposes into ammonia and hydrogen chloride and these two gases combine to form ammonium chloride on cooling. The reaction between ammonia and hydrogen chloride, therefore, is reversible:

$$NH_{3(g)} + HCl_{(g)} \underset{heat}{\overset{cool}{\rightleftharpoons}} NH_4Cl_{(s)}$$

Most ammonium salts do this, but do not try it with ammonium nitrate—it explodes.

This type of reaction is a reversible decomposition and is sometimes called a *dissociation*. If the reversible decomposition is brought about by heat, as in this case, it is called a *thermal dissociation*.

More about acids and bases

The action between ammonia and hydrogen chloride results in the formation of ammonium chloride. Since this compound is ionic, the reaction can be represented:

$$NH_3 + HCl \rightarrow NH_4^+Cl^-$$

Hydrogen chloride has acted as an acid by giving a hydrogen ion to the ammonia:

$$\begin{cases} HCl \quad\quad \rightarrow H^+ + Cl^- \\ \quad\text{acid} \\ \\ NH_3 + H^+ \rightarrow NH_4{}^+ \end{cases}$$

This should remind you of the action between hydrogen chloride and water (p. 103):

$$HCl + H_2O \rightarrow H_3O^+ + Cl^-$$
$$\text{acid}$$

$$\begin{cases} HCl \quad\quad \rightarrow H^+ + Cl^- \\ \\ H_2O + H^+ \rightarrow H_3O^+ \end{cases}$$

Note that both reactions are reversible, which indicates that both the ammonium ions and the hydronium ions can give hydrogen ions back to the chloride ions:

$$NH_4^+ + Cl^- \rightarrow NH_3 + HCl$$
$$H_3O^+ + Cl^- \rightarrow H_2O + HCl \quad \text{(p. 107)}$$

What is a base?

The idea that an acid is something which can give a hydrogen ion should, by now, be firmly established. But, so far, the term 'base' has been confined to the basic oxides or hydroxides of metals which form salts with acids.

The definition of a *base* may now be extended to include *all substances which accept hydrogen ions from an acid*. Thus, ammonia can act as a base:

$$NH_3 + H^+ \rightarrow NH_4^+$$

Water can also act as a base:

$$H_2O + H^+ \rightarrow H_3O^+$$

To sum up: *When a substance gives hydrogen ions, it is acting as an acid. When a substance accepts hydrogen ions, it is acting as a base.*

Note the expression 'acting as a base' rather than 'is a base'. There is a good reason for this; when ammonia reacts with water, ammonium ions and hydroxide ions are formed:

$$NH_3 + H_2O \rightarrow NH_4^+ OH^-$$

In this reaction, ammonia is acting as a base and water is acting as an acid:

$$\begin{cases} \underset{\text{acid}}{H_2O} \quad\;\; \rightarrow H^+ + OH^- \\[2em] \underset{\text{base}}{NH_3} + H^+ \rightarrow NH_4^+ \end{cases}$$

So water can act either as a base or as an acid depending on the substance with which it is reacting. Many substances have this dual nature (including ammonia), so that it is unwise to classify substances rigidly as acids or bases.

Of course, some substances have a stronger tendency one way than the other; for example, nitric acid can give hydrogen ions to water:

$$\underset{\text{acid}}{HNO_3} + \underset{\text{base}}{H_2O} \rightarrow H_3O^+ + NO_3^-$$

but when mixed with concentrated sulphuric acid it receives hydrogen ions:

$$\underset{\text{base}}{HNO_3} + \underset{\text{acid}}{H_2SO_4} \rightarrow H_2NO_3^+ + HSO_4^-$$

In the first reaction it is acting as an acid, in the second it is acting as a base. But because its tendency to undergo the first kind of reaction is much stronger than its tendency to the second and because we shall meet it mostly in aqueous solutions, it is reasonable to call it an acid.

Ammonium compounds and ammonia

These two are sometimes confused. Ammonia (NH_3) is a compound which can exist uncombined with anything else. Ammonium does not exist on its own; it always forms part of a compound, for example in ammonium hydroxide and ammonium salts; and usually it is in the form of a positive ion, the ammonium ion (NH_4^+), which is formed when ammonia receives a hydrogen ion ($NH_3 + H^+ \rightarrow NH_4^+$).

Ammonium salts are the first salts you have met which do not contain a metallic element. They are all derived from the base, ammonia, as a result of its action with an acid. Both in appearance and properties they are typical salts and they are rightly included in this class of compound.

Bases of the ammonia type are common in the chemistry of living things. Some important aspects of the chemistry of proteins and amino acids are concerned with the ability of these compounds to give and receive hydrogen ions (p. 261).

The reaction between ammonia and oxygen

Experiment 17.8

To investigate the action between ammonia and copper oxide (C)

Put one large measure of ammonium chloride and one large measure of powdered soda-lime into a dry side-arm tube. (Soda-lime is made from

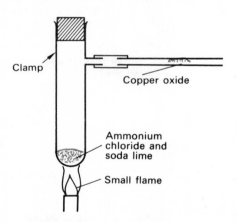

Clamp

Copper oxide

Ammonium chloride and soda lime

Small flame

Figure 70

calcium oxide and a concentrated solution of sodium hydroxide; it acts as a strong alkali and has the advantage of not being deliquescent). Put one small measure of copper oxide half way along a 15 cm piece of dry glass tubing. Fit this to the side arm by a short stiff rubber tube.

Warm the mixture of ammonium chloride and soda-lime gently until ammonia comes out of the side tube. Now heat the copper oxide with a small flame and continue to pass ammonia over it. Look for changes in colour in the copper oxide and the formation of water at the end of the side arm.

Does ammonia burn? Try to ignite the excess ammonia which issues from the delivery tube.

Experiment 17.8 indicates that ammonia will reduce copper oxide to copper. If the apparatus drawn below in *figure 71* is used, it can be shown that nitrogen is a product of this reduction, in addition to copper and water:

$$3CuO + 2NH_3 \rightarrow 3Cu + 3H_2O + N_2$$

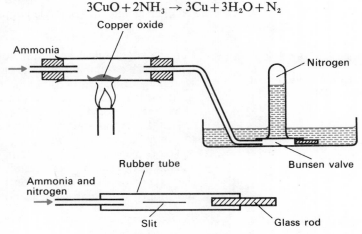

Figure 71 and Figure 72

The bunsen valve is simply a slit in a piece of rubber tubing, which allows gas to come through from inside the tube, but does not allow water to enter; thus it prevents 'sucking back' which would otherwise occur because of the great solubility of ammonia.

Although ammonia will react with the oxygen in copper oxide, it will not burn in air.

If the air is enriched with oxygen, however, ammonia will burn. This can be demonstrated by using the apparatus drawn in *figure 73*. The products of this combustion are nitrogen and water:

$$4NH_3 + 3O_2 \rightarrow 2N_2 + 6H_2O$$

Note that the products are those which would have been expected if the ammonia had first decomposed. The hydrogen forms water, but the nitrogen remains unchanged. Compare this with the burning of hydrocarbons (p. 31).

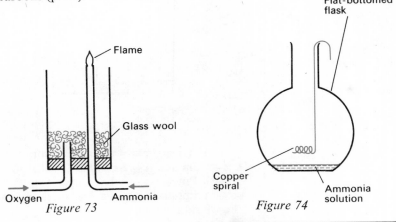

Figure 73

Figure 74

If ammonia and oxygen are passed over a heated catalyst (usually platinum/rhodium alloy) a different reaction takes place; instead of nitrogen and water, nitrogen monoxide and water are formed:

$$4NH_3 + 5O_2 \rightarrow 4NO + 6H_2O$$

Other metals, for example copper, will also catalyse this reaction.

Experiment 17.9

The catalytic oxidation of ammonia (D)

Put 25 cm³ of 0·880 ammonia solution into a 250 cm³ flat-bottomed flask. Make a tight spiral in the end of a 30 cm piece of copper wire by wrapping it three times round the end of a bunsen burner. Make a hook on the other end of the wire so that it will hang centrally, about 1 cm above the ammonia solution.

Heat the spiral until it glows white hot and immediately hang it over the ammonia solution (*figure 74*).

The copper should continue to glow white hot for several minutes. This indicates that it is catalysing the action between the ammonia and the oxygen and that this action is sufficiently exothermic to maintain the copper at its high temperature.

The action of ammonia on the salts of metals

Experiment 17.10

To investigate the action of ammonia on anhydrous salts (C)

Weigh two small dry beakers; add one large measure of anhydrous copper sulphate to each and weigh again. Stand one beaker in a larger beaker containing about 0·5 cm of concentrated ammonium hydroxide solution. Stand the other in a similar beaker containing water. Cover each of the larger beakers with a filter paper. Look for colour changes in the copper sulphate.

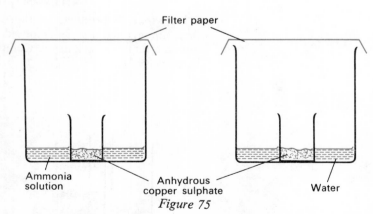

Filter paper

Ammonia solution

Anhydrous copper sulphate

Water

Figure 75

After about 45 minutes remove the two beakers; dry the outside of them and re-weigh them. Which shows the greatest increase in weight?

Put some of the copper sulphate which has been in contact with ammonia gas into a dry, small test tube. Warm the tube gently and test for ammonia.

Experiment 17.10 indicates that anhydrous copper sulphate combines with ammonia. The salts of several elements will do this. If you have time, you can investigate similar actions of ammonia on anhydrous salts of calcium, zinc, and cobalt. The reaction between ammonia and calcium chloride explains why the latter is not used to dry ammonia gas.

Problems

(1) Dissolve the substance A in water. Investigate the action on the solution of (a) dilute sodium hydroxide (b) hydrochloric acid and aqueous barium chloride (c) blue litmus paper. Record your observations and deduce the nature of A. What explanation can you offer for its reaction with (c)?

(2) You are given a mixture containing sodium chloride and ammonium chloride only. Devise an experiment by which you can determine the % by weight of sodium chloride in the mixture.

(3) Calculate what fraction of a g-molecule 3·4 g of ammonia is. What is the volume of this weight of ammonia at s.t.p.?

With what volume (s.t.p.) of hydrogen chloride will this volume of ammonia exactly combine?

(4) (a) Calculate the formula weight of ammonium chloride. (b) If this weight of ammonium chloride is heated to 273°C, calculate the total volume of gas formed (assume it to be completely decomposed).

(5) When 50 cm³ of ammonia are decomposed completely, 25 cm³ of nitrogen and 75 cm³ of hydrogen are formed.

Deduce (a) the simple ratio of reacting volumes and (b) the equation for the decomposition of ammonia.

(6) The gas B, which resembles ammonia, contains carbon, hydrogen, and nitrogen. It has a molecular weight of 31. Deduce its molecular formula.

B reacts with hydrogen chloride to form the salt C. Investigate the action of (a) heat and (b) dilute aqueous sodium hydroxide on C. Explain, as far as you can, the reactions which have taken place and deduce equations for them.

Summary

(1) The molecular formula for ammonia is NH_3.

(2) Ammonia is manufactured by combining nitrogen and hydrogen in the presence of a catalyst at pressures above 200 atm and at temperatures between 475°C and 600°C.

(3) Ammonia is very soluble in water, with which it forms ammonium hydroxide by a reversible reaction. Ammonium hydroxide is a weak alkali, being slightly ionized in aqueous solution:

$$NH_3 + H_2O \rightleftharpoons NH_4OH \rightleftharpoons NH_4^+ + OH^-$$

(4) Ammonium hydroxide exists only in aqueous solution; the pure substance has not been isolated.

(5) The definition of a base has been extended to include all substances which can accept hydrogen ions. The reaction of ammonia with hydrogen chloride is an example of this:

$$\begin{cases} \underset{\text{acid}}{\text{HCl}} & \rightarrow \text{H}^+ + \text{Cl}^- \\ \\ \underset{\text{base}}{\text{NH}_3} + \text{H}^+ \rightarrow \text{NH}_4^+ \end{cases} \qquad \underset{\text{base}}{\text{NH}_3} + \underset{\text{acid}}{\text{HCl}} \rightarrow \text{NH}_4^+\text{Cl}^-$$

(6) The terms 'acids' and 'bases' are not rigid; many substances can act as either acids or bases depending on the other reactants and the conditions of the reaction.

(7) When ammonia accepts hydrogen ions from an acid, the resulting compound is called an ammonium salt.

(8) Most ammonium salts decompose on heating:

$$\text{NH}_4^+\text{Cl}^-_{(s)} \underset{\text{cool}}{\overset{\text{heat}}{\rightleftharpoons}} \text{NH}_{3(g)} + \text{HCl}_{(g)}$$

This type of reversible decomposition is called *thermal dissociation*.

(9) Ammonia can act as a reducing agent; for example it reduces heated copper oxide to copper. It burns with difficulty, forming nitrogen and water. It reacts with oxygen in the presence of a catalyst to form nitrogen monoxide and water.

(10) Some anhydrous salts of metals react with ammonia much as they react with water.

Section 18

Nitric acid-oxides of nitrogen-equilibria

Manufacture and uses of nitric acid

Nitric acid is usually manufactured by the following series of reactions:

(i) The catalytic oxidation of ammonia to nitrogen monoxide (p. 164):

$$4NH_3 + 5O_2 \rightarrow 4NO + 6H_2O$$

(ii) The atmospheric oxidation of the nitrogen monoxide to nitrogen dioxide:

$$2NO + O_2 \rightarrow 2NO_2$$

(iii) The reaction of the nitrogen dioxide with water:

$$3NO_2 + H_2O \rightarrow 2HNO_3 + NO$$

Nitric acid is mainly used to manufacture fertilizers and explosives. The bulk of it is sold as concentrated nitric acid, which is a mixture of 70% acid and 30% water.

Laboratory preparation

Experiment 18.1

To prepare fuming nitric acid and to investigate some of its properties (D)

Fuming nitric acid is very corrosive and should therefore be made in apparatus connected by ground glass joints (*figure 76*). Its unpleasant toxic fumes should be led away to a sink or to a fume cupboard.

(i) Put 50 g of potassium nitrate into a 250 cm³ round-bottomed flask and add 50 cm³ of concentrated sulphuric acid. Replace the thermometer and, using a small flame, heat the mixture so that it boils and a liquid distils into the receiving vessel. Note the temperature of the vapour which distils over.

(ii) Thoroughly dry some sawdust by warming it very gently on an iron pan for about $\frac{3}{4}$ hr. Arrange the sawdust, which must be cool enough to handle, into a cone shape; pour 4–5 cm³ of fuming nitric acid on to the top and stand back.

(iii) Cut off a piece of phosphorus about the size of a match head (the phosphorus should be under water when this is done) and transfer it to a dry evaporating dish. Leave the phosphorus to dry for about a minute, then add 2–3 cm³ of fuming nitric acid and stand back.

Note the formation of the brown gas, nitrogen dioxide, in both these reactions.

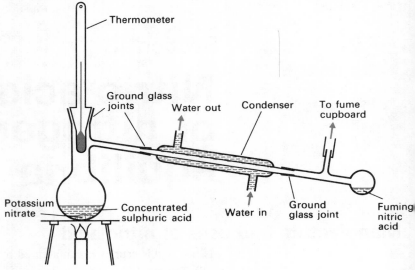

Figure 76

The yellow distillate in Experiment 18.1 is fuming nitric acid. It decomposes slightly, even at room temperature, into nitrogen dioxide; this dissolves in the acid and causes the yellow colour.

Nitric acid is a strong acid—it gives hydrogen ions almost as readily as sulphuric acid; the reason for its displacement from one of its salts must lie in its greater volatility compared with that of sulphuric acid (see the action of concentrated sulphuric acid on chlorides—p. 107):

$$KNO_3 + H_2SO_4 \rightarrow KHSO_4 + HNO_3$$

Concentrated sulphuric acid will displace nitric acid from any nitrate; potassium nitrate is used simply because it is one of the easiest to keep dry—many of the others are hygroscopic.

The action of fuming nitric acid on dry sawdust and on phosphorus indicates its very powerful oxidizing properties. Nearly 80% of its weight consists of oxygen and this is readily available for the combustions you have just witnessed.

Properties of nitric acid

The concentrated nitric acid which is used in the laboratory consists of approximately 70% acid and 30% water; a litre of it contains 16 g-formulae of nitric acid (16 M HNO_3). The concentration of dilute nitric acid referred to in this book is 2 M; i.e. 2 g-formulae per litre.

Experiment 18.2

Some properties of dilute
nitric acid (C)

By now, you should be familiar with the technique for investigating simple reactions. Investigate the action of dilute nitric acid on (a) aqueous sodium hydroxide coloured with litmus solution (b) oxides of metals (copper oxide and lead monoxide are suggested) (c) carbonates (d) metals (including magnesium and copper).

Experiment 18.3

The action of concentrated
nitric acid on copper (C)

Put one or two pieces of copper turnings into a small tube and add six drops of dilute nitric acid. Add concentrated nitric acid drop by drop, shaking the tube after each drop, until a reaction starts. Note that the gas which is given off is colourless in the tube, but brown at the mouth of the tube. Add a further six drops of concentrated nitric acid and note that the gas which is now evolved is brown from the moment it is formed.

The action of nitric acid on oxides, hydroxides, and carbonates

Experiments 18.2 and 18.3 indicate:

(i) The action between nitric acid and the oxides, hydroxides, and carbonates of metals is similar to that of the other strong acids. The salts of nitric acid, nitrates, are formed in each reaction. Work out equations for the action of nitric acid on (a) sodium hydroxide (b) copper oxide (c) calcium carbonate.

The action of nitric acid on metals

These reactions can be summarized as follows:

(i) Hydrogen is rarely a product.
(ii) Oxides of nitrogen are frequently formed.
(iii) Concentrated nitric acid produces a brown gas, nitrogen dioxide.
(iv) Dilute nitric acid produces mostly nitrogen monoxide. Nitrogen monoxide is a colourless gas; it reacts with oxygen in the air to form nitrogen dioxide: $(2NO + O_2 \rightarrow 2NO_2)$.
(v) In all the reactions the metal is oxidized: $Cu \rightarrow Cu^{2+} + 2e^-$

This implies that the nitric acid is reduced and that, when this happens, oxides of nitrogen form part of the products.

It is obvious that the outstanding property of nitric acid, in addition to its acidity, is its oxidizing power. This we will now consider further.

Nitric acid as an oxidizing agent

In each of the following reactions the volume of dilute nitric acid used will be eight times that of concentrated nitric acid. This ensures that the same number of g-formulae (HNO_3) will be present in each reaction.

Experiment 18.4

The oxidizing action of nitric
acid on (a) potassium iodide
and (b) iron (II) sulphate (C)

(a) Put 2 drops of potassium iodide solution into each of two small test tubes. To one tube add one drop of concentrated nitric acid and to the other add 8 drops of dilute nitric acid.
(b) Put 2 drops of aqueous iron (II) sulphate into each of two small test tubes. To one tube add 2 drops of concentrated nitric acid and to the

other add 16 drops of dilute nitric acid. Test the tube containing the concentrated nitric acid for iron (III) ions by adding ammonium hydroxide (p. 113).

Divide the contents of the other tube into two parts. Raise one part to boiling point, then test both parts for iron (III) ions.

Experiment 18.4 indicates that both dilute and concentrated nitric acid oxidize iodide ions to iodine:

$$I^- \rightarrow \tfrac{1}{2}I_2 + e^-$$

and iron (II) ions to iron (III) ions:

$$Fe^{2+} \rightarrow Fe^{3+} + e^-$$

and that the effectiveness of the oxidation increases with (i) the concentration of the acid and (ii) the temperature of the acid.

Nitrates
Experiment 18.5

The action of heat on nitrates (D)

This investigation should be carried out with three groups of nitrates: (i) sodium and potassium nitrates; (ii) calcium, strontium, and barium nitrates; and (iii) copper, cobalt, lead, and nitrates.

For the first two groups use about 0·5 cm of the nitrate in a dry, small test tube; for the last group use about half this quantity. Look for the formation of nitrogen dioxide and test for the formation of oxygen. Do not put your eyes, ears or nose near to the mouth of the tube.

After allowing the residue to cool, add hydrochloric acid, warm gently and look for rapid effervescence of oxides of nitrogen.

Arrange the nitrates in the order of ease with which they decompose. How does this relate to the position of the metals in the Periodic Table?

All nitrates decompose to some extent when heated; but Experiment 18.5 indicates that the ease with which this happens and the nature of the products is not the same for all nitrates:

(i) Nitrates decompose to form a residue of the metal itself, or its oxide, or its nitrite (nitrites react with hydrochloric acid to form oxides of nitrogen).

(ii) The nitrates of the most reactive metals (sodium and potassium) decompose to give off oxygen and to leave a residue of nitrite:

$$2NaNO_3 \rightarrow 2NaNO_2 + O_2$$

(iii) The nitrates of the least reactive metals (silver and mercury) decompose to give off oxygen and nitrogen dioxide and leave a residue of the metal itself:

$$2AgNO_3 \rightarrow 2Ag + 2NO_2 + O_2$$

(iv) The majority of nitrates decompose to give off oxygen and nitrogen dioxide and leave a residue of the oxide of the metal:

$$2Pb(NO_3)_2 \rightarrow 2PbO + 4NO_2 + O_2$$

(v) The nitrates of the metals in group II of the Periodic Table may first form nitrites, but these finally decompose to the oxides as in (iv).

N.B. It is useful to know that all nitrates are soluble in water.

Nitrogen dioxide

Nitrogen dioxide is conveniently prepared by the action of heat on a nitrate. Since nitrogen dioxide reacts readily with water, it should be made in dry apparatus and from a nitrate which contains no water of crystallization and which is not deliquescent.

Experiment 18.6

The preparation and some properties of nitrogen dioxide (D)

A convenient apparatus is shown in *figure 77*.

$$2Pb(NO_3)_2 \rightarrow 2PbO + 4NO_2 + O_2$$

Most of the nitrogen dioxide collects in the U-tube as a straw-coloured liquid.

Note how the colour of the gas darkens with increasing temperature.

Pour some of the liquid into a beaker of cold water and test the resulting solution with blue litmus paper.

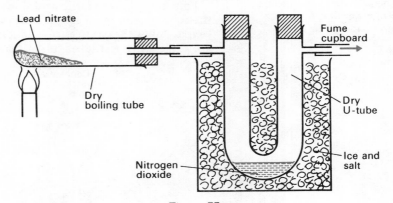

Figure 77

Nitrogen dioxide has a boiling point of 22°C. Both the gas and the liquid react with water at low temperatures to give a mixture of nitric and nitrous acids; hence, it is called a mixed acid anhydride:

$$H_2O + 2NO_2 \rightarrow HNO_2 + HNO_3$$

The formula of nitrogen dioxide

The ratio by weight of nitrogen to oxygen in nitrogen dioxide is 14:32, which indicates that NO_2 is the simplest formula for the gas. This has a formula weight of 46.

To deduce the molecular formula of the gas, the obvious step is to find out the weight the volume of which would be 22·4 litres (after conversion to s.t.p.). If the molecular formula is NO_2, the weight of 22·4 litres would be 46 g; but if the formula is N_2O_4, then the weight of 22·4 litres would be 92 g. It is found at temperatures below 154°C that the weight of 22·4 litres of the gas is neither of these two figures; it always lies between them.

The explanation is that the gas is a mixture, consisting of N_2O_4 molecules and NO_2 molecules, the two gases being in dynamic equilibrium:

$$N_2O_4 \rightleftharpoons 2NO_2$$

The molecular weight is the mean molecular weight of the two.

As the temperature goes up, the molecular weight goes down until at 154°C it is 46. This indicates that a rise in temperature favours the formation of NO_2, until at 154°C all the gas consists of molecules of this formula.

Nitrogen monoxide

Nitrogen monoxide can be prepared by the reduction of nitric acid under conditions designed to give the maximum yield of nitrogen monoxide and the minimum of the other oxides of nitrogen.

Experiment 18.7

The preparation and some properties of nitrogen monoxide (C or D)

The usual gas generator can be used and the gas collected over water (*figure 78*).

Pour concentrated nitric acid slowly down the thistle funnel, shaking the tube to mix the acid with the water, until a steady effervescence begins. Allow the gas to escape until it changes to brown as it enters the air. Collect two test tubes full of the gas.

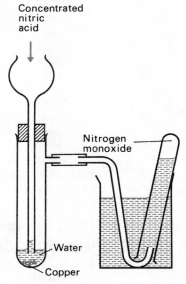

Concentrated nitric acid

Nitrogen monoxide

Water

Copper

Figure 78

Expose the contents of one of the tubes to the atmosphere. Keep your face well away from the nitrogen dioxide which is formed.

The action between nitrogen monoxide and oxygen

These two gases combine spontaneously at room temperature to form nitrogen dioxide:

$$2NO + O_2 \rightarrow 2NO_2$$

This reaction is a fundamental part of the manufacture of nitric acid (p. 167) and it was used to illustrate Gay Lussac's Law (p. 147). At higher temperatures the reaction is reversible.

Equilibria

In Section 15 we discussed how *fast* chemical reactions go: it is equally important to know how *far* they will go.

Many reactions, for most practical purposes, can be regarded as having gone to completion; that is, all the reactants have been converted to the products. But many others are reversible; that is, the products can reform the reactants; these do not go to completion unless one or more of the products is continuously removed. Here is a summary of some of the reversible reactions which you have already studied:

$$HCl_{(g)} + H_2O_{(l)} \rightleftharpoons H_3O^+_{(aq)} + Cl^-_{(aq)}$$
$$H_2S_{(aq)} \rightleftharpoons 2H^+_{(aq)} + S^{2-}_{(aq)}$$
$$NH_{3(g)} + H_2O_{(l)} \rightleftharpoons NH_4OH_{(aq)}$$
$$NH_4OH_{(aq)} \rightleftharpoons NH_4^+_{((aq)} + OH^-_{(aq)}$$
$$NH_4Cl_{(s)} \rightleftharpoons NH_{3(g)} + HCl_{(g)}$$
$$N_2O_{4(g)} \rightleftharpoons 2NO_{2(g)}$$

Another reversible change, although not a chemical one, was studied in Section 8. In this the two way change was that of a liquid into its vapour and the vapour back into the liquid:

$$H_2O_{(l)} \rightleftharpoons H_2O_{(g)}$$

If water is left in a sealed space, a situation is reached in which liquid is changing into a gas and gas into a liquid continuously, but the total amounts of each remain the same. We described this as a *position of equilibrium*. Furthermore, this equilibrium was *dynamic*, implying that change from one to the other goes on all the time even though the amounts remain the same.

It is important to realize that equilibrium can only occur in a *closed system*; that is, a situation in which none of the component substances are being added or taken out. For example, if water were left open to the atmosphere so that its vapour could escape continuously, it would dry up and never reach an equilibrium.

If the components of a reversible chemical change are left in a closed system under constant conditions, they, too, will reach a position of equilibirum in which the amounts of all the substances will remain the same although they are continuously changing one into the other.

Experiment 18.8

To investigate the equilibrium of iodine between aqueous and trichloroethane solutions (C)

Put trichloroethane into a test tube to a depth of about 2 cm, and an aqueous solution of potassium iodide in another test tube to about the same depth. Add a crystal of iodine to each test tube. Shake both tubes and note the colour of the solutions of iodine. (N.B. Iodine dissolves more readily in water containing potassium iodide than it does in plain water.)

Add an equal amount of trichloroethane to the aqueous solution and an equal volume of aqueous potassium iodide solution to the trichloroethane solution. Shake each test tube for about five minutes.

(i) What is the colour of the aqueous iodine solution?
(ii) What is the colour of the solution of iodine in trichloroethane?
(iii) Describe and explain the change which takes place when trichloroethane is added to the aqueous solution of iodine.
(iv) Describe and explain the change which takes place when water containing potassium iodide is added to the solution of iodine in trichloroethane.

Suck off the aqueous layer from one of the test tubes with a teat pipette. Add a fresh quantity of water containing potassium iodide, shake the tube for a few minutes, remove the aqueous layer again and repeat several times. What eventually happens to the concentration of iodine in the trichloroethane layer?

Experiment 18.8 shows that an equilibrium can be reached from either direction.

$$I_{2(aq)} \rightleftharpoons I_2 \text{ (trichloroethane)}$$

In this equilibrium can be attained starting from either an aqueous solution of iodine or a solution of iodine in trichloroethane.

Changing the position of an equilibrium

We have already seen that an ionic equilibrium can be altered by removing one or more of its components (pp. 132 and 158). Thus, hydrogen sulphide in aqueous solution will continue to ionize if sulphide ions are removed by precipitation. Similarly ammonium hydroxide will continue to ionize if the hydroxide ions are removed by precipitation. Here is another example:

Experiment 18.9

To investigate the equilibrium between bismuth chloride and bismuth oxychloride (C)

Weigh 0·4 g of bismuth oxychloride (BiOCl) and put it into a test tube together with 4 cm³ of water. Shake the tube.

(i) Does the bismuth oxychloride appear to dissolve?

To the contents of the tube add 2 cm³ of a solution of hydrochloric acid made by mixing equal volumes of concentrated acid and water. Add more of the acid, dropwise, until a clear solution is just obtained. Now add water, dropwise and shaking the tube, until a precipitate is formed. Continue this alternate addition of acid and water for as long as time allows.

The changes which take place can be represented:

$$BiCl_{3(aq)} + H_2O_{(l)} \rightleftharpoons BiOCl_{(s)} + 2HCl_{(aq)}$$

(ii) Which change encourages the position of equilibrium to move to the left?
(iii) Which change encourages the position of equilibrium to move to the right?

In Experiment 18.9 it appears that an increase in the concentration of hydrochloric acid moves the position of equilibrium to the left (as it is represented in the equation) and an increase in the amount of water (the same as a decrease in the concentration of hydrochloric acid) moves the position of equilibrium to the right. A general statement on the effect on an equilibrium of changing the concentrations of the components is made in the Summary.

Problems

(1) The nitrate of an unknown metal decomposes when heated to form oxygen and a white solid only. The white solid evolves nitrogen dioxide when treated with hydrochloric acid. The atomic number of the element lies between 31 and 38 (inclusive). From your knowledge of the general

behaviour of nitrates and the Periodic Table, deduce—giving your reasons—the name of the metal.

(2) Investigate the accuracy of the statement that potassium nitrate decomposes to form potassium nitrite and oxygen only.

Weigh a small dry tube, add about 0·3 g of potassium nitrate and weigh again. Heat the potassium nitrate and follow the course of the reaction by cooling and weighing it on three occasions: (a) when, after gentle heating, the evolution of oxygen appears to stop (b) when, after stronger heating, a brown gas first appears (c) after heating for a further five minutes.

After cooling the final residue examine its action with dilute hydrochloric acid.

(3) Mix one small measure each of sodium nitrate and sodium hydrogen sulphate; add a small piece of copper and warm gently. Identify the gas evolved and explain the reactions which have taken place.

(4) At 27°C and 1 atm pressure, 92 g of nitrogen dioxide have a volume of 32 litres. Correct this volume to s.t.p. and hence calculate the apparent molecular weight of nitrogen dioxide at 27°C (to the nearest whole number).

(5) 42 cm³ of nitrogen monoxide reacted exactly with 100 cm³ of air to form nitrogen dioxide. Deduce the % by volume of oxygen in the air.

(6) It is sometimes said that copper reacts with nitric acid (made by mixing 1 volume of concentrated nitric acid with 1 volume of water) to form nitrogen monoxide in accordance with the equation $3Cu + 8HNO_3 \rightarrow 3Cu(NO_3)_2 + 2NO + 4H_2O$. This implies that no gas other than nitrogen monoxide is formed in the reaction. Devise an experiment by which you could check the truth of the last statement.

(7) You are given an aqueous solution of bromine in which the bromine is in an equilibrium:

$$Br_{2(aq)} + H_2O_{(l)} \rightleftharpoons H^+_{(aq)} + Br^-_{(aq)} + HOBr_{(aq)}$$

Devise a practical method by which you can move the position of this equilibrium to the right and then back to the left. What observations enable you to decide in which direction the position of equilibrium moves?

Summary

(1) Nitric acid is made commercially by the catalytic oxidation of ammonia and, in the laboratory, by the action of concentrated sulphuric acid on a nitrate.

(2) Nitrates can be formed by the action of nitric acid on metals and on the oxides, hydroxides, and carbonates of metals. Hydrogen is rarely formed by the action of a metal on nitric acid.

(3) Nitric acid is an oxidizing agent and, when it acts as such, it is usually reduced to oxides of nitrogen. The products of the reduction of nitric acid depend on (i) the reducing agent, (ii) the concentration of the acid, and (iii) the temperature.

(4) All nitrates decompose when heated. The products of decomposition fall into three groups:

  (i) The nitrates of the most reactive metals (e.g. sodium and potassium) decompose to the nitrites plus oxygen.

(ii) The nitrates of most metals decompose to an oxide of the metal plus nitrogen dioxide and oxygen.

(5) Nitrogen dioxide can be made by the action of heat on most nitrates or by the action of concentrated nitric acid on copper. It can exist in two molecular forms in equilibrium with each other:

$$N_2O_4 \rightleftharpoons 2NO_2$$

High temperatures favour the reaction left to right, and low temperatures favour the reaction right to left. Nitrogen dioxide reacts with water to form a mixture of nitric and nitrous acids.

(6) Nitrogen monoxide can be made by the action of copper on diluted nitric acid. It combines with oxygen to form nitrogen dioxide.

(7) If the components of a reversible change are left under constant conditions in a closed system (one in which material is not added or removed), a dynamic equilibrium is established in which the concentration of each component remains constant.

(8) If the concentration of a component is increased, the position of equilibrium moves in a direction which tends to decrease the concentration of that component.

(9) If the concentration of a component is decreased, the position of equilibrium moves in a direction which tends to increase the concentration of that component.

Section 19
The electrical nature of matter (2)

The structure of atoms

So far we have used a theory concerning the electrical nature of matter which can be summarized as follows:

(1) Metallic elements can give one or more electrons to non-metallic elements.

(2) This results in the formation of ionic compounds in which the ions of metals are positively charged and the ions of non-metals are negatively charged.

(3) The electron is the smallest unit of electricity and it has a negative charge.

This adequately explains some of the properties of metals and non-metals and some of the properties of their compounds. In the past few sections, however, new facts have been studied which this simple theory does not explain. Here are some of them:

  (i) the formation of non-ionic compounds
  (ii) the formation of molecules by combination of two or more atoms of the same element (H_2, O_2, etc.)
  (iii) the conversion of some non-ionic compounds into ions by the action of water
  (iv) the action between acids and bases
  (v) the variation of combining capacity from one element to another
  (vi) the variation in reactivity from one element to another
  (vii) the source of the positive charge in ions
  (viii) the classification of similar elements into groups (the Periodic Table)
  (ix) the differing volumes occupied by 1 g-atom of solid elements
  (x) the difference in electrical conductance between metallic and non-metallic elements
  (xi) the differences between the atomic weights of elements.

Before extending our theory to explain some of these facts, more experimental evidence is required.

J. J. Thomson's experiments

Towards the end of the nineteenth century, at the Cavendish Laboratory in Cambridge, J. J. Thomson produced evidence which pointed to the existence of electrons. When a high voltage is applied to a gas at a very low pressure, electricity flows through the gas in the form of rays (cathode rays) which move from the cathode towards the anode. These rays can be detected by allowing them to strike a fluorescent screen. You must have seen this effect either in your work in physics or on televisions screens; the latter are illuminated by cathode rays striking their fluorescent surface.

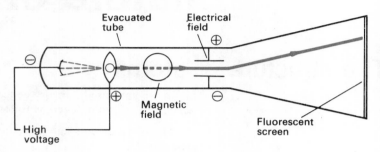

Figure 79

Thomson measured the deflection which a magnetic field and an electrical field produced on the rays (*figure 79*). He found that his measurements could be explained by assuming that the rays consisted of very small particles (electrons) which carried a negative charge. He was able to determine the speed of these particles and the ratio of their charge to their mass (e/m). He also found that the latter was the same no matter which gas was in the tube.

Further work by Millikan, who observed the effect of these small charged particles on tiny oil drops which were slowly falling, led to the determination of the charge on the electron (e). Since e/m was already known, it was possible to calculate the mass of the electron. This was found to be $\frac{1}{1836}$ of that of a hydrogen atom.

Electrons can be produced in other ways; for example, by strongly heating a piece of metal. This is the basis of the thermionic valve.

It is now accepted that electrons are an essential part of the structure of atoms.

Rutherford's experiments

At the beginning of the twentieth century, Rutherford, working first at Manchester and then at Cambridge, produced evidence about the structure of that part of the atom which does not consist of electrons.

His work was made possible by the investigation of radioactivity and the isolation of the radioactive element, radium, by Madame Curie. Radioactive elements spontaneously give off rays which can be of three types:

(i) Gamma (γ) rays, which resemble light waves except that they have a much shorter wave-length

(ii) beta (β) rays, which are moving electrons like cathode rays

(iii) alpha (α) rays, which have a mass of 4 and carry two positive charges; these can, therefore, be regarded as charged helium atoms (He^{2+}).

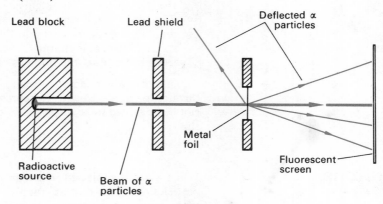

Figure 80

Rutherford directed a beam of α particles at a piece of very thin metal foil. He was able to follow the path of the particles by observing their point of impact on a fluorescent screen.

He observed that most of the α particles went straight through the foil and continued their straight-line path; a much smaller number were deflected from the straight line; and a still smaller number bounced off the metal foil.

Rutherford then proceeded to imagine a model of an atom which would fit in with these facts. This model can be summarized as follows:

(i) Since most of the α particles pass unobstructed through the solid metal and since the physical properties of metals indicate that their atoms are closely packed together, there must be a great deal of space within the atoms.

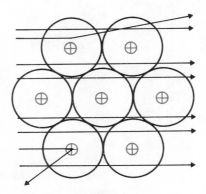

Figure 81

(ii) The deflection of a small number of α particles can be explained by assuming that there is a *nucleus* in the centre of each atom in which most of the mass and all the positive charge of the atom is concentrated. If an α particle passes near to this nucleus, the positive charges will repel each other and the α particle will be deflected.

(iii) Since only a tiny fraction of the α particles are deflected, the size of the nucleus must be much smaller than that of the whole atom.

(iv) The electrons, because they are the easiest part of an atom to remove, appear to surround the nucleus at various distances from it. Since the total charge on an atom is zero, the number of electrons must equal the number of positive charges on the nucleus.

Figure 81, which is not to scale, illustrates the passage of α particles through a solid element. ⊕ represents the nucleus, and the electrons can be imagined to be dispersed in the much larger volume surrounding this.

Protons

When a gas is subjected to a high voltage in a discharge tube, positive particles are formed in addition to electrons. In other words, the electrical energy causes the gas to ionize.

If hydrogen, which has the smallest atoms of any element, is ionized in this way it is found that never more than one electron per atom can be removed from it. This indicates that the hydrogen atom contains only one electron.

The positive particles formed when hydrogen ionizes in this way are called *protons*:

$$H \rightarrow H^+ + e^-$$
hydrogen atom → 1 proton + 1 electron

The proton has one positive charge and a mass of one; it is what, up to now, we have called a hydrogen ion.

Protons are now regarded as one of the fundamental particles of which the nucleus of an atom is made. The hydrogen atom appears to consist of one electron and a nucleus of one proton (*figure 82*).

1 electron
somewhere in here

1 proton

Figure 82

This is a very simple model of a hydrogen atom. It does not show exactly where the electron is, what movement and energy the electron has, or the relative sizes of the electron and proton. None of these are necessary at this level of chemistry, so, for the moment, this simple model will suffice.

The structure of other atoms

The evidence for the detailed structure of atoms comes from several sources, the following being the most important:

(i) The mass spectrograph, in which the masses of atoms are determined.

(ii) Nuclear reactions, in which the nuclei of atoms are changed—generally by bombarding them with other particles.

(iii) The energy required to remove one or more electrons from an atom. This is called *ionization energy* and is measured in units of electron volts. (An electron volt is the energy required to move one electron through a potential difference of 1 volt.)

(iv) The wavelengths of the radiant energy which comes from atoms when they are excited by the action of heat or electricity. These can be analysed into patterns, known as spectra, from which information about parts of the internal structure of atoms can be deduced.

(i) and (ii) give information chiefly about the nuclei of atoms, and (iii) and (iv) give information chiefly about the electrons in atoms.

The number of protons in the nucleus

The number of protons in the nucleus of an atom is called its *atomic number*.

Each element has its own atomic number and no two elements have the same atomic number. In the Periodic Table the elements are arranged in the order of their atomic numbers. Starting from hydrogen, there is an increase of one proton in each atom from one element to the next. The arrangement of the elements according to their atomic numbers is almost the same as the arrangement according to their atomic weights—but not quite. Examine the Periodic Table to discover where the two arrangements differ.

The electrons surrounding the nucleus

In an electrically neutral atom, the number of electrons must equal the number of protons (the atomic number). It has been shown that all electrons are identical in charge and mass, but it seems that they also have energy and the amount and form of this energy can vary from one electron to another within an atom.

The information provided by the spectra and the ionization energy of atoms indicates that the electrons within an atom can be divided into groups, each group consisting of electrons with similar energy.

Various names have been given to these groups of electrons; they can be called shells, or energy levels. There appears to be a maximum number of electrons which can exist in a given shell:

1st electron shell—a maximum of 2 electrons

2nd electron shell—a maximum of 8 electrons

3rd electron shell—a maximum of 18 electrons

4th electron shell—a maximum of 32 electrons

The electrons can be subdivided into smaller groups, but we shall only consider these major groups here. The shells are numbered in the order of their increasing distance from the nucleus: the 1st shell being nearest to the nucleus. The higher the number of the shell, the greater is the energy of an electron contained in the shell.

The arrangement of electrons in shells

We shall discuss the arrangement of the electrons in the first twenty elements only. Evidence from spectra and ionization energies points to the following arrangements:

Table 10

	Atomic Number	1st Shell	2nd Shell	3rd Shell	4th Shell
hydrogen	1	1			
helium	2	2			
lithium	3	2	1		
beryllium	4	2	2		
boron	5	2	3		
carbon	6	2	4		
nitrogen	7	2	5		
oxygen	8	2	6		
fluorine	9	2	7		
neon	10	2	8		
sodium	11	2	8	1	
magnesium	12	2	8	2	
aluminium	13	2	8	3	
silicon	14	2	8	4	
phosphorus	15	2	8	5	
sulphur	16	2	8	6	
chlorine	17	2	8	7	
argon	18	2	8	8	
potassium	19	2	8	8	1
calcium	20	2	8	8	2

There is also some evidence for this pattern from chemical properties. Turn to the Periodic Table and see if you can find any relationship between the arrangement of the first twenty elements and the arrangement of their electrons:

(i) Elements with similar chemical properties have a similar arrangement of electrons: for example, atoms of the halogen elements all have seven electrons in the outer shell.

(ii) The charge on the ions of metallic elements equals the number of electrons in the outer shell of the atoms from which they are formed, and the charge on the ions of non-metallic elements equals eight minus the number of electrons in the outer shell. It seems likely that the electrons in an atom of an element and the way in which they are arranged round the nucleus account for the chemical properties of the element.

It must be emphasized that this simple theory of atomic structure explains only some of the properties of some of the elements. This theory is only the beginning; as you progress in chemistry, it will be necessary to modify and enlarge it.

Neutrons

If you compare the atomic weights of the elements with their atomic numbers—shown in Appendix C—you will see that for all the elements except hydrogen the atomic weight is greater than the atomic number. Oxygen, for example, has an atomic weight of 16 and an atomic number of 8. It seems, therefore, that the protons in the nucleus of an atom account for only part of its mass.

In 1932, the English physicist, Chadwick, discovered evidence which pointed to the existence of another particle, in addition to the proton, which made up the nuclei of atoms. The particle has a mass of 1; but, unlike the proton, it has no electrical charge and for this reason it is called the *neutron*.

It appears that the mass of an atom is concentrated almost entirely in its nucleus and is approximately equal to the number of protons (the atomic number) plus the number of neutrons. Thus the atomic weight of oxygen (16) is the sum of the weight of 8 protons and 8 neutrons in each atom.

Isotopes

All atoms of the same element have the same number of protons in the nucleus (atomic number), but the number of neutrons in the nucleus may differ. Hydrogen atoms, for example, may have one of three different nuclei:

$$
\begin{aligned}
&\text{(i)} \quad \text{1 proton only} &&\text{mass 1} \\
&\text{(ii)} \quad \text{1 proton} + \text{1 neutron} &&\text{mass 2} \\
&\text{(iii)} \quad \text{1 proton} + \text{2 neutrons} &&\text{mass 3}
\end{aligned}
$$

These forms of elements, which have differing numbers of neutrons in their nuclei, are called *isotopes*. Isotopes of an element have differing atomic weights, but they have the same atomic number and the same arrangement of electrons; their chemical properties, therefore, are the same.

The formation of ionic compounds

Our work so far has indicated that when metallic elements combine with non-metallic elements the resulting compound frequently consists of positive ions from the metal and negative ions from the non-metal. Let us examine these facts in the light of the simple theory of atomic structure; for example, the action between sodium and chlorine to form sodium ions and chloride ions (sodium chloride):

$$Na + \tfrac{1}{2}Cl_2 \rightarrow Na^+Cl^-$$

This can be explained by assuming that each sodium atom gives one electron to each chlorine atom:

$$
\left\{
\begin{aligned}
&Na \rightarrow Na^+ + e^- \\[2em]
&\tfrac{1}{2}Cl_2 + e^- \rightarrow Cl^-
\end{aligned}
\right.
$$

G

Or, in the form of a diagram showing the electrons in the outer shell only:

$$Na\bullet + {}^{\times}_{\times}\overset{\times\times}{Cl}{}^{\times}_{\times} \rightarrow Na^+ + {}^{\bullet}_{\times}\overset{\times\times}{Cl}{}^{\times}_{\times}{}^-$$

($\bullet$ represents a sodium electron, $\times$ represents a chlorine electron)

The sodium, which as an atom had 11 positive charges (protons) balanced by 11 negative charges (electrons), now has only 10 electrons. Therefore, because the positive charge on the nucleus is unchanged, there is an overall charge on the sodium ion of one positive.

Similarly, each chloride ion has one negative charge in excess of the positive charges and its overall charge is one negative.

Here are some examples:

(i)   magnesium + chlorine → magnesium chloride

$$Mg{}^{\bullet}_{\bullet} \quad + \quad {}^{\times}\overset{\times\times}{Cl}{}^{\times}_{\times\times} \\ {}^{\times}\overset{\times\times}{Cl}{}^{\times}_{\times\times} \rightarrow \quad Mg^{2+} + 2\left[{}^{\bullet}_{\times}\overset{\times\times}{Cl}{}^{\times}_{\times\times}\right]^-$$

($\bullet$ represents a magnesium electron; $\times$ represents a chlorine electron)

(ii)   calcium + oxygen → calcium oxide

$$Ca{}^{\bullet}_{\bullet} \quad + \quad \overset{\times\times}{O}{}^{\times}_{\times} \rightarrow Ca^{2+} + {}^{\bullet}_{\bullet}\overset{\times\times}{O}{}^{\times}_{\times\times}{}^{2-}$$

($\bullet$ represents a calcium electron; $\times$ represents an oxygen electron)

(iii)   sodium + sulphur → sodium sulphide

$$2Na\bullet \quad + \quad \overset{\times\times}{S}{}^{\times}_{\times\times} \rightarrow 2Na^+ + {}^{\bullet}_{\bullet}\overset{\times\times}{S}{}^{\times}_{\times\times}{}^{2-}$$

($\bullet$ represents a sodium electron; $\times$ represents a sulphur electron)

It is clear that the number of positive charges on the ion of a metal equals the number of electrons which it has lost, and the number of negative charges on the ion of a non-metal equals the number of electrons which it has gained.

N.B. Although different symbols are used here to distinguish between the electrons from different atoms, it must be remembered that all electrons are the same in mass and charge.

Notice that in all the examples of the combination of elements given above the arrangement of electrons in the products is that of a noble gas. For example the sodium ion Na$^+$ has the arrangement 2·8 which is the same as that of neon which *precedes* sodium in the Periodic Table. Also the chloride ion Cl$^-$ has the arrangement 2. 8. 8 which is the same as that of argon which *follows* chlorine in the Table.

It is significant that the noble gases are very stable, indicating that when elements combine their products attain a more stable electron structure. This electron structure is often, *but not always*, that of a noble gas.

The ionic (electrovalent) bond

If some compounds consist of closely-packed ions, there must be a strong attractive force between the positive ions and the negative ions. It is this electrostatic attractive force, called the *ionic bond*, which keeps the ions in their fixed positions in a solid compound (it is sometimes called the *electrovalent bond*).

Electrostatic forces increase as the distance between the ions decreases. In a tightly packed mixture of ions the forces must be very strong and it must be difficult to separate the ions from each other. This explains why ionic substances usually have higher melting points and crystals which are much harder than those of most non-ionic substances.

When an ionic compound forms crystals either from the molten compound or from a solution, it seems likely that the ions will tend to arrange themselves so that oppositely charged ions are nearest to each other. This means that a positively charged ion will tend to have negatively charged ions closest to it, and vice versa. Thus, one ion is not bonded solely to one other ion; it is bonded to several ions. In other words, the ionic bond is an attraction which acts all round each ion and not in one particular direction. In a crystal of sodium chloride, for example, each sodium ion is bonded to several chloride ions.

We shall see later (p. 200) that the ions in solid ionic compounds usually arrange themselves in a definite pattern and this accounts for the regular shape of the crystals of these compounds.

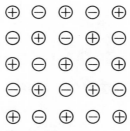

Figure 83

The gram ion (g-ion)

The particles of an ionic compound are a mixture of oppositely charged ions; they are not molecules. It is possible, therefore, to state the concentration of a solution of an ionic compound in terms of the number of g-ions per litre. *The weight of Avogadro's number of ions is called 1 g-ion.*

Example 1 A molar solution of sodium chloride contains 1 g-formula (NaCl) per litre.

$$NaCl \text{ contains } Na^+ + Cl^-$$

i.e. 1 formula of sodium chloride contains 1 sodium ion + 1 chloride ion
1 g-formula of sodium chloride contains 1 g-ion of sodium ion + 1 g-ion of chloride ion.

$\therefore$ M NaCl solution consists of 1 g-ion Na$^+$ per litre + 1 g-ion Cl$^-$ per litre.

Example 2 A molar solution of ammonium sulphate contains 1 g-formula $(NH_4)_2SO_4$ per litre.

$$(NH_4)_2SO_4 \text{ contains } 2NH_4{}^+ + SO_4{}^{2-}$$

i.e. 1 formula of ammonium sulphate contains 2 ammonium ions + 1 sulphate ion.

1 g-formula of ammonium sulphate contains 2 g-ions of ammonium ion + 1 g-ion of sulphate ion.

$\therefore$ M $(NH_4)_2SO_4$ solution consists of 2 g-ions NH$_4{}^+$ per litre + 1 g-ion SO$_4{}^{2-}$ per litre.

The mole

So far in our work, the gram ion is the fourth expression which represents the weight of Avogadro's number (N_A) of particles; the others are gram atom, gram formula, and gram molecule.

One *mole* is Avogadro's number of any particles—atoms, ions, molecules, protons, electrons etc. Thus, the weight of 1 mole of iron is the weight of N_A atoms of iron; it is 1 g-atom (56 g). Similarly, the weight of 1 mole of sodium chloride is the weight of N_A NaCl units; it is 1 g-formula (58·5 g). 1 mole of electrons = 1 faraday.

The formation of non-ionic compounds

The properties of non-ionic substances

We have studied many substances in which atoms have combined together without forming ions. Some of these substances are compounds: water, alcohol, sugar, hydrogen chloride, ammonia, carbon dioxide, and sulphur dioxide. Some of them are diatomic elements: hydrogen, oxygen, nitrogen, and the halogens.

Before going on to develop a theory to explain the way in which the atoms in these substances are bonded together, it may be helpful to summarize what we already know of their properties and structure:

(i) Their electrical conductance is low and the pure substances cannot be electrolysed even when they are liquids. It appears that they do not contain ions.

(ii) Most of them have low melting points and boiling points; many, in fact, are gases at room temperature. This indicates that their individual particles are easily separated from each other and dispersed.

(iii) Although they are not ionic, the compounds are often very stable: it requires a great deal of energy to decompose water into its elements or hydrogen molecules into hydrogen atoms.

The covalent bond theory

Let us take hydrogen chloride as an example. Hydrogen chloride gas appears to be in the form of molecules, each molecule consisting of one hydrogen atom and one chlorine atom. These two atoms must be bonded strongly together because hydrogen chloride is difficult to decompose, but they are not in the form of ions. When hydrogen chloride is dissolved in water, however, it readily forms hydrogen ions and chloride ions.

All this can be explained if we make two assumptions:

(i) The bond between the two atoms is electrical; i.e. it is concerned with electrons.

(ii) Two electrons, one from each atom, are shared; they are not completely given or received.

Because it is formed by the *sharing* of electrons, the bond is called a *covalent bond*. Here are some examples in the form of diagrams:

(i)   1 hydrogen + 1 chlorine → 1 hydrogen chloride
         atom   atom   molecule

$$H\bullet \quad + \quad \overset{\times\times}{\underset{\times\times}{\times Cl \times}} \quad \rightarrow \quad H \boxed{\bullet} \overset{\times\times}{\underset{\times\times}{Cl \times}}$$

(the dots and crosses in all the examples represent the outer shell electrons and ☐ encloses the pair of shared electrons)

(ii)   2 hydrogen atoms → 1 hydrogen molecule

$$H\bullet + H\bullet \quad \rightarrow \quad H \boxed{\overset{\bullet}{\times}} H$$

(iii)   2 hydrogen atoms + 1 oxygen atom → 1 water molecule

$$2H\bullet \quad + \quad \overset{\times\times}{\underset{\times\times}{O \times}} \quad \rightarrow \quad H \boxed{\times} \overset{\times\times}{\underset{\boxed{\times\bullet}}{O \times}} \atop H$$

(iv)   3 hydrogen atoms + 1 nitrogen atom → 1 ammonia molecule

$$3H\bullet \quad + \quad \overset{\times}{\underset{\times}{\times N \times}} \quad \rightarrow \quad \overset{H}{\underset{H}{H \boxed{\times} N \times \atop \boxed{\times\bullet}}}$$

(v) 4 hydrogen atoms + 1 carbon atom → 1 methane molecule (CH_4)

$$4H\bullet \quad + \quad \overset{\times}{\underset{\times}{\times C \times}} \quad \rightarrow \quad \overset{H}{\underset{H}{H \boxed{\bullet} C \boxed{\bullet} H}}$$

In each of these examples each covalent bond is shown as a shared pair of electrons.

Covalent molecules

In the discussion on ionic compounds it was stressed that each ion is bonded by electrostatic attraction to many other ions. This is not so in compounds formed by the covalent bond. In hydrogen chloride, for example, each hydrogen atom is bonded to one chlorine atom only. It follows that in covalent compounds the individual particles are usually molecules containing a fixed number of atoms.

Intermediate bonds

The simple conclusions to which these discussions have led are only the beginnings of very much more elaborate theories about the forces which hold together the elements in compounds. Although some substances are clearly held together by either ionic bonds or covalent bonds, many more do not fit rigidly into either of these classes of bonding. The bonds in many substances show some of the characteristics of both types. Hydrogen chloride, for example, is largely covalent in character, but there must be some tendency for the chlorine atom to take over the pair of shared electrons completely, because hydrogen chloride very readily forms ions when it dissolves in water. In other words, the bond in hydrogen chloride must be partly ionic in character and becomes completely so when the compound is dissolved in certain solvents.

The ease with which elements form ions

Much of our work has shown that the tendency to form ions is not equal in all elements. On p. 114, for example, we discovered that chlorine forms chloride ions ($Cl + e^- \rightarrow Cl^-$) more readily than iodine forms iodide ions ($I + e^- \rightarrow I^-$). This is shown by the fact that chlorine is a better oxidizing agent than iodine.

Similarly, sodium reacts more readily than silver when it combines with non-metallic elements. Our theory of the formation of the ionic bond indicates that a sodium atom loses an electron more readily than a silver atom does.

A list can be drawn up to show how the ease with which ions are formed varies from one element to another. The measurement of ionization energy (p. 181) is one way of doing this, but it is done on the elements in their gaseous state and the techniques are rather too difficult for demonstration in an elementary laboratory. Many of the reactions of elements, however, take place in the presence of water, and it is possible to show the relative tendency of some of the elements to change into ions when they are in contact with water or aqueous solutions.

Experiment 19.1

To investigate the relative tendency of copper and zinc to form ions (C or D)

To standardize the conditions, the metals are placed in contact with a solution containing a fixed concentration of their own ions.

Three-quarters fill a 250 cm³ beaker with an M/5 solution of copper sulphate and three-quarters fill a small porous pot with an M/5 solution of zinc sulphate. Stand the pot inside the beaker. The porous pot allows the solutions to join and thus complete an electrical circuit between the zinc and the copper; at the same time it prevents complete mixing of the two solutions.

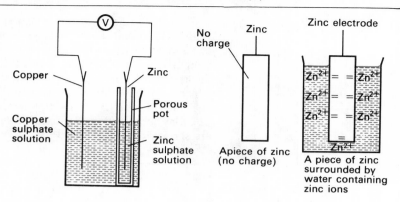

Figure 84   *Figure 85*

Put a piece of copper sheet into the copper sulphate solution and a piece of zinc sheet into the zinc sulphate solution. By means of crocodile clips and wire, attach the zinc and the copper to the terminals of a voltmeter to measure the potential difference between them. Note which one is positive and which one is negative. Do not allow the crocodile clips to touch the solutions. This is an example of a chemical cell.

The experiments can be repeated using various pairs of metals, for example: iron/copper, magnesium/copper, magnesium/zinc, and zinc/silver. Each metal is put into an M/5 solution of its own ions.

The electrochemical series

Experiment 19.1 indicates that the zinc electrode is at a lower potential (it is more negative) than the copper electrode. Let us see if our theory of ion formation can explain this.

A piece of metal by itself carries no overall positive charge; but, if it is put into a solution and some of it dissolves in the form of positive ions, the metal itself will retain an equal negative charge (*figure 85*).

The greater the tendency to form positive ions, the greater will be the negative charge on the metal. Therefore, the difference in potential between a zinc electrode and a copper electrode is a measure of the greater tendency of zinc to form zinc ions than the tendency of copper to form copper ions.

The same sort of argument can be applied to non-metallic elements, except that in this case the elements tend to form negative ions and leave themselves positively charged (*figure 86*).

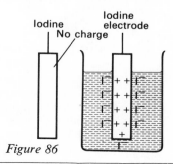

Figure 86

From experiments such as this, the metallic elements can be arranged (Table 11) so that those which form positive ions most readily are at the top and those which form positive ions least readily are at the bottom. Similarly, the non-metallic elements can be arranged (Table 12) so that those which form negative ions most readily are at the top and those which form negative ions least readily are at the bottom.

Tables 11 and 12 are a simplified form of the electrochemical series. The ions contained in the standard solution in contact with the element are shown in brackets.

Table 11 *Table 12*

Metals (electropositive elements)			Non-metals (electronegaitive elements)		
K	(K^+)	Positive ion formed most readily	Cl_2	(Cl^-)	Negative ion formed most readily
Ca	(Ca^{2+})		Br_2	(Br^-)	
Na	(Na^+)				
Mg	(Mg^{2+})		I_2	(I^-)	
Al	(Al^{3+})				
Zn	(Zn^{2+})		O_2	(OH^-)	Negative ion formed least readily
Fe	(Fe^{2+})				
Sn	(Sn^{2+})				
Pb	(Pb^{2+})				
H_2	(H_3O^+)				
Cu	(Cu^{2+})				
Ag	(Ag^+)				
Hg	(Hg^{2+})	Positive ion formed least readily			

The experiments which must be carried out to decide the position of some of the elements in the series present some technical difficulties; it is obviously difficult to make a direct electrical connection with the gaseous elements. This can be overcome by coating a piece of platinum with bubbles of the gas; for example, in the hydrogen electrode (*figure 87*).

The hydrogen electrode is actually used as a standard to which the electrical potentials of all other electrodes are compared.

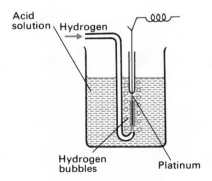

Figure 87

The discharge of ions (electrolysis)

Positive ions

The position of an element in the electrochemical series indicates the ease with which its atoms can change into ions. If an atom forms an ion easily, the reverse process—the changing of an ion into an atom—is likely to be difficult. Therefore the position of an element in the electrochemical series will indicate the ease with which its ions can be discharged. For example, sodium is near the top of the series, therefore it will form a positive ion readily, but the reverse process, the formation of a sodium atom from a sodium ion, will be difficult:

$$Na \rightarrow Na^+ + e^- \qquad \text{easy}$$
$$Na^+ + e^- \rightarrow Na \qquad \text{difficult}$$

On the other hand copper, which is lower in the series, forms a positive ion less readily than sodium does; therefore, it will be easier to discharge a copper ion than to discharge a sodium ion:

$$Cu \rightarrow Cu^{2+} + 2e^- \qquad \text{difficult}$$
$$Cu^{2+} + 2e^- \rightarrow Cu \qquad \text{easy}$$

So, in the electrolysis of a solution containing both copper ions and sodium ions, copper ions will be discharged at the cathode rather than sodium ions. This is called *selective discharge*.

Negative ions

Chlorine forms negative ions more readily than iodine:

$$\tfrac{1}{2}Cl_2 + e^- \rightarrow Cl^- \qquad \text{easy}$$
$$\tfrac{1}{2}I_2 + e^- \rightarrow I^- \qquad \text{difficult}$$

Reversing the process, it follows that the discharge of iodide ions is easier than the discharge of chloride ions:

$$Cl^- \rightarrow \tfrac{1}{2}Cl_2 + e^- \qquad \text{difficult}$$
$$I^- \rightarrow \tfrac{1}{2}I_2 + e^- \qquad \text{easy}$$

Therefore in the electrolysis of a solution containing both chloride and iodide ions, iodide ions will be discharged at the anode rather than chloride ions.

N.B. The relative position of two elements in the electrochemical series is not a sure guide to which of them will be formed by the electrolysis of a solution containing ions of them both. There are at least two other factors which decide this: (i) the concentration of the ions and (ii) the material of which the electrode is made.

The relationship between chemical properties and the electrochemical series

If the electrochemical series indicates the general tendency of elements to form ions, it should be a good guide to some of the chemical activity of the elements. It is helpful at this stage to use the electrochemical series to forecast some of the chemical properties of elements and their compounds, but it must be emphasized that it is based on ionization in aqueous solution and that water itself plays a part in the ionization process.

Metals

(i) Elements at the top form positive ions most readily; they are the most reactive metals. They combine with non-metals most readily and the resulting compounds are the most stable.

(ii) Elements at the top lose electrons most readily, therefore they are the best reducing agents.

(iii) Descending the series, the reactivity and reducing power of the metals decreases and the stability of their compounds decreases.

Non-metals

(i) Elements at the top form negative ions most readily; they are the most reactive non-metals.

(ii) Elements at the top accept electrons most readily; therefore, they are the best oxidizing agents.

(iii) Descending the series, the reactivity and oxidizing powers of the non-metals decrease.

Problems

(1) Suggest reasons for the following: (i) the atomic weight of many elements is not a whole number (ii) water molecules and ammonia molecules, when they act as bases, combine readily with protons.

(2) You are given a solution containing equal concentrations in mole units of copper ions and zinc ions. In electrolysis, which of the metals do you think will be formed at the cathode? Test your theory by experiment.

(3) You are given a solution containing equal concentration (in mole units) of iodide ions and bromide ions. In electrolysis, which of the elements will be formed at the anode? Test your theory by experiment.

(4) Calculate the concentration of the ions in the following solutions in terms of g-ions/litre:

(a) $M/5$ $NaCl$ (b) $M/5$ $CaCl_2$ (c) $M/10$ $AgNO_3$ (d) $M/4$ Na_2CO_3 (e) $M/10$ $Al_2(SO_4)_3$ (f) 2 M HCl (g) M H_2SO_4.

(5) What weight (in grams) of sodium hydroxide would you dissolve to form 1 litre of a solution containing $0 \cdot 1$ g-ion OH^- per litre?

(6) What weight (in grams) of copper sulphate crystals ($CuSO_4.5H_2O$) would you dissolve to form 1 litre of a solution containing $0 \cdot 2$ g-ion Cu^{2+} per litre?

Summary

(1) Atoms seem to be made up of three fundamental particles:

	Mass	Charge
electrons	1/1836	-1
protons	1	$+1$
neutrons	1	0

(2) The positive charge and the mass of an atom are concentrated in a small nucleus. It seems, therefore, that all the neutrons and protons are in the nucleus.

(3) The number of protons in the nucleus of an atom is called the atomic number. Each element has its own fixed atomic number.

(4) In an electrically neutral atom the number of electrons must equal the number of protons.

(5) The electrons appear to surround the nucleus in a series of shells. Electrons with similar energy are said to occupy the same shell.

(6) Elements with similar chemical properties have a similar arrangement of electrons.

(7) For the first twenty elements, the charge on the ion of a metal equals the number of electrons in the outer shell of the atom from which it is formed; the charge on the ion of a non-metal equals eight minus this number.

(8) Isotopes of an element differ in the number of neutrons in their nuclei; they differ, therefore, in their atomic weight but not in their atomic number.

(9) The ionic bond is an electrostatic attraction between oppositely charged ions. The ions are formed by metallic atoms giving electrons to non-metallic atoms. Each ion will have oppositely charged ions as its nearest neighbours.

(10) One mole is Avogadro's number of any particles. 1 g-ion is the weight of Avogadro's number of ions.

(11) The covalent bond is formed by the sharing of a pair of electrons between two atoms. Most covalent compounds consist of separate particles called molecules in which each atom is bonded to a small fixed number of other atoms.

(12) The electrochemical series has been arranged so that those elements which form ions most readily are at the top and those which form ions least readily are at the bottom.

Section 20
Energy changes and structure

We must now amplify the work you have done on the energy changes which accompany the changes in materials. Your work so far can be summarized:

(1) As a result of some chemical changes, energy is given out to the surroundings (*exothermic*); in others energy is taken from the surroundings (*endothermic*).

(2) Exothermic changes such as the oxidation of starch, sugar, coal and oil, are a source of much of our body, domestic, and industrial energy.

(3) Transfer of energy in chemical changes can be in the form of heat, mechanical, or electrical energy.

Experiment 20.1

To measure the heat given out when sodium hydroxide and hydrochloric acid solutions react (C)

Pour 50 cm³ of 2 M hydrochloric acid from a measuring cylinder into a light plastic beaker. Have ready 50 cm³ of 2 M sodium hydroxide in another measuring cylinder or in the same measuring cylinder after rinsing. Take the temperature of both solutions to the nearest 0·5°C. If you use the same thermometer, rinse it before putting it into the other solution.

Pour the sodium hydroxide solution quickly into the hydrochloric acid. Briefly stir the mixture with the thermometer and quickly take the temperature.

Sample results

Temperature of hydrochloric acid = 21°C
Temperature of sodium hydroxide = 21°C
(If these two temperature were not the same, their mean would have to be used in the calculation.)
Temperature after mixing   = 34°C
Approximate weight of mixed solutions = 100 g (0·1 kg)
Specific heat capacity of solution = 4·2 kilojoules per kilogramme per °C, or 1 kilocalorie per kilogramme per °C.

∴ If the products of the reaction had been allowed to cool to the original temperature (21°C) the amount of energy given to the surroundings = wt. of solution × specific heat capacity × change in temperature

= 0·1 kg × 4·2 kJ (1 kcal) × 13°C
= 5·46 kJ or 1·3 kcal

In 50 cm³ of 2 M solution there is $\frac{50 \times 2}{1000}$ g-formula NaOH

$$= 0\cdot1 \text{ g-formula NaOH}$$

Similarly in 50 cm³ of 2 M solution there is 0·1 g-formula HCl ∴ when 1 g-formula (1 mole) each of sodium hydroxide and hydrochloric acid are mixed, the energy given to the surroundings when the products have cooled to the original temperature will be: $10 \times 5\cdot46$ kJ ($1\cdot3$ kcal).

$$= 54\cdot6 \text{ kJ or 13 kcal}$$

N.B. These results are of an actual experiment. More accurate measurement would give 57 kJ or 13·6 kcal.

It must be emphasized that the energy generated in a chemical change is not given completely to the surroundings until the products have cooled to the original temperature of the reactants. All material has energy and it follows that if energy is given to the surroundings as a result of a chemical change the energy of the products must be less than the energy of the reactants. Taking Experiment 20.1 as an example this energy difference can be shown in an energy diagram in which the energies of the reactants and the products are shown at two different levels:

Energy level $NaOH_{(aq)} + HCl_{(aq)}$

57 kJ | 13·6 kcal
Energy level $NaCl_{(aq)} + H_2O_{(l)}$

This energy difference is given the symbol ΔH, Δ stands for difference and H for energy.

ΔH = Energy of products—energy of reactants.

In our example the energy of the reactants is greater than the energy of the products. Therefore, ΔH is negative. This can be conveniently written as part of the equation for the reaction, and has the advantage that an equation represents mole quantities of reactants and products:

$$NaOH_{(aq)} + HCl_{(aq)} \rightarrow NaCl_{(aq)} + H_2O_{(l)} \ \Delta H = -57 \text{ kJ/mol}$$
$$\text{or} -13\cdot6 \text{ kcal/mol}$$

In words this means: when 1 g-formula of sodium hydroxide reacts with 1 g-formula of hydrogen chloride, both in aqueous solution, a dilute aqueous solution of sodium chloride is formed and 57 kJ are transferred to the surroundings when the products have cooled to the original temperature of the reactants.

ΔH is called the *heat of the reaction*.

Notice that in an exothermic reaction ΔH will be negative, because the energy of the products is lower than that of the reactants; conversely, in an endothermic reaction ΔH will be positive.

If this experiment is repeated with similar strong acids and alkalis, the same heat of reaction is obtained. This is because the reaction is the same no matter which strong acids and alkalis are used:

$$H^+_{(aq)} + OH^-_{(aq)} \rightarrow H_2O_{(l)} \ \Delta H = -57 \text{ kJ or } -13\cdot6 \text{ kcal/mol}$$

Experiment 20.2

To measure the heat transferred when ammonium nitrate dissolves in water **(D)**

Measure 95 cm³ of water from a measuring cylinder into a light plastic beaker and take its temperature. Add 8 g of ammonium nitrate and stir briskly with a thermometer to dissolve it; this should take 20 to 30 seconds. Take the temperature again.

Calculate the heat which would be transferred if 1 g-formula of ammonium nitrate were dissolved in water to form a solution of similar concentration, the solution being allowed to return to the original temperature of the water. (8 g of ammonium nitrate dissolved in 95 cm³ of water forms about 100 cm³ of solution and this has approximately the same specific heat as that of water.)

In Experiment 20.2 the temperature dropped when ammonium nitrate was added to water. To return to the original temperature, the solution must take in heat from its surroundings. The change is therefore endothermic, the products being at a higher energy level than the reactants at the same temperature, and ΔH is positive.

energy level $NH_4NO_{3(aq)}$
$\uparrow$ 21 kJ or 5 kcal
Energy level $NH_4NO_{3(s)} + aq$

$$NH_4NO_{3(s)} + aq \rightarrow NH_4NO_{3(aq)} \quad \Delta H = 21 \text{ kJ or } 5 \text{ kcal/mol}$$

Experiment 20.3

To measure the heat of the reaction between zinc and aqueous copper sulphate (C)

Measure 50 cm³ of 0·4 M copper sulphate solution into a light plastic beaker from a measuring cylinder and take its temperature Add about 2 g of powdered zinc quickly and stir with the thermometer vigorously but taking care not to splash. Record the highest temperature which the mixture reaches; this should take about one minute.

Calculate the heat of the reaction

$$Zn_{(s)} + Cu^{2+}_{(aq)} \rightarrow Zn^{2+}_{(aq)} + Cu_{(s)}$$

You can neglect the heat taken by the metals and the beaker. Assume that the specific heat of the solution is approximately that of water for the same volume.

Heat of combustion

Most of the energy which we get from chemical sources comes from reactions in which substances are burned, particularly substances containing carbon and hydrogen. We saw in Section 3 that our body energy comes from the oxidation of food and can be regarded as a form of burning. So that the heat given out by the combustion of substances is very important to us.

Heat of combustion can be defined as the heat given out when 1 mole of a substance is completely burned in oxygen.

For example:

(i) The burning of carbon:
$$C_{(s)} + O_{2(g)} \rightarrow CO_{2(g)} \quad \Delta H = -393 \text{ kJ or } -94 \text{ kcal/mol}$$

(ii) The burning of ethanol (alcohol)
$$C_2H_6O_{(l)} + 3O_{2(g)} \rightarrow 2CO_{2(g)} + 3H_2O_{(l)} \quad \Delta H = -1370 \text{ kJ/mol}$$
$$\text{or } -328 \text{ kcal/mol}$$

(iii) The burning of octane:
$$C_8H_{18(l)} + 12\tfrac{1}{2}O_2 \rightarrow 8CO_{2(g)} + 9H_2O_{(l)} \quad \Delta H = -5450 \text{ kJ/mol}$$
$$\text{or } -1300 \text{ kcal/mol}$$

The heat of combustion of a substance is sometimes called its calorific value. (It will be interesting to see what new word will be invented to replace calorific when the calorie finally becomes an obsolete unit.) The relative calorific values of foods and fuels are of obvious importance, but you should be careful when interpreting relative calorific values that the amounts of substances are expressed in appropriate units. For example, the relative calorific value of alcohol and octane given above is about 1:4, but this is in mole units. You will get a different ratio as you compare their calorific values per gramme. Try it. Commercially, it is perhaps more important to compare calorific values per unit of money.

Structure

In Section 19 we discussed the ways in which atoms can combine with each other. But the product of the combination of a small number of atoms cannot be directly observed; direct observation can be made only on much larger quantities of material, and it is the general structure of observable quantities of materials which will be the subject of the present Section.

There are four main questions to be answered when investigating the structure of a substance:

(1) What is the nature of the individual particles of which the substance is composed?
(2) What forces hold the particles together in liquids and solids?
(3) Are the particles arranged in a regular or a random manner?
(4) Can the individual particles exist separately (molecular) or do they form part of a much larger continuous structure (giant structure)?

Gases

The structure of gases has been studied in some detail in Sections 8 and 16. There is little more to be said at this level except to emphasize that gases appear to consist of very small molecules, moving more or less freely, and with little or no attraction between them.

Liquids

The condensation of gases into liquids can be explained by assuming that the molecules slow down and come closer to each other; this can be brought about by cooling and by increasing the pressure. The closer the molecules get together, the greater becomes the attractive force between them and in a liquid this attractive force is sufficiently large to limit the independent movement of the molecules to those which can escape at the surface. The rest of the molecules are still capable of some movement, but it is much more restricted than it is in gases. It is important to note, however, that an essential characteristic of a liquid is that it will flow and take up the shape of the vessel containing it; it has no permanent and definite shape of its own.

One way of studying the structure of anything is to take it to pieces. Applying this to chemistry, one way of measuring the forces which hold the particles of a liquid together is to measure the energy required to separate all the particles of a liquid from each other. In other words, measure the energy required to change a certain amount of liquid into a gas. The forces holding particles together will vary from liquid to liquid and in comparing them it is obviously important to use the same amount of each liquid; but you will notice that this amount is the same number of particles, not necessarily the same weight. We shall measure the energy required to change 1 *mole* of a liquid into a gas.

Experiment 20.4

To measure the amount of energy required to convert 1 mole of water into steam (C)

Pour 50 cm³ of water from a measuring cylinder into a 100 cm³ conical flask. Support the flask in a clamp so that it is about 5 cm above the top of a bunsen and arrange asbestos mats round it to prevent the flame being blown by draughts when you light the bunsen. Put a thermometer into the water. Take the bunsen from under the flask; light it and arrange the flame so that it is about 5 cm high and with just enough air to take the yellow colour out of it.

Place the bunsen flame under the flask and immediately start a stop-clock. Stir the water gently with the thermometer and take the temperature every 15 seconds—you will probably need a partner to help you to do this. Do not rest the bulb of the thermometer on the bottom of the flask when taking the temperature. Do not alter the bunsen flame. Keep as still as possible, and persuade your classmates to do likewise, to avoid causing draughts.

Note the time at which the water starts to boil. Allow it to boil for between 5 and 10 minutes, then remove the bunsen. Note the length of the *boiling* time. When the flask is cool enough to handle, pour the water into a measuring cylinder and calculate how much has been boiled away.

Plot a graph of temperature (vertically) against time. You should find that the points between about 30 and 70°C lie almost on a straight line. Draw the best straight line through these points and measure its gradient, dividing the temperature rise by the time it takes. The gradient gives the rate at which the temperature rises in °C per minute.

Sample results
Rate at which temperature rises = 37°C in 2 minutes
= 18·5°C per minute
Weight of water = 50 g (0·05 kg)

Specific heat capacity = 4·2 kJ (1 kcal) per kilogramme per °C.
∴ Heat supplied to water per minute

= wt. × temperature rise × specific heat capacity
= 0·05 × 18·5 × 4·2 kJ (1 kcal)
= 3·9 kJ or 0·925 kcal

Time for which water boiled = 10 minutes
Weight of water evaporated in this time = 15 g
Total amount of heat supplied during boiling time = 3·9 kJ (1 kcal) × 10
∴ Amount of heat required to change 1 g of water into steam

$$= \frac{39}{15} \text{ kJ (9·25 kcal)}$$

∴ Amount of heat required to change 1 mole (1 g-molecule = 18 g)

$$\text{of water into steam} = \frac{39 \text{ kJ (9·25 kcal)}}{15} \times 18$$

= 47 kJ or 11 kcal

The results given for Experiment 20.4 are those of a school experiment. More accurate work gives 41 kJ/mol or 9·8 kcal/mol. (N.B. This is the result for evaporation at 100°C; it differs slightly for evaporation at other temperatures.)

The change from water into steam is endothermic and can be represented:

$$H_2O_{(l)} \rightarrow H_2O_{(g)} \quad \Delta H = 41 \text{ kJ or } 9\cdot 8 \text{ kcal/mol}$$

ΔH is called *Mole Heat of Vaporization* and it indicates the energy required to separate Avogadro's number of molecules of water from each other. In other words, it indicates the strength of the forces which hold Avogadro's number of molecules together in water.

The strength of the forces holding particles of substances together is one important part of our study of the structure of substances. It is interesting therefore to compare the heats of vaporization of a number of substances:

Table 13

	State at 25°C, 1 atm	ΔHvap kJ/mol	ΔHvap kcal/mol
hydrogen, H_2	gas	0·8	0·2
carbon dioxide, CO_2	gas	13	3·1
hydrogen chloride, HCl	gas	16	3·9
bromine, Br_2	liquid	30	7·2
chloroform, $CHCl_3$	liquid	29	7·0
octane, C_8H_{18}	liquid	34	8·1
sulphur, S	solid	12	3·0
phosphorus, P (white)	solid	12	3·0
phosphorus, P (red)	solid	29	7·0
naphthalene, $C_{10}H_8$	solid	40	9·6
sodium chloride, NaCl	solid	172	41
sodium fluoride, NaF	solid	201	48
copper, Cu	solid	331	79
iron, Fe	solid	357	85
carbon, C (graphite)	solid	600	143

You should notice that these substances can be divided roughly into two types:

(A) Those which are solid or liquid or gas at room temperature and have a low heat of vaporization.

(B) Those which are solid at room temperature and have a high heat of vaporization.

It seems that in type A the forces holding the particles together are very much less than those in type B. Furthermore, all the quoted substances in type B are solids at room temperature, but type A can be solids or liquids. This brings us to the study of the structure of solids.

The structure of solids

Most of the solid substances which we have studied can have a definite regular shape; they are said to be *crystalline*. You have seen crystals with a low heat of vaporization (e.g. ice, sulphur, naphthalene) and crystals of high heat of vaporization (e.g. sodium chloride, silver, carbon).

The crystalline nature of metals is not always obvious, although you can see regular crystal shapes on a piece of freshly galvanized iron; these are crystalline zinc with which the iron is coated. The following experiment enables you to make small crystals of metals yourselves.

Experiment 20.5
To make crystals of metals
(C)

Hang a clean strip of sheet copper, about 1 cm wide into a solution of 0·1 M silver nitrate. Cork the flask, to hold the strip steady and to keep out the dust, and leave it for about half an hour.

The crystals of silver should be visible to the naked eye, but can be seen to better advantage with a low powered microscope. Why does the solution change colour? Write an ionic equation for the reaction.

Repeat the experiment using a strip of zinc and a 0·1 M solution of lead acetate. Again write an equation.

Why have solids got regular crystalline shapes?

An explanation could be that the particles of which solids are constructed are arranged in regular patterns. For example the sodium and chloride ions in sodium chloride could be arranged in the pattern of a cube (*figure 88*) and the extension of this pattern many millions of times could finally become a crystal of sodium chloride which is visibly a cube. This regular arrangement of the particles of a solid is called a *lattice*. Some typical lattices are shown in *figures 88 to 94*.

○ Represents a chloride ion
● Represents a sodium ion
(not to scale)

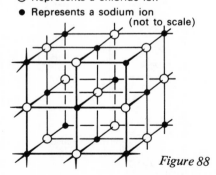

Figure 88

The structure of these lattices is of great interest not only to chemists but also to engineers, metallurgists, physicists and biologists, because in the lattices lies the secret of both physical and chemical properties of substances. But the particles of which substances are made up are too small to be seen, and the distances between particles are equally small in solids and liquids; how, then, can the patterns in which they are arranged be deduced?

Diffraction patterns

Fine fabrics have a regular structure of threads too small to be seen with the naked eye. If you look through such a fabric at a single point of light, you will notice that the point of light appears to be broken up into several points of light. This phenomenon is called diffraction and the pattern of light spots is called a *diffraction pattern*.

You can see a diffraction pattern if you look through the fabric of an umbrella at a distant street lamp (at night!). More conveniently, perhaps, look through a handkerchief at a bright point source of light a few feet away in the laboratory. Try stretching and tilting the handkerchief and notice how a change in the structure of the fabric causes a change in the diffraction pattern.

It is important to realize that the points of light which make up the diffraction pattern are not in the same pattern as that of the threads in the fabric which causes the diffraction. But from a diffraction pattern it is possible to *deduce* the pattern of the structure which causes it. This deduction will not be attempted at your present level of study; it is sufficient to know that it forms the basis for our knowledge of the unseen structure of solids.

X-ray diffraction

The arrangement of particles in a solid is much closer and the particles themselves are much smaller than the thread structure of a fabric. Light waves may be diffracted by a fine fabric or similar structures, but not by the much finer structures of particles of atomic and molecular size in solids. It was discovered, however, that X-rays, having a much shorter wave length than light waves, do form a diffraction pattern when they pass through solids. These X-ray diffraction patterns can be photographed and subsequently measured. It was from these photographs and measurements that W. L. Bragg was able to deduce the arrangement of particles in solids.

The technique of X-ray diffraction has brought about a great increase in our knowledge of the structure of solids. Three main pieces of information can be deduced:

(i) the geometric arrangement of the particles,
(ii) their distance apart,
(iii) and whether the particles form a continuous (giant) structure or can exist separately from all the other particles (molecular).

Molecular structures and giant structures

In a molecule atoms are combined together to form a particle of definite size which can have a stable existence by itself, for example:

a molecule of hydrogen—H_2
a molecule of sulphur—S_8
a molecule of benzene—C_6H_6

In a solid of molecular structure the molecules are held together in a lattice by attractive forces between them.

In a giant structure atoms are also combined together. But in this case the number combined together is not definite and, in theory at least, the number could be infinite.

This distinction between molecular and giant lattices is an important one and explains many differences in the physical properties of solids. Here are some examples:

(i) Giant ionic lattice

This lattice is typical of ionic compounds such as metallic salts and oxides. One example is sodium chloride (*figure 88*); the main characteristics of its lattice are as follows:

(1) The individual particles are ions.

(2) The force holding the particles together is the electrical attraction between positive and negative ions.

(3) The particles are arranged in a regular cubic pattern. Each ion has six oppositely charged ions nearest to it (the six sodium ions nearest to the central chloride ion in *figure 88* are numbered).

(4) *Figure 88* shows only a small part of the lattice; it could be extended in all directions. There is no molecule of sodium chloride (NaCl) in the lattice; no one sodium ion is linked to only one chloride ion. Sodium chloride, and the other ionic solids, are giant structures of ions.

Turn to Table 13 and you will see that the heat of vaporization of sodium chloride is very high. This is characteristic of substances which have a giant structure and indicates the strong forces of the bonds holding the particles together.

$$Na^+Cl^-_{(s)} \rightarrow Na^+_{(g)} + Cl^-_{(g)} \quad \Delta H = 172 \text{ kJ (41 kcal)/mol}$$

High melting and boiling points are also characteristic of compounds of this type of structure.

Another characteristic of this type of compound is that they conduct electricity when they are molten but not when they are solid. This is further evidence for the rigid model of the solid compound, in which the ions are not free to move, and the mobile ions which result from the partial breaking of the attractive force between the ions when the compound is melted.

Ionic solids are usually hard because of the strong forces between ions in every direction. But if they are given a blow—say from a hammer—they often prove to be brittle; a possible explanation being that the blow produces a slight distortion so that ions of like charge are brought nearest to each other and the resulting repulsion between them causes the crystal to split. This is sometimes called cleaving.

In *figure 88* the ions are diminished in size so that the general shape can be better seen. A more accurate model would show the ions actually touching each other and also drawn to scale.

(ii) Giant metallic lattice

One of the differences between the structure of a metallic element and that of an ionic compound is that in the former all the particles are of the same size, being atoms of the same element. In many metals, the atoms seem to behave as spheres packed as closely together as possible. There are two ways in which this close packing can be done:

Experiment 20.6

To investigate the close
packing of spheres **(C)**

You will require 35 polystyrene spheres of uniform diameter (about
2 cm). Arrange 15 of them in a 5-sided triangle holding them in place
with three thin books. Add a second layer of 10 spheres, each fitting into
a hollow formed by a triangle of spheres in the first layer. The second
layer is shown in *figure 89*.

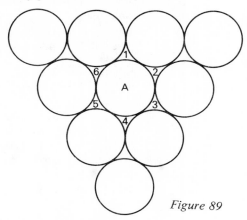

Figure 89

Notice that the sphere marked A is touching 6 other spheres arranged
round it in a regular hexagon. It is also touching the three spheres in the
first layer in whose hollow it rests. At this stage it is touching 9 spheres.

A third layer of three spheres can now be added so that each touches
sphere A. But they can be added in two different ways: resting in
spaces 1, 3 and 5, or in spaces 2, 4, and 6. Either way a close packed
arrangement of spheres is the result in which sphere A is touching 12
other spheres. Imagine your model extended indefinitely and you should
realize that all the spheres except those on the edges and sides, are
surrounded by 12 nearest neighbours.

Similarly there are two ways in which atoms of metals can be close
packed to form a giant structure. In these two kinds of close packed
lattices the atoms themselves occupy 74% of the available space. In a
third type of lattice the atoms occupy 68% of the available space, so
they are nearly, but not quite, close packed. There is so little unoccupied
space in all three lattices that it is not surprising that the density of
metals tends to be high, particularly if the size of the atoms themselves
is small compared with their weight.

The forces holding the particles of a metal together are those of the
metallic bond. Some electrons seem to be free to leave their parent atoms,
leaving the latter in the form of positive ions. The electrons seem to be
able to move freely between the positive ions of the metal and this explains the high conductivity of metals.

Most metals have high melting and boiling points and high heat of
vaporization (see Table 13). Again, this is characteristic of a giant structure and indicates that the metallic bond, like the ionic bond, is strong.

Another characteristic of metal elements is that they are tough
without being brittle; they can be distorted into thin wire or sheets
without breaking. When subjected to stress they tend to bend before
they break.

(iii) **Giant covalent lattices**

Diamond has a typical covalent lattice. In it the individual particles are carbon atoms held together by covalent bonds, each bond being formed by sharing a pair of electrons. The same pattern extends indefinitely in three dimensions, so that a diamond crystal is virtually one giant molecule its size governed only by the size of the crystal. The great hardness, high melting point, and high heat of vaporization, all reflect the great strength of the bonds in the diamond type of lattice.

Each carbon atom is bonded to four other carbon atoms; the general pattern being that of a regular tetrahedron (*figures 90 and 91*) with a carbon at the centre bonded to one carbon atom at each of the four corners.

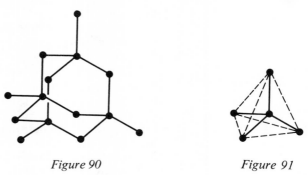

Figure 90 *Figure 91*

In a giant covalent lattice, as in the other two types of giant lattice, there is nothing which can be called a molecule composed of a definite number of atoms and being able to lead a separate existence.

(iv) **Molecular lattices**

Refer to Table 13. Those substances which can form crystalline solids with low melting and boiling points and low heats of vaporization (Type A) have lattices in which the component particles are molecules. They also tend to be soft, non-conductors, with a low density.

A typical example is that of solid carbon dioxide (dry ice), in which the basic pattern is a molecule at each corner of a cube and a molecule at the centre of the face of each cube (*figure 92*).

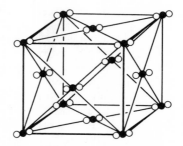

○ ● ○ Represents a molecule of carbon dioxide

Figure 92

Each molecule consists of one carbon atom joined to two oxygen atoms by two pairs of covalent bonds ($O=C=O$). Neither the carbon atom nor the oxygen atoms have the capacity to form any more covalent bonds between each other. Furthermore, the molecules have no electrostatic attraction for each other as in the case of oppositely charged ions.

But there must be some forces holding the molecules of carbon dioxide together, or it would not remain a solid. These forces must be very weak compared with those which operate in the giant structures described above and this is reflected in the low subliming point and low heat of vaporization of solid carbon dioxide. In carbon dioxide and in many other molecular structures these forces are called *van der Waals'* forces.

X-ray diffraction patterns reveal that the distance between molecules in a molecular lattice is much greater than the distance between the particles in the types of giant lattice. This is a further indication of a weak binding force and explains the general softness and low density of compounds with this type of structure.

At this stage it is important to realize that when a molecular structure is melted or vaporized the forces which are being overcome are those *between* molecules not those *within* molecules. Thus, when dry ice vaporizes the carbon—oxygen ($C=O$) bonds are not being broken. In other words, the molecules of carbon dioxide are being separated from each other; they are not being decomposed and they can lead a stable existence on their own.

Allotropy

You have already studied two elements, carbon and sulphur, which can exist in more than one allotropic form. It is now possible to explain the existence of these allotropes by reference to their structure.

Graphite

The giant covalent structure of diamond is described above. The second crystalline form of carbon is interesting in that it has some characteristics of a giant covalent lattice, in which the forces are those of the covalent bond, and some of the characteristics of a molecular lattice, in which the forces are van der Waals' forces.

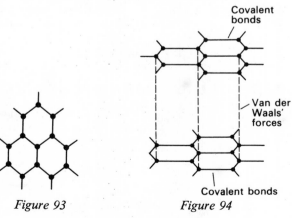

Figure 93   *Figure 94*

The carbon atoms appear to be bonded together in flat layers in a pattern of six carbon atoms joined by covalent bonds in a regular hexagon (*figure 93*).

The layers appear to be bonded together by the much weaker van der Waals' forces (*figure 94*). This means that, although the carbon atoms in each layer are strongly bonded together, the layers themselves are easily separated. Because of this, graphite is much softer than its allotrope, diamond.

Sulphur

The two crystalline forms of sulphur are described on p. 120 Both have molecular structures in which the unit of structure is the sulphur molecule which consists of a ring of eight atoms.

Crystalline sulphur has a low melting point and a low heat of vaporization, typical of a molecular solid. You will remember that when sulphur first melts it forms mobile liquid which presumably consists of S_8 molecules moving freely. Why then does sulphur liquid become more viscous as the temperature increases?

The bonds holding the eight sulphur atoms together in the molecule are quite strong and are not broken at the temperature at which sulphur melts. But at higher temperatures it seems that the ring of eight atoms is broken forming a chain of atoms. These chains link up to form much longer chains, containing many thousands of atoms. The very long chains can no longer move freely; their size and shape does not allow it. Hence the liquid becomes viscous and when cooled quickly forms the rubbery solid, plastic sulphur.

The shapes of molecules

So far we have discussed the shape of crystal lattices. We have also mentioned that atoms of elements can be regarded as spherical in shape and you have built up models of spheres to represent the close packing of atoms in metallic elements. But we have not yet mentioned the shapes of molecules.

Modern experimental techniques have revealed much information about the geometric patterns in which atoms *within* molecules are arranged. These arrangements of atoms give rise to a number of differently shaped molecules.

The shape of a carbon dioxide molecule

The three atoms in a molecule of carbon dioxide are in one straight line (*figure 95*). The angle between the two C=O bonds is 180° and the shape of molecules of this type is said to be *linear*.

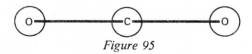

Figure 95

The shape of a methane molecule

Methane has the molecular formula CH_4, having four covalent bonds from the central carbon atom, one to each of the four hydrogen atoms. The arrangement of the four bonds is in three dimensions. The carbon atom appears to be at the centre of a regular tetrahedron with a hydrogen atom at each of the four corners (*figure 96*).

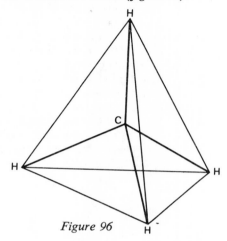

Figure 96

The four covalent bonds are directed from the central carbon atom to the four corners and this gives an angle between the bonds of 109°28′. You should notice that the same tetrahedral structure is present in the giant covalent structure of a diamond.

A theory to explain molecular shape

A simple theory to explain why molecules have certain shapes can be summarized as follows:

Covalent bonds consist of pairs of negatively charged electrons. Being of the same charge, the electron pairs in the bonds repel each other. The molecule therefore adopts a shape in which its bonds are as far apart from each other as possible.

Thus, in carbon dioxide there are two double covalent bonds. To get as far apart as possible the two bonds must point in completely opposite directions, so the angle between the bonds is 180° and the molecule has a linear form.

In methane there are four single covalent bonds. When four equal bonds repel each other the maximum angle which they can get between them is 109°28′; that is why they point from the centre to the four corners of a regular tetrahedron.

Ions, as well as molecules, have definite shapes. Thus, the ammonium ion, NH_4^+, having four equal N—H bonds adopts the same shape as a methane molecule. The ammonia molecule, however, is different.

The shape of an ammonia molecule

In an ammonia molecule three of the five outer electrons of the nitrogen atom form three N—H bonds. This leaves one pair of nitrogen electrons not bonded. A *non-bonded pair* of electrons is sometimes called a *lone pair*.

You might expect that the three N—H bonds would point from the centre to three of the corners of a regular tetrahedron, with the lone pair of electrons directed towards the fourth corner. But measurements show that the angle between the N—H bonds is about 107° not 109°28′. It seems that the three N—H bonds are slightly squeezed together. This can only be explained by extending our original theory, assuming that the repulsion between a lone pair and a bonded pair of electrons is greater than the repulsion between two bonded pairs of electrons.

Thus the lone pair of electrons in the ammonia molecule pushes the three bonded pairs in the N—H bonds through about $2\frac{1}{2}°$ against their natural repulsion. Therefore the ammonia molecule has a pyramid shape, the lone pair completing a tetrahedron which is not quite regular.

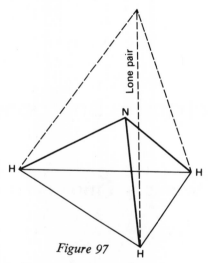

Figure 97

Our theory can be extended to other molecules and it is suggested that before you read further you should try to deduce the shape of a water molecule.

The shape of a water molecule

Oxygen has six electrons which can be used in bonding. In a water molecule two of the electrons are used in forming two O—H bonds, leaving two non-bonded pairs of electrons.

The two covalent bonds repel each other, and, if it were not for the two lone pairs, the two O—H bonds would take up a linear position. But, using the extension of our theory, the two lone pairs of electrons will repel the two O—H bonds pushing the latter closer together. And, as there are *two* lone pairs, the covalent bonds will be pushed even closer together than they are in the ammonia molecule. The angle between the two O—H bonds is about $104\frac{1}{2}°$. A water molecule, therefore, is a V-shape, the two lone pairs completing an irregular tetrahedron (*figure 98*).

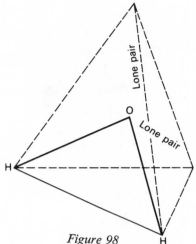

Figure 98

Energy changes and bond changes

A discussion of energy changes and structure has been put into the same Section deliberately. When substances react some bonds are broken and others are made; energy is usually required to break bonds and energy is usually evolved when bonds are made.

The various stages of bond breaking and bond making are called the mechanism of a reaction and they are not apparent from the simple equation for a reaction. But the overall energy change for a reaction is the sum of the energies involved in the complex bond breaking and making which goes on in the reaction.

Electrical energy

In all the experiments in this Section the energy of the reactions has shown itself as heat. In Experiment 20.3 and in many others the energy of a chemical change can be in the form of electrical energy. You should be aware that the electrical energy which can be derived from a chemical change is not usually the same as the heat energy which can be derived from the same change. For example in Experiment 20.3 the chemical change is:

$$Zn_{(s)} + Cu^{2+}{}_{(aq)} \rightarrow Zn^{2+}{}_{(aq)} + Cu_{(s)}$$

The heat energy which can be derived from this reaction is 12·5 kJ/mol, but the electrical energy which can be derived from the same reaction is 12·1 kJ/mol.

The law of conservation of energy

The total amount of energy before and after a chemical reaction is the same if one takes into account the energy changes in the surroundings as well as in the reactants and products. This is an example of the Law of Conservation of Energy. But it is important to note that the *usefulness* of the energy is *not conserved*. Many chemical reactions have the potential to give energy as useful work; Experiment 20.3, for example, could be used to drive an electric motor. But once the reaction has taken place and the energy has been dissipated as heat causing a negligible temperature rise in the surroundings its availability for useful work is also dissipated.

The total amount of energy may be conserved but its availability to do useful work is not conserved. An incomplete understanding of the Law of Conservation of Energy has dangerous implications if we think that we can use our resources of chemical energy recklessly.

Summary

(1) When the products of an *exothermic* reaction return to the original temperature, their energy content is *less* than that of the reactants, energy having been lost to the surroundings.

(2) When the products of an *endothermic* reaction return to the original temperature their energy content is *greater* than that of the reactants, energy having been gained from the surroundings.

(3) ΔH represents the Heat of a Reaction for the mole quantities shown in the equation.

(4) ΔH = energy of products − energy of reactants; it is negative for an exothermic reaction and positive for an endothermic reaction.

(5) Heat of combustion is the heat given out when one mole of a substance is completely burned in oxygen.

(6) A description of the structure of a substance may include:

    (i) The nature of the individual particles.

    (ii) The forces holding the particles together.

    (iii) The arrangement of the particles, the lattice.

    (iv) Whether it is a molecular or a giant structure.

(7) The forces which hold the particles of a substance together can be measured by determining the energy required to vaporize one mole of it. This is called the Mole Heat of Vaporization.

(8) Lattice structures can be determined by the manner in which they diffract X-rays.

(9) In a molecular structure the individual particles are molecules; that is small groups of atoms, combined together in a fixed composition, with the ability to have a stable, independent existence.

The forces *between* molecules are not strong. As a result, molecular substances usually have low melting and boiling points and a low heat of vaporization. They also tend to be soft, non-conductors, with a low density.

(10) In a giant lattice, the particles form a continuous structure in which there are no molecules. The bonds holding the particles together may be ionic (as in salts), metallic, or covalent (as in diamond). The bonds

are much stronger than the forces between molecules; as a result, substances of giant structure usually have high melting and boiling points and heat of vaporization.

(11) The ions in a giant ionic structure are only free to move and carry electricity when the substance is molten or dissolved. The electrons in a giantmetallic structure are free to move in solids or liquids. The electrons in a giant covalent structure of the diamond type are fixed in covalent bonds and are not free to carry electricity. Substances of molecular structure are non-conductors.

(12) The bonds *within* a molecule are usually much stronger than those *between* molecules.

(13) The shape of a molecule is largely determined by the repulsion between the bonds which bind its component atoms together. The repulsion between a lone pair (non-bonded pair) of electrons and a covalent bond is greater than that between two covalent bonds.

Section 21
Periodic table– alkali metals

The periodic table

The Periodic Table has already been mentioned in your study of valency and of the halogen elements. The main purpose of the Table is to classify the elements to assist the orderly study of them. The principal characteristics of a classification of the elements, like that of any other numerous group of things, should be:

(1) The elements should be arranged in an order which depends on one of their fundamental characteristics.

(2) The elements should be divided into groups in such a way that similar elements lie in the same group.

(3) The elements within the same group will not have identical properties. But the way in which properties differ from one element to another (the gradation of properties) should conform to some pattern; so, knowing the properties of one element in a group, it should be possible to predict the properties of another in the same group.

(4) Similarly, the gradation of properties from one group of elements to the next group should conform to some pattern.

The general structure of the table

(1) The elements are arranged in the order of their atomic numbers starting with hydrogen, atomic number 1. Earlier Periodic Tables were based on atomic weights, but this produced some anomalies; for example, argon and potassium would not be in groups of similar elements. (Check this.)

(2) You will notice that the metals lie on the left-hand side of the Table and the non-metals on the right. The actual dividing line runs roughly from element 5 to element 84.

(3) The elements are divided into eight groups running vertically. Some groups of elements are given names:

Group I—the Alkali metals.

Group II—the Alkaline Earth metals.

Group VII—the Halogens.

Group O—the Noble (or inert) gases.

(4) The three rows of elements forming the large block in the centre of the Table are called the Transition Metals.

(5) The elements are also divided into periods which run horizontally. The number of elements in each complete period is significant:

Period 1—2 elements.
Period 2—8 elements.
Period 3—8 elements.
Period 4—18 elements.
Period 5—18 elements.
Period 6—32 elements.

Turn to Table 10 (p. 182) and you will see that this arrangement corresponds to the number of electrons in succesive energy levels for the first twenty elements.

General characteristics of halogens (group VII)

A detailed study of the halogens was done in Section 12. It will be useful, at this stage, to summarize their similarities and gradation of properties.

Table 14

	Electron configuration	Atomic radius Å	Ionic radius Å	Boiling point °C	ΔHvap kJ/mol	↑ Increasing reactivity and oxidizing power
F_2	2.7	0·71	1·36	−188	13·4	
Cl_2	2.8.7	0·99	1·81	− 35	20·1	
Br_2	2.8.18.7	1·14	1·95	58	30·2	
I_2	2.8.18.18.7	1·33	2·16	183	42·0	

Notice that each element has the same number of electrons in the outer shell; this explains their similarity of properties.

The gradation in properties arises from the increase in size and charge on the nucleus and the number of electrons which shield the outer seven electrons from the positive attraction of the nucleus. This, in turn, affects the tendency of the atoms to accept electrons, i.e. oxidize. Hence the relative oxidizing power and reactivity of the halogens.

The atomic and ionic radii are calculated from X-ray diffraction evidence and are based on the assumption that the atoms and ions are spheres, but not solid spheres. The radii increase with increasing atomic weight and number—as might be expected. Notice the big increase in size when an atom gains a single electron to become an ion.

The low boiling points and mole heats of vaporization are characteristic of molecular substances. Notice that the increasing size of the atoms of which the diatomic molecules are composed seems to increase the forces which bind the molecules together and hence increases the energy required to separate them and change them into vapours.

General characteristics of alkali metals (group 1)

The alkali metals have a characteristic single electron in the outer shell. When they react they tend to lose this electron and this tendency increases with increasing atomic size, indicating that the further the outer electron is from the nucleus, and the greater the number of electrons between it and the nucleus, the more readily is it separated from

Table 15

	Electron configuration	Atomic radius Å	Ionic radius Å	Boiling point °C	ΔHvap kJ/mol	increasing reactivity and reducing power
Li	2.1	1·52	0·60	1,331	134	
Na	2.8.1	1·86	0·95	890	86	
K	2.8.8.1	2·27	1·33	766	78	

the atom. Hence the increasing reactivity and the increasing reducing powers of the alkali metals as the atomic size increases.

Characteristics of period 3

Leaving out argon, the following table summarizes the trends in properties from one group to the next along a period.

Table 16

Group	I	II	III	IV	V	VI	VII
Element	Na	Mg	Al	Si	P	S	Cl
Electrons	2.8.1	2.8.2	2.8.3	2.8.4	2.8.5	2.8.6	2.8.7
Atomic radius Å	1·86	1·60	1·34	1·18	1·10	1·02	0·99
Ionic radius Å	$0·95^+$	$0·65^{2+}$	$0·50^{3+}$			$1·84^{2-}$	$1·81^-$
Maximum valency	1	2	3	4	5	6	7

Metallic structure   ←   →   Molecular structure

← Increasing tendency to form positive ions

← Increasing reducing power

Increasing tendency to form negative ions →

Increasing oxidizing power →

Notice the decrease in atomic size from left to right despite the increasing number of electrons.

The maximum valency (oxidation state) corresponds to the number of electrons in the outer shell and to the number of the group; but remember that a frequently used valency for elements in groups V, VI, and VII, is eight minus that number.

Oxides tend to become more ionic and basic to the left of the Period: more molecular and acidic to the right.

Chlorides tend to become more ionic to the left of the Period: more molecular to the right.

The alkali metals

The alkali metals have a metallic structure. Sodium will serve as an example, but remember that lithium will be less reactive and potassium will be more reactive.

Physical properties

Sodium is a good conductor of heat and electricity. It is shiny (when freshly cut), malleable and ductile but, unlike most metals, it is soft and has a low density (0.97 g/cm^3).

Chemical properties

Sodium reacts readily to form stable ionic compounds. Many of these reactions have been studied before, so they are only summarized here:

(i) with oxygen, $4Na + O_2 \rightarrow 2Na_2O$
(ii) with the halogens, e.g. $2Na + Cl_2 \rightarrow 2NaCl$
(iii) with water, $2Na + 2H_2O \rightarrow 2NaOH + H_2$

The position of sodium in the electrochemical series accords with these properties. It readily loses electrons to form positive ions and so combines readily with non-metallic elements to form ionic compounds; it is a strongly electropositive element.

A large amount of energy, mainly in the form of heat, is given out when sodium reacts with other elements. To decompose the resulting compounds this energy must be applied. It is not surprising, therefore, that sodium compounds are stable; compounds easily formed are usually difficult to decompose.

Sodium as a reducing agent

Sodium readily gives one electron from each of its atoms. Since reduction is the giving of electrons, it is to be expected that sodium, together with the other elements high in the electrochemical series, will be a good reducing agent. Titanium has been made by reducing titanium tetrachloride with sodium.

$$TiCl_4 + 4Na \rightarrow Ti + 4NaCl$$

Magnesium is now used instead of sodium.

The properties of alkali metal compounds

Electrical properties

Most of the common alkali metals compounds are ionic in all states; they conduct electricity when they are liquid or dissolved, but not when they are solid.

When molten sodium compounds are electrolysed, sodium is formed at the cathode (p. 50), but when aqueous solutions of sodium compounds are electrolysed, hydrogen, not sodium, is formed at the cathode. When aqueous sodium hydroxide is electrolysed using platinum electrodes, hydrogen is formed at the cathode and oxygen at the anode in the ratio 2 vol.:1 vol., corresponding to the electrolysis of water.

H

Solubility

Most alkali metal compounds are soluble in water, but they do not dissolve in liquid hydrocarbons. (Lithium carbonate is sparingly soluble in water.)

Flame tests
Experiment 21.1

The flame test (C)

Put a small quantity of any sodium compound on to a watch glass. Clean a platinum wire by dipping it into concentrated hydrochloric acid and then heating the wire in a bunsen flame (heat the tip of the wire only; if the flame touches the glass rod which holds the wire, the glass may crack).

Dip the platinum wire into the sodium compound and then heat the tip of the wire in the edge of a bunsen flame.

Note the characteristic colour of the flame.

Much of chemistry is concerned with identifying substances. Each substance has its own characteristic properties and some of these serve to distinguish it from every other substance. The most useful properties for the purpose of identification are those in which each substance differs from all other substances and which are easily observed. We have seen that melting and boiling points can be used; but, as the number of known substances has grown, it is no longer possible to identify substances by these simple properties alone; too many of them have almost identical melting and boiling points.

Use is made of many other chemical and physical properties and two of these are worth special mention: (i) the wavelengths of the radiation which is given out when a substance is submitted to heat or electrical energy, and (ii) the wavelengths which are absorbed when radiation is passed through a substance. The first gives rise to an emission spectrum and the second to an absorption spectrum. The wavelengths are not confined to visible radiation: ultra-violet, infra-red, and X-ray radiation are all used. These methods can detect not only single substances but also parts of single substances such as the sodium ions in sodium compounds.

The flame test is a crude example of the use of the visible radiation emitted from substances which are excited by heat. Under these conditions sodium ions emit yellow light only and they do so with sufficient intensity to be obvious without the use of instruments.

Many other ions show characteristic wavelengths strong enough to be detected with the naked eye and which can be used for identification in a flame test: potassium (lilac), calcium (red), strontium (crimson), copper (green).

Sodium hydroxide (caustic soda)

Sodium hydroxide is a white, corrosive, deliquescent solid which dissolves readily in water with the evolution of heat.

It is a strong alkali and its aqueous solution exhibits the usual properties of hydroxide ions.

(i) It will precipitate insoluble hydroxides of metals:

$$Fe^{3+}_{(aq)} + 3OH^-_{(aq)} \rightarrow Fe(OH)_{3(s)}$$

(ii) It will displace ammonia from ammonium salts:

$$NH_4^+{}_{(aq)} + OH^-{}_{(aq)} \rightarrow NH_4OH_{(aq)} \rightarrow NH_3{}_{(g)} + H_2O_{(l)}$$

(iii) It gives the usual alkaline reactions with indicators.

Sodium chloride (common salt)

Sodium chloride occurs naturally in enormous quantities in the sea and in rock salt deposits. It forms part of the body fluids of many animals, including man, and is an essential part of their diet. It is used as a starting material for the manufacture of most other sodium compounds.

Most of the important reactions of sodium chloride have already been studied: e.g. with concentrated sulphuric acid (p. 100) and with aqueous silver nitrate (p. 100).

Sodium carbonate (soda ash, Na_2CO_3)

Sodium carbonate is a white powder. It dissolves in water to form an alkaline solution and, when its aqueous solution is crystallized below 32°C, it forms a hydrate: $Na_2CO_3.10H_2O$ (washing soda). Large quantities are manufactured from sodium chloride by the Ammonia-Soda (Solvay) process described on p. 272.

It is one of the most stable carbonates; it can be melted without decomposition. Carbon dioxide is displaced from it when it is treated with acids stronger than carbonic acid:

$$CO_3{}^{2-}{}_{(aq)} + 2H^+{}_{(aq)} \rightarrow H_2CO_3{}_{(aq)} \rightarrow H_2O_{(l)} + CO_2{}_{(g)}$$

Sodium hydrogen carbonate (baking powder, $NaHCO_3$)

Sodium hydrogen carbonate is an intermediate product in the ammonia-soda process for making sodium carbonate (p. 272).

It contains acidic hydrogen and could be classified as an acid salt but, in fact, its solution is slightly alkaline—test it with universal indicator. This is a common feature of the salts derived from strong alkalis and weak acids.

It is one of the few hydrogen carbonates which can exist at room temperature. Even so, it decomposes readily when heated:

$$2NaHCO_3 \rightarrow Na_2CO_3 + H_2O + CO_2$$

It shows the usual reaction with acids stronger than carbonic acid:

$$HCO_3{}^-{}_{(aq)} + H^+{}_{(aq)} \rightarrow H_2CO_3{}_{(aq)} \rightarrow H_2O_{(l)} + CO_2{}_{(g)}$$

Sodium sulphate (Na_2SO_4)

Like the carbonate, it forms a decahydrate with water: $Na_2SO_4.10H_2O$ (Glauber's salt).

In the laboratory it can be made by mixing a 2 M solution of sodium hydroxide with an equal volume of an M solution of sulphuric acid:

$$2NaOH + H_2SO_4 \rightarrow Na_2SO_4 + 2H_2O$$

Problems

(1) Devise a theory to explain why the atomic radius of elements in a single period of the Periodic Table decreases as the size of the nucleus and the number of electrons increases.

(2) Devise a theory to explain why the ionic radius of metal ions is smaller than the atomic radius of the same element, while the ionic radius of non-metal ions is larger than the atomic radius of the same element.

(3) Carry out the following tests on substance *A*:

 (i) The flame test.

 (ii) The action of heat—test for oxygen.

 (iii) The brown ring test.

   Record your observations and identify *A*.

(4) Carry out the following tests on the salt *E*:

 (i) The flame test.

 (ii) The action of its solution on litmus.

 (iii) Add dilute sulphuric acid; warm gently; smell the resulting gas and test it with moist blue litmus paper.

 (iv) Add solid ammonium chloride and a few drops of water; warm gently; smell the resulting gas and test it with moist red litmus paper.

   Record your observations and explain as far as you can the reactions which have taken place.

Summary

The best summary is to be found in the general structure of the Periodic Table at the beginning of this section.

Section 22
Group II–calcium and magnesium

Calcium and magnesium do not occur naturally, but their compounds are abundant:

(i) Chalk, limestone, and marble, are all forms of calcium carbonate.
(ii) Magnesite is magnesium carbonate.
(iii) Dolomite is a mixed carbonate of calcium and magnesium.
(iv) Anhydrite is calcium sulphate, $CaSO_4$.
(v) Gypsum is hydrated calcium sulphate, $CaSO_4.2H_2O$.

Sea water contains both calcium and magnesium ions in solution. Magnesium ions are second only to sodium ions in their abundance in sea water and they are in sufficient concentration to make sea water a profitable source of the metal. The concentration of calcium ions in sea water is less than one-fifth of the concentration of magnesium ions.

Magnesium mixed with aluminium forms light alloys which are extensively used for aircraft.

Calcium is not made in such large quantities as magnesium because it is not used as a structural metal. Some calcium is used to reduce uranium tetrafluoride to uranium:

$$UF_4 + 2Ca \rightarrow U + 2CaF_2$$

Both metals are light (specific gravity: calcium 1·5, magnesium 1·7), otherwise their physical properties are those of typical metals (p. 203).

Chemical properties
Reaction with water

Calcium reacts readily with cold water; magnesium reacts slowly with cold water, but rapidly when heated in steam:

$$Ca + 2H_2O \rightarrow Ca(OH)_2 + H_2$$
$$Mg + H_2O \rightarrow MgO + H_2$$

With oxygen

Both elements burn readily:

$$2Ca + O_2 \rightarrow 2CaO$$
$$2Mg + O_2 \rightarrow 2MgO$$

With the halogens

Both elements combine readily:

$$Ca + Cl_2 \rightarrow CaCl_2$$
$$Mg + Cl_2 \rightarrow MgCl_2$$

This chemical activity is to be expected from the position of the metals in the electrochemical series. Both are high in the series and from this is to be expected that they will readily form positive ions and be very reactive.

Compounds of calcium and magnesium

Carbonates
Experiment 22.1

To investigate the action of heat on the carbonates of calcium and magnesium (C)

Make a small loop in a length of Eureka (Constantan) wire so that it will hold a piece of marble in the centre of a tripod (*figure 99*).

Weigh a watch glass; put the piece of marble on to it and weigh again. Fix the piece of marble into the loop of wire and heat it strongly for twenty minutes. While this is going on, heat two small measures of magnesium carbonate in a small dry tube for two or three minutes and test for the evolution of carbon dioxide.

Allow the residue from the marble to cool and, without touching it, release it from the wire loop on to the weighed watch glass. Weigh the two together.

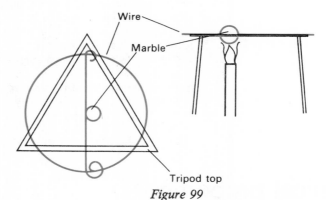

Figure 99

Specimen results

Weight of watch glass	= 12·60 g
Weight of watch glass + marble	= 13·80 g
Weight of watch glass + residue	= 13·27 g

Wt. of marble	Loss in weight	Wt. of residue
= 1·20 g	= 0·53 g	= 0·67 g

If these weights are converted into g-formulae, they correspond to a decomposition of the calcium carbonate into calcium oxide and carbon dioxide:

Divide each weight by the formula weight of the appropriate substance.

No. of g-formulae of $CaCO_3$	No. of g-formulae of CO_2	No. of g-formulae of CaO
$=\dfrac{1\cdot20}{100}$	$=\dfrac{0\cdot53}{44}$	$=\dfrac{0\cdot67}{56}$
$=0\cdot012$	$=0\cdot012$	$=0\cdot012$

∴ 1 g-formula of calcium carbonate decomposes to form 1 g-formula of carbon dioxide plus 1 g-formula of calcium oxide.

From this it follows that the equation for the reaction is:

$$CaCO_3 \rightarrow CO_2 + CaO$$

Experiment 22.2

To investigate the action of water on the oxides of calcium and magnesium (C)

To the cold residue of the heated marble from the previous experiment, add water drop by drop. Tip the resulting powder into a small beaker; add a further 10 cm³ of water; swirl it to dissolve as much as possible, then filter it.

Test the filtrate with (a) red litmus paper and (b) carbon dioxide generated from another piece of marble.

Investigate the action of water on the residue of the heated magnesium carbonate.

Both calcium and magnesium carbonates decompose when strongly heated, but calcium carbonate is more stable than magnesium carbonate:

$$CaCO_3 \rightarrow CaO + CO_2$$
$$MgCO_3 \rightarrow MgO + CO_2$$

Calcium oxide, which is also called quicklime, reacts exothermically with water to form calcium hydroxide. There is very little reaction between magnesium oxide and water:

$$CaO + H_2O \rightarrow Ca(OH)_2$$

Calcium hydroxide (slaked lime) forms a suspension in water (milk of lime). Some of it dissolves in water to form an alkaline solution (limewater). Limewater reacts with carbon dioxide to form a white precipitate of calcium carbonate:

$$Ca(OH)_{2(aq)} + CO_{2(g)} \rightarrow CaCO_{3(s)} + H_2O_{(l)}$$

Both calcium carbonate and magnesium carbonate are insoluble in water.

Sulphates

Magnesium sulphate is readily soluble in water whereas calcium sulphate is only slightly soluble. Calcium sulphate can be formed by precipitation when solutions containing sulphate ions and calcium ions are mixed:

$$Ca^{2+}_{(aq)} + SO_4^{2-}_{(aq)} \rightarrow CaSO_{4(s)}$$

Magnesium sulphate can be made by the usual methods for making soluble salts: the action of dilute sulphuric acid on the metal, or its oxide, or its carbonate.

Chlorides

Both calcium and magnesium chlorides are very soluble in water. Anhydrous calcium chloride absorbs water vapour rapidly; it is deliquescent and it can be used as a drying agent (not for ammonia—see p. 165).

Hardness of water

Soap

Soap is a mixture of sodium salts of various acids (p. 254). These acids are all made from fats—they are sometimes called fatty acids; all of them contain carbon and have high molecular weights. A typical example is palmitic acid ($C_{15}H_{31}COOH$); sodium palmitate ($C_{15}H_{31}COONa$) forms part of most soaps.

For simplicity, soap will be represented here by the formula Na^+X^-. X^- represents the various ions which are derived from fatty acids.

Hard water

Hard water is water with which it is difficult to form a lather with ordinary soap. Much of the soap is wasted in forming an insoluble scum.

Experiment 22.3

To investigate the causes of hardness in water **(C)**

Put 10 cm³ of distilled water into each of three test tubes. To the first test tube add about 1 cm³ of soap solution and shake it. To the second tube add about 1 drop of a molar solution of any calcium salt, then add 1 cm³ of soap solution and shake the tube. To the third tube add 1 drop of a molar solution of any magnesium salt, then add 1 cm³ of soap solution and shake the tube.

In which tube does the best lather form? In which tube does the scum form?

It is clear from Experiment 22.3 that solutions which contain calcium and magnesium ions react with soap solution to form a precipitate. This wastes the soap and makes the formation of a lather difficult. The precipitate seems to be formed from the calcium or magnesium ions and the ions from the fatty acids:

$$Mg^{2+}_{(aq)} + 2X^-_{(aq)} \rightarrow MgX_{2(s)}$$
$$Ca^{2+}_{(aq)} + 2X^-_{(aq)} \rightarrow CaX_{2(s)}$$

It follows that calcium or magnesium ions in solution can cause hardness of water.

In many parts of the United Kingdom the water supply contains calcium compounds in solution—the presence of magnesium compounds is rare. The calcium compounds are ionized and therefore the water is hard. The two chief compounds found in solution are calcium hydrogen carbonate and calcium sulphate.

Calcium hydrogen carbonate in water

If you look back to Experiment 7.6 (p. 60) you will remember that, when carbon dioxide is passed into a suspension of calcium carbonate, insoluble calcium carbonate is changed into soluble calcium hydrogen carbonate:

$$CaCO_{3(s)} + H_2O_{(l)} + CO_{2(g)} \rightarrow Ca(HCO_3)_{2(aq)}$$

This is typical of the conversion of an insoluble normal salt into a soluble acid salt by the action of an excess of the acid.

The same reaction occurs in nature. Calcium carbonate occurs as limestone and chalk, both of which are porous to water. The water which passes through the rock contains some carbon dioxide, which has dissolved as the rain filters through the soil. The water, therefore, is a dilute solution of carbonic acid. This reacts with the limestone or chalk to form a solution of calcium hydrogen carbonate.

Calcium sulphate in water

Much of our water is pumped from supplies which are stored naturally deep underground. If this water has been in contact with gypsum or anhydrite, some of the rock will have dissolved to form a solution of calcium sulphate. The concentration of calcium sulphate will not be large, because calcium sulphate is not very soluble, but it will cause a sufficient concentration of calcium ions to make the water hard.

Water softening

Hard water not only causes difficulties when washing with soap, it can also lead to the blockage of hot water pipes by the precipitation of insoluble calcium salts in them. The difficulty in washing can be avoided by using synthetic detergents instead of soap, but the second problem can be a serious one and methods for softening the water have to be used extensively in some areas.

The essential part of any softening process is to remove the calcium or magnesium ions from their solution in water by converting them into insoluble calcium and magnesium compounds. The following methods can be used.

(i) *Sodium carbonate*. The addition of sodium carbonate to the water produces carbonate ions which remove calcium and magnesium ions by precipitating them as their carbonates:

$$Ca^{2+}_{(aq)} + CO_3^{2-}_{(aq)} \rightarrow CaCO_{3(s)}$$
$$Mg^{2+}_{(aq)} + CO_3^{2-}_{(aq)} \rightarrow MgCO_{3(s)}$$

(ii) *Ion-exchange*. In this process certain insoluble ionic substances, which can be either naturally occurring (zeolites) or synthetic (ion-exchange resins), are used. These substances consist of very large negative ions, which do not move, linked with small mobile positive ions such as sodium ions (*figure 100*).

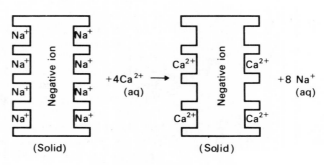

Figure 100

223

The ion-exchange compound is contained in a cylinder through which all the water passes. Sodium ions pass from the solid into the solution and are replaced by calcium ions, which form an ionic bond with the giant negative ions.

In this way the calcium ions remain in the solid in the cylinder. The water which flows through contains an equivalent number of sodium ions.

Methods (i) and (ii) will soften all types of hard water. Water which contains calcium hydrogen carbonate can be softened by two further methods.

(iii) By adding just sufficient calcium hydroxide to convert the soluble hydrogen carbonate into insoluble calcium carbonate:

$$Ca(HCO_3)_{2(aq)} + Ca(OH)_{2(aq)} \rightarrow 2CaCO_{3(s)} + 2H_2O_{(l)}$$
$$\text{acid salt} \quad + \quad \text{base} \quad \rightarrow \quad \text{normal salt}$$

(iv) If the water is heated, calcium hydrogen carbonate decomposes into insoluble calcium carbonate:

$$Ca(HCO_3)_{2(aq)} \rightarrow CaCO_{3(s)} + H_2O_{(l)} + CO_{2(g)}$$

(This process is not suitable for large-scale use)

Problems

(1) You are provided with the substance A, a salt of a metal which is in either group I or group II of the Periodic Table. Investigate the nature of A by the following tests:

(i) Heat a small quantity of A in a small dry test tube. If a liquid is formed, test it for the presence of water.
(ii) The flame test.
(iii) To a few drops of an aqueous solution of A add an equal volume of aqueous sodium carbonate.
(iv) Add one drop of the solution of A to dilute sulphuric acid.
(v) To the solution of A add dilute nitric acid followed by aqueous silver nitrate.

(2) B is a compound of calcium. Devise an experiment which will tell you whether B is soluble in water or not.

Warm a little of B with the substance C and test the resulting gas with moist red litmus paper.

What conclusions can you draw about the nature of B and C from these experiments alone?

(3) D is either sodium carbonate, calcium carbonate, calcium sulphate, or sodium chloride. By the shortest possible method deduce which of these four.

(4) Shake a small quantity of E with distilled water. Centrifuge or filter off the excess solid. Treat the clear solution with soap solution. What conclusions can you draw about the nature of E?

(5) You are supplied with magnesium and M sulphuric acid. Weigh out about 1 g of magnesium and calculate the volume of the acid solution which will just react with it. Add 5% to the calculated volume and then use this quantity of acid to prepare crystals of magnesium sulphate.

(6) You are supplied with calcium carbonate, 2 M hydrochloric acid, and M sulphuric acid. Weigh out about 5 g of calcium carbonate and from it prepare a sample of calcium sulphate. Use the calculated volumes of acid plus 5%.

Thoroughly dry the calcium sulphate in an oven, below 100°C. Determine whether the calcium sulphate is hydrated and, if so, determine how many g-molecules of water it contains per g-formula.

Summary

(1) The reactivity of the elements of group II of the Periodic Table increases with increasing atomic number, atomic weight, and atomic size. This is related to an increasing tendency to form positive ions.

(2) Calcium displaces hydrogen from cold water. Magnesium displaces hydrogen readily from steam, but only slowly from cold water.

(3) The carbonates of calcium and magnesium are insoluble in water; when strongly heated, they decompose to the oxides.

(4) Calcium oxide reacts exothermically with water to form calcium hydroxide. Calcium hydroxide dissolves slightly in water to form an alkaline solution. Magnesium oxide has little reaction with water.

(5) Hardness in water is caused by calcium or magnesium ions in solution. These ions undergo a precipitation reaction with soap. In the United Kingdom calcium hydrogen carbonate and calcium sulphate are the compounds usually found in hard water.

(6) Water is softened by precipitating the calcium ions either as calcium carbonate or in an ion-exchange resin.

Section 23
Aluminium and zinc

There is more aluminium, in the combined state, than any other metal in the earth's crust. Unfortunately it is not easily extracted from its most abundant compounds, the silicates of aluminium of which clay and many rocks are composed. The two commercially important ores are bauxite, $Al_2O_3.2H_2O$, and cryolite, Na_3AlF_6.

Zinc is found as zinc blende, ZnS, and calamine, $ZnCO_3$.

Aluminium, alone or alloyed, is one of the most important structural metals. Because of its low density, it is used for structures in which lightness is important: aircraft, ships' superstructure, cooking utensils and overhead cables. Powdered aluminium is used in some paints and aluminium foil is used for containing foodstuffs. It is a fashionable metal amongst sculptors.

Zinc is largely used as a thin protective coat on iron. In this form it can be seen on dust-bins, buckets, and metal roofs. Brass is an alloy of copper and zinc.

Both metals have the physical properties typical of metals; zinc is a little unusual in its low boiling point ($905°C$).

Chemical properties

Action with oxygen The surface of both metals becomes oxidized when they are exposed to air. This causes a thin protective coat of oxide to form on the metal, which prevents further corrosion.

Both metals burn when heated in air. Combustion takes place more readily if they are in the powdered or vapour state; in fact, mixtures of finely powdered aluminium and air can explode.

The reaction of aluminium with oxygen is strongly exothermic: more so than that of iron and oxygen.

$$2Al + 1\tfrac{1}{2}O_2 \rightarrow Al_2O_3 \quad \Delta H = -1680 \text{ kJ } (-400 \text{ kcal})/\text{mol}$$
$$2Fe + 1\tfrac{1}{2}O_2 \rightarrow Fe_2O_3 \quad \Delta H = -840 \text{ kJ } (-200 \text{ kcal})/\text{mol}$$

This difference in the energy evolved when the two oxides are formed indicates the difference in the affinities of the two metals for oxygen. Aluminium combines more readily with oxygen than iron does. This is strikingly illustrated in the next experiment.

Experiment 23.1

The 'Thermit' Reaction (D)

Mix 18 g of iron (III) oxide with 6 g of aluminium powder on a piece of paper (do not grind them). These quantities are in the ratio of 1 g-formula of iron (III) oxide to 2 g-atoms of aluminium ($Fe_2O_3 : 2Al$).

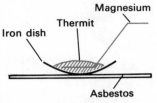

Figure 101

Pile the mixture on to an iron dish standing on an asbestos mat. Insert a 20 cm piece of magnesium ribbon which has been bent as shown in *figure 101*

Light the end of the magnesium and move at least ten feet away. When everything has cooled down, examine the pieces of iron which remain in the dish.

The violence of the 'Thermit' reaction will be apparent. The reduction of iron (III) oxide by aluminium is strongly exothermic and the pieces of iron show signs of having been molten:

$$Fe_2O_3 + 2Al \rightarrow 2Fe + Al_2O_3$$

Actions with acids and alkalis

Experiment 23.2

To investigate the action of aluminium and zinc on hydrochloric acid and sodium hydroxide (C)

Put one small measure of aluminium powder into the bottom of each of two small test tubes. Add six drops of dilute hydrochloric acid to one tube; shake the tube and wait for a minute or two to see if any reaction takes place. If no reaction takes place, add six drops of concentrated hydrochloric acid. Test for hydrogen.

To the second tube add six drops of dilute sodium hydroxide; shake the tube and, when effervescence occurs, test for hydrogen.

Repeat the experiment using zinc dust.

Aluminium and zinc react readily with hydrochloric acid, particularly if it is concentrated:

$$2Al + 6HCl \rightarrow 2AlCl_3 + 3H_2$$
$$Zn + 2HCl \rightarrow ZnCl_2 + H_2$$

The hydrochloric acid and the chlorides are ionized in aqueous solution. This can be shown in an ionic equation; and the chloride ions, being the same on both sides, can be cancelled:

$$2Al_{(s)} + 6H^+_{(aq)} \rightarrow 2Al^{3+}_{(aq)} + 3H_{2(g)}$$
$$Zn_{(s)} + 2H^+_{(aq)} \rightarrow Zn^{2+}_{(aq)} + H_{2(g)}$$

Notice that the metal atoms are losing electrons ($Al \rightarrow Al^{3+} + 3e^-$ $Zn \rightarrow Zn^{2+} + 2e^-$) and the hydrogen ions are gaining electrons ($H^+ + e^- \rightarrow \frac{1}{2}H_2$). Therefore, the metals are being oxidized and the hydrogen ions are being reduced. Zinc, but not aluminium, reacts in a similar manner with dilute sulphuric acid.

Aluminium also reacts readily with aqueous sodium hydroxide; it dissolves and hydrogen is evolved. Zinc has little apparent action under the conditions of Experiment 23.2; it does, however, dissolve in hot aqueous sodium hydroxide. The products of these reactions are sodium aluminate and sodium zincate; these two compounds will also be made in the next experiment.

Compounds of aluminium and zinc

Hydroxides
Experiment 23.3

To investigate the formation and some reactions of the hydroxides of aluminium and zinc (C)

You are supplied with an M/10 aqueous aluminium sulphate and M/10 aqueous zinc sulphate.

Put four drops of the aluminium sulphate solution into a small tube. Add four drops of dilute sodium hydroxide solution, one drop at a time, shaking the tube after adding each drop. Look carefully for the appearance and disappearance of a precipitate. Now add four drops of a dilute acid in the same way.

Repeat the experiment with the zinc sulphate solution (you may need one or two more drops of the sodium hydroxide solution).

Repeat the experiment with both solutions, using ammonium hydroxide instead of sodium hydroxide.

The first action of solutions of hydroxides on solutions of aluminium and zinc salts is to precipitate the hydroxides of the two metals:

$$Al^{3+}_{(aq)} + 3OH^-_{(aq)} \rightarrow Al(OH)_{3(s)}$$
$$Zn^{2+}_{(aq)} + 2OH^-_{(aq)} \rightarrow Zn(OH)_{2(s)}$$

There is a further reaction with excess sodium hydroxide, in which both the hydroxides dissolve:

$$Al(OH)_3 + NaOH \rightarrow \underset{\substack{\text{sodium}\\\text{aluminate}}}{NaAlO_2} + 2H_2O$$

$$Zn(OH)_2 + 2NaOH \rightarrow \underset{\substack{\text{sodium}\\\text{zincate}}}{Na_2ZnO_2} + 2H_2O$$

This is an unfamiliar reaction for the hydroxides of metals; they are both behaving as acids by reacting with alkalis to form salts; and in these salts both metals form part of negative ions: AlO_2^- and ZnO_2^{2-}.

When acid is added to solutions of sodium aluminate and sodium zincate, precipitates of the two hydroxides are first re-formed and then dissolve in excess acid:

$$2Al(OH)_3 + 3H_2SO_4 \rightarrow Al_2(SO_4)_3 + 6H_2O$$
$$Zn(OH)_2 + H_2SO_4 \rightarrow ZnSO_4 + 2H_2O$$

The last reaction is the usual reaction of the basic hydroxides of metals. Aluminium and zinc hydroxides, therefore, can dissolve both in acids and strong alkalis. Hydroxides which do this are said to be *amphoteric*.

The action of excess ammonium hydroxide on the hydroxides of the two metals is different from that of a strong alkali such as sodium hydroxide. Both hydroxides can be precipitated by ammonium hydroxide, but only zinc hydroxide dissolves in excess ammonium hydroxide. Furthermore, zinc hydroxide does not reappear when the solution is acidified. You will meet similar reactions in the work on copper (p. 236).

Oxides

Aluminium oxide, also called alumina, and zinc oxide can be made in the laboratory by heating the appropriate hydroxide, or, in the case of zinc oxide by heating zinc carbonate:

$$2Al(OH)_3 \rightarrow Al_2O_3 + 3H_2O$$
$$Zn(OH)_2 \rightarrow ZnO + H_2O$$
$$ZnCO_3 \rightarrow ZnO + CO_2$$

Both oxides are amphoteric, dissolving in acids to form aluminium and zinc salts and in strong alkalis to form aluminates and zincates respectively.

Zinc oxide changes from white to yellow when heated and back to white on cooling.

Chlorides

Solutions of the chlorides can be made by the usual action of hydrochloric acid on the metals, oxides, hydroxides, and, for zinc only, the carbonate. Anhydrous aluminium chloride is made by the direct combination of chlorine and aluminium. A laboratory preparation is described on p. 114.

$$2Al + 3Cl_2 \rightarrow 2AlCl_3$$

Aluminium chloride which has been freshly made in this way exhibits some unusual properties for the chloride of a metal:

(i) It readily sublimes.
(ii) Its solutions in some non-aqueous solvents do not readily conduct electricity.
(iii) It reacts violently with water to form an acidic solution which conducts electricity.

It appears that aluminium chloride is molecular, not ionic, and that the bonds between the aluminium and the chlorine are covalent. Like hydrogen chloride, however, aluminium chloride reacts with water to form ions. We shall meet a similar compound in iron (III) chloride (p. 235).

Problems

(1) Identify the substances A and B by means of the following experiments:

(i) Heat small quantities separately in dry test tubes and test for the formation of water.
(ii) Make separate solutions of A and B and investigate their action on (a) sodium hydroxide solution and (b) ammonium hydroxide solution (start with four drops of the solutions each time and add the alkalis a drop at a time).
(iii) To the aqueous solutions add hydrochloric acid followed by barium chloride solution.

(2) You are given aluminium powder, dilute sulphuric acid, ammonium hydroxide, and hydrochloric acid (concentrated acid diluted with an equal volume of water). Prepare crystals of aluminium sulphate.

(3) Subject the substance C to the following tests:

(i) Heat it strongly in a dry tube.

(ii) Treat it with dilute hydrochloric acid and identify the gas evolved.

(iii) Investigate the action of ammonium hydroxide on the solution from (ii). What can you deduce about the nature of C?

(4) Calculate the amount of heat evolved when 1 g-formula of iron (III) oxide is reduced by aluminium powder. Use the information given on p. 226.

Summary

In so short a section a summary is hardly necessary, but it is worth while emphasizing some new features:

(i) Aluminium and zinc dissolve in strong alkalis to form aluminates and zincates.

(ii) The oxides and hydroxides of aluminium and zinc are amphoteric; they dissolve in both acids and alkalis.

(iii) Aluminium chloride is the first non-ionic chloride of a metal which we have studied. It reacts with water to form ions in a manner similar to that of hydrogen chloride.

Section 24
Transition metals– iron and copper

The characteristics of transition metals

Refer to the three rows of elements which form a large block in the centre of the Periodic Table. Their main characteristics can be summarized as follows:

(1) Typical metallic structure and physical properties.
(2) Most of their compounds are coloured.
(3) Each exhibits more than one valency (oxidation state).
(4) Their ions readily form complex ions.
(5) Many of the elements and their compounds are used as catalysts.

Occurrence

Of all the metals we have studied so far, copper is the first to occur as the free metal. It does so in small scattered quantities and these are not important sources of the metal. Copper is found in a variety of ores, chiefly its sulphides, carbonates, and oxides.

Free iron is found only in meteorites, although it may be present in large quantities beneath the earth's crust. Like copper, its ores are chiefly sulphides, carbonates, and oxides. It is an essential element in haemoglobin, the red substance which acts as an oxygen carrier in blood.

Manufacture

In the United Kingdom iron is largely made from its oxide and carbonate ores by heating them in a blast furnace with coke. The iron ores are reduced to iron and the coke is oxidized to carbon dioxide—details are given on p. 279.

The sulphide ores of copper are roasted in air and then smelted in a blast of air. Copper (I) sulphide is formed and this then reacts with oxygen to form copper and sulphur dioxide:

$$Cu_2S + O_2 \rightarrow 2Cu + SO_2$$

Notice that the extraction of copper, unlike the extraction of iron, requires no reducing agent.

The electrolytic purification of copper

A piece of impure copper is made into an anode in a solution of copper sulphate; the cathode is a sheet of pure copper. When electricity is passed through the solution, pure copper is deposited on the cathode:

$$Cu^{2+}_{(aq)} + 2e^- \rightarrow Cu_{(s)}$$

At the same time the impure copper of which the anode is made dissolves (you may remember that this happened in Experiment 10.1 on p. 88).

We have already found that at an anode a substance in the liquid can be oxidized by having electrons removed from it. But when the anode is made of copper it appears that the copper itself is oxidized:

$$Cu_{(s)} \rightarrow Cu^{2+}_{(aq)} + 2e^-$$

Thus the copper anode is oxidized to form copper (II) ions at the same rate as copper (II) ions are reduced to form copper at the cathode.

The effect is to transfer copper from the anode ot the cathode, where it is deposited in a pure form. The concentration of the solution of copper (II) ions is unchanged.

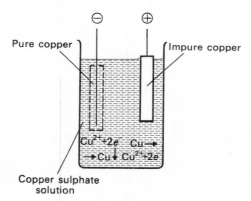

Pure copper

Impure copper

$Cu^{2+} + 2e$ $Cu \rightarrow$
$\rightarrow Cu$ $Cu^{2+} + 2e$

Copper sulphate
solution

Figure 102

Uses of iron

Iron, particularly when mixed with small quantities of other elements, is a very versatile metal; because of this and its cheapness, abundance, and ease of extraction, it is our chief structural metal. Here is a brief description of some of its forms:

(i) *Cast iron.* This is the iron which either comes directly from the blast furnace (*pig iron*) or a mixture made by melting pig iron with scrap iron. It contains up to 5% of carbon in addition to other impurities.

Cast iron melts at a temperature about 400°C lower than that of pure iron. As it solidifies it expands slightly, so that when it is poured into a mould it accurately fills every detail of it. Articles made in this way are known as *castings*. Cast iron is useful for making structures which must be hard and strong but which are not subjected to sudden strains and shocks—it is rather brittle.

(ii) *Wrought iron*. This is the purest form of iron normally used. It is tough and malleable. It is not suitable for casting, but is easily welded and hammered into shape (forged). Although it is softer than other forms of iron, it is used for chains, couplings, and decorative ironwork.

(iii) *Steel*. 'Steel' loosely describes many iron alloys. All steels contain up to $1 \cdot 5\%$ of carbon and their physical properties change considerably with small changes in their carbon content.

Stainless steel contains chromium and nickel. Steel which contains tungsten is very hard and is used for making cutting tools. Manganese steel is used to make machinery for crushing hard substances such as rock.

Uses of copper

Pure copper is a very good conductor of electricity and, as it is easily ductile, large quantities are used in electrical wiring. It is also easily made into sheets and pipes, which makes it useful for roofing and for pipes carrying liquids and vapours. It is particularly good for carrying water and steam, because it does not react with either of them.

Alloys of copper include the coinage metals (with nickel), bronze (with tin), phosphor-bronze (with tin and phosphorus), and brass (with zinc).

Chemical properties

Many of the chemical properties of these metals have been discussed in other parts of this book; they are summarized below. When studying them, keep in mind the relative positions of the metals in the electrochemical series: it is to be expected that iron will be more reactive than copper; its compounds will be more stable and it will more readily displace hydrogen from water and acids. Both metals have the physical properties typical of metals.

Iron

(i) *With air*. Iron burns when strongly heated to form a black oxide, tri iron tetroxide:

$$3Fe + 2O_2 \rightarrow Fe_3O_4$$

In the presence of moisture and air at room temperature, iron rusts. This is an oxidation, which results in the formation of iron (III) oxide.

$$4Fe + 3O_2 \rightarrow 2Fe_2O_3$$

(ii) *With water*. In the absence of air, iron has little reaction with cold water. When it is treated in steam, it is oxidized to tri iron tetroxide and hydrogen is formed:

$$3Fe_{(s)} + 4H_2O_{(g)} \rightleftharpoons Fe_3O_{4(s)} + 4H_{2(g)}$$

(iii) *With acids*. Iron reacts with dilute hydrochloric and sulphuric acids, forming hydrogen and the appropriate iron (II) salt:

$$Fe_{(s)} + 2H^+_{(aq)} \rightarrow Fe^{2+}_{(aq)} + H_{2(g)}$$

There is little worthy of note in its action with concentrated acids.

(iv) *With some non-metallic elements.* With chlorine it readily forms iron (III) chloride (p. 114):

$$2Fe + 3Cl_2 \rightarrow 2FeCl_3$$

Copper

(i) *With air.* When it is heated in air, copper can be slowly oxidized to copper (II) and copper (I) oxides:

$$2Cu + O_2 \rightarrow 2CuO$$
$$4Cu + O_2 \rightarrow 2Cu_2O$$

Copper, after prolonged exposure to air at ordinary temperatures, acquires a green coating (patina). The nature and cause of this green coating is outside the scope of this book, but you may find it interesting to investigate it yourself.

(ii) *With water.* Copper has no action on water and steam.

(iii) *With acids.* In the absence of air, copper has no action on dilute acids except nitric acid (p. 169). Copper is oxidized by nitric acid and it goes into solution in the form of copper (II) nitrate. Oxides of nitrogen are evolved as a result of the reduction of the nitric acid; nitrogen monoxide is the chief product from dilute nitric acid, nitrogen dioxide the chief product from concentrated nitric acid.

Compounds of iron and copper

Oxidation states

In its simple compounds iron shows combining capacities of either two or three. The compounds are known respectively as *iron (II)* and *iron (III)*. In iron (II) compounds each atom of iron appears to have been oxidized by the removal of two electrons:

$$Fe \rightarrow Fe^{2+} + 2e^-$$

In iron (III) compounds further oxidation appears to have taken place by the removal of another electron:

$$Fe \rightarrow Fe^{3+} + 3e^-$$
$$\text{or}$$
$$Fe^{2+} \rightarrow Fe^{3+} + e^-$$

Thus iron (II) and iron (III) ions can be described as *oxidation states* of iron. In iron (II) compounds the oxidation state is two and in iron (III) compounds it is three.

Copper, in its simple compounds, shows oxidation states of one and two:

copper (I) compounds $Cu \rightarrow Cu^+ + e^-$
copper (II) compounds $Cu \rightarrow Cu^{2+} + 2e^-$

To change iron (II) and copper (I) compounds to iron (III) and copper (II) compounds, an oxidation is required. Conversely, to change iron (III) and copper (II) compounds to iron (II) and copper (I) compounds, a reduction is required.

Iron (II) compounds

Iron (II) sulphate is the most familiar iron (II) compound. It is soluble in water from which it crystallizes as a heptahydrate ($FeSO_4.7H_2O$). It forms a brown compound ($FeSO_4.NO$) with nitrogen monoxide.

When soluble iron (II) salts are treated with alkaline solutions, iron (II) hydroxide is precipitated:

$$Fe^{2+}_{(aq)} + 2OH^-_{(aq)} \rightarrow Fe(OH)_{2(s)}$$

The precipitate rapidly changes from green to a rust colour because of oxidation by the air.

It is not possible to keep iron (II) oxide under normal conditions, because it spontaneously oxidizes in air.

Iron (II) compounds can be oxidized to iron (III) compounds by the action of bromine or chlorine water, nitric acid, hydrogen peroxide, or potassium permanganate.

Iron (III) compounds

Iron (III) oxide is conveniently made by heating iron (III) hydroxide:

$$2Fe(OH)_3 \rightarrow Fe_2O_3 + 3H_2O$$

This equation will remind you of the equation for the action of heat on aluminium hydroxide.

Iron (III) hydroxide can be formed as a rust-coloured precipitate by adding an alkaline solution to a solution of any iron (III) salt:

$$Fe^{3+}_{(aq)} + 3OH^-_{(aq)} \rightarrow Fe(OH)_{3(s)}$$

Iron (III) chloride and aluminium chloride also resemble each other: both are made in a similar way (p. 114) and both appear to be non-ionic until they are dissolved in water.

Experiment 24.1

To investigate the action between an iron (III) salt and iron **(C)**

Put one small measure of reduced iron into a small test tube and add eight drops of a solution of a iron (III) salt. Shake the tube occasionally over a period of five minutes. Allow the iron to settle; suck off some of the solution with a teat pipette and test it for iron (II) ions.

Iron (III) salts are converted into iron (II) salts by reduction:

$$Fe^{3+} + e^- \rightarrow Fe^{2+}$$

This can be done by many reducing agents; Experiment 24.1 shows that iron itself is a convenient one:

$$2Fe^{3+} + Fe \rightarrow 3Fe^{2+} \begin{cases} Fe \rightarrow Fe^{2+} + 2e^- \\ \\ 2Fe^{3+} + 2e^- \rightarrow 2Fe^{2+} \end{cases}$$

Copper (II) compounds

Copper (II) oxide is already familiar. It is a typical basic oxide which reacts with acids to form solutions of copper (II) salts. In the laboratory it is more convenient to make it by heating copper (II) nitrate than by heating the metal in air:

$$2Cu(NO_3)_2 \rightarrow 2CuO + 4NO_2 + O_2$$

Copper (II) hydroxide can be made by adding an alkaline solution to a solution of a copper (II) salt:

$$Cu^{2+}_{(aq)} + 2OH^-_{(aq)} \rightarrow Cu(OH)_{2(s)}$$

Copper (II) hydroxide dissolves in excess ammonium hydroxide, but not in excess sodium hydroxide; compare this with the action of zinc hydroxide (p. 229). The solution so formed is deep blue and this reaction serves as a test for copper (II) ions in solution.

Copper (II) sulphate is the most familiar copper (II) salt. It crystallizes as a pentahydrate ($CuSO_4 . 5H_2O$) and is usually called simply copper sulphate.

Reduction of copper (II) compounds

Experiment 24.2

To investigate the action of iron on a solution of a copper (II) salt (C)

Weigh a dry boiling tube; add approximately 1 g of reduced iron and weigh again. Heat 20 cm³ of a M solution of copper (II) sulphate until it is just too hot to hold in the hand; add it to the iron.

Shake the contents of the tube for about 5 minutes. Allow the copper which is formed to settle, then decant the solution from it. Half fill the tube with water and allow the copper to settle and decant again. Repeat this washing process at least once more. Take care that none of the copper is lost during the decantations.

Drain off as much water as possible. Lay the boiling tube on a tripod and gauze and heat it gently with a moving bunsen until its contents are dry. Allow the tube to cool and then weigh it.

Specimen results

Weight of tube	= 39·67 g
Weight of tube and iron	= 40·68 g
Weight of tube and copper	= 40·82 g
Weight of iron	= 1·01 g
Weight of copper	= 1·15 g

These weights will give us more information if they are converted into mole units—g-atoms of iron and g-atoms of copper:

$$1\cdot01 \text{ g of iron} = \frac{1\cdot01}{56} \text{ g-atoms of iron} = 0\cdot018 \text{ g-atoms}$$

$$1\cdot15 \text{ g of copper} = \frac{1\cdot15}{64} \text{ g-atoms of copper} = 0\cdot018 \text{ g-atoms}$$

It follows that the ratio of iron to copper in mole units is

$$1 \text{ g-atom} : 1 \text{ g-atom}$$

$$\therefore \ 1 \text{ atom of iron forms 1 atom of copper}$$

The results of Experiment 24.4 indicate that one atom of iron reduces 1 copper (II) ion to form 1 atom of copper:

$$Fe_{(s)} + Cu^{2+}_{(aq)} \rightarrow Fe^{2+}_{(aq)} + Cu_{(s)}$$

The copper (II) ions have been reduced to copper and the iron has been oxidized to iron (II) ions:

$$\begin{cases} Fe \rightarrow Fe^{2+} + 2e^- & \text{(oxidation)} \\ Cu^{2+} + 2e^- \rightarrow Cu & \text{(reduction)} \end{cases}$$

Copper (I) compounds

Experiment 24.3

To investigate the action between a copper (II) salt and an iodide (C)

To 4 drops of copper (II) sulphate solution add an excess (8 drops) of potassium iodide solution. Allow the precipitate so formed to settle and take note of the characteristic brown colour of the iodine solution.

Add sodium thiosulphate solution drop by drop until the colour of the iodine has gone and the true colour of the precipitate can be seen. Divide the suspension into two parts; investigate the action of ammonium hydroxide on one part and the action of more sodium thiosulphate solution on the other.

We have learned already (p. 114) that an iodide is converted to iodine by oxidation:

$$I^- \rightarrow \tfrac{1}{2}I_2 + e^-$$

As this happens with any copper (II) salt, it is reasonable to infer that the copper (II) ions have acted as the oxidizing agent and have themselves been reduced to copper (I) ions:

$$Cu^{2+} + e^- \rightarrow Cu^+$$

The white precipitate formed in Experiment 24.3 is copper (I) iodide formed from the copper (I) ions and the excess iodide ions:

$$Cu^+ + I^- \rightarrow CuI$$

Usually copper (II) compounds are more stable than the corresponding copper (I) compounds; but copper (I) iodide is an exception. You will have observed that it dissolves readily in ammonium hydroxide and in sodium thiosulphate solution. This resembles the action of these two reagents on silver chloride (p. 105).

The protection of iron from rusting

The rusting of iron is a complex process, but essentially it involves:

(1) The dissolving of iron: $Fe_{(s)} \rightarrow Fe^{2+}_{(aq)} + 2e^-$.
(2) Further oxidation to iron (III): $Fe^{2+}_{(aq)} \rightarrow Fe^{3+}_{(aq)} + e^-$.
(3) The precipitation of iron (III) as hydrated iron (III) oxide.

Two widely used methods of protecting iron from rusting are to coat it with either zinc (galvanizing) or tin (tin plating). You may have noticed that the former is used for structures which may be knocked or scratched (roofing, buckets, dustbins etc.), the latter for domestic goods which do not, or should not, get rough handling. There is a good reason for this.

If protected iron is scratched and an aqueous solution forms in the scratch, a chemical cell is set up (*figure 103*).

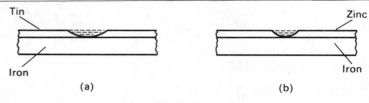

Figure 103

In A iron is higher in the electrochemical series than tin; it therefore has a greater tendency to dissolve as ions. Therefore, iron is the negative terminal of the cell; stage 1 takes place and finally rust forms.

In B it is zinc which is higher in the series and has the greater tendency to dissolve as ions. Therefore, iron is the positive terminal; it does not dissolve and rusting does not take place.

Problems

(1) Subject the substance A to the following tests:

 (i) Warm a small quantity in a dry test tube.

(ii) Make an aqueous solution of A and divide it into two parts; to one part add sodium hydroxide solution, warm very gently and test the gas evolved with moist red litmus paper.

(iii) To the second part of the solution A add dilute hydrochloric acid followed by barium chloride solution.

What can you deduce about A?

(2) Weigh about $\frac{1}{50}$ mole of iron (II) sulphate crystals ($FeSO_4 . 7H_2O$) and $\frac{1}{50}$ mole of ammonium sulphate [$(NH_4)_2SO_4$]. Dissolve the two salts in 10 cm³ of warm dilute sulphuric acid and set the solution aside to form crystals of the substance B.

Investigate the action of a solution of B on (a) sodium hydroxide solution (b) hydrochloric acid followed by barium chloride solution (c) bromine water followed by sodium hydroxide solution.

Give an explanation of each of these reactions. What do they tell you about the nature of B?

(3) You are given a solution containing iron (II) and iron (III) ions in the ratio $Fe^{2+} : 2Fe^{3+}$. Add a slight excess of ammonium hydroxide to the solution and filter off the resulting precipitate. Using a spatula, scrape the precipitate into a small evaporating basin and heat it gently. Record and explain your observations.

(4) Dissolve a small piece of copper in the minimum of 5 M nitric acid to form a solution of the substance C. Add aqueous sodium hydroxide to the solution of C to form the precipitate D. Centrifuge D; wash it and dissolve it in the minimum of dilute hydrochloric acid to form a solution of the substance E. Add potassium iodide solution to the solution E to form the precipitate F.

Identify C, D, E, and F, and explain all the reactions which have taken place.

(5) You are given iron, ammonium hydroxide solution, dilute sulphuric acid, and chlorine or bromine water. Prepare a solution containing iron (III) ions and from this prepare iron (III) oxide.

(6) You are given zinc dust, dilute sulphuric acid, and copper carbonate. Prepare a sample of copper.

(7) The divalent metal M is above copper in the electrochemical series. A piece of M weighing 3·4 g was put into 20 cm³ of a molar solution of copper (II) sulphate until reaction ceased. M was then found to weigh 2·1 g. Calculate:

(a) the fraction of a g-formula of copper (II) sulphate in 20 cm³ of molar solution,

(b) the fraction of a g-ion of copper (II) ion in the same solution,

(c) the equation for the action between M and copper (II) ions,

(d) the fraction of a g-atom of M which has reacted,

(e) the atomic weight of M.

(8) It would appear that zinc protects iron from rusting better than tin does. Why, then, is tin used to coat tin cans?

Summary

Only new work is included in this summary; the routine chemistry of the metals is excluded.

(1) During electrolysis, a copper anode is oxidized to form copper (II) ions:

$$Cu \rightarrow Cu^{2+} + 2e^-$$

(2) Iron can be oxidized to the iron (II) state (oxidation state 2):

$$Fe \rightarrow Fe^{2+} + 2e^-$$

and further oxidized to the iron (III) state (oxidation state 3):

$$Fe^{2+} \rightarrow Fe^{3+} + e^-$$

(3) Copper can be oxidized to the copper (I) state (oxidation state 1):

$$Cu \rightarrow Cu^+ + e^-$$

and further oxidized to the copper (II) state (oxidation state 2):

$$Cu^+ \rightarrow Cu^{2+} + e^-$$

(4) Iron (II) compounds are converted to iron (III) compounds by oxidation. Iron (III) compounds are converted to iron (II) compounds by reduction.

(5) Iron, and most metals above copper in the electrochemical series, will reduce a solution containing copper (II) ions to copper:

$$Cu^{2+} + Fe \rightarrow Cu + Fe^{2+}$$

(6) Rusting involves the dissolving of iron in the oxidation state 2; its oxidation to the 3 state; its precipitation as hydrated iron (III) oxide.

Section 25
Lead and silicon

Lead

Lead is typically metallic except that it has low melting points compared with other metals.

Lead has been known and used for over two thousand years. Its chief use has been in the form of sheets for roofing and pipes for carrying water. It is resistant to chemical attack and for this reason is used in laboratories for pipes, bench surfaces, and containers. It is also increasingly used as a shield against harmful rays.

Alloys of lead include solder and pewter (with tin), lead shot (with arsenic), and type metal (with tin and antimony). A compound of lead with carbon and hydrogen, lead tetraethyl $Pb(C_2H_5)_4$, is added to petrol to decrease 'knocking' in car engines.

Lead in its normal physical state resists attack by air and water. It reacts slowly with hydrochloric acid to form lead chloride:

$$Pb + 2HCl \rightarrow PbCl_2 + H_2$$
$$Pb + 2H^+ \rightarrow Pb^{2+} + H_2$$

Nitric acid dissolves lead to form lead (II) nitrate and is itself reduced to oxides of nitrogen—compare this with the action of copper on nitric acid.

Compounds of lead
Oxidation states

Lead shows combining capacities of two and four; for example $PbCl_2$ and $PbCl_4$.

If these compounds were ionic, the oxidation of the metal could be represented thus:

$$Pb \rightarrow Pb^{2+} + 2e^-$$
$$Pb \rightarrow Pb^{4+} + 4e^-$$

This indicates that lead has oxidation states of 2 and 4.

Many of the compounds of lead are not ionic, but the oxidation state of the metals in these compounds is still said to be 2 and 4, even though the electrons are shared and not given up completely.

Lead (II) oxide and hydroxide

The oxide, which is a yellow powder, can be made by heating molten lead strongly in air, but in the laboratory it is best made by heating lead nitrate (p. 171).

The hydroxide is precipitated when an alkaline solution is added to a solution of a lead (II) salt:

$$Pb^{2+}{}_{(aq)} + 2OH^-{}_{(aq)} \rightarrow Pb(OH)_{2(s)}$$

The hydroxide decomposes to the oxide when heated:

$$Pb(OH)_2 \rightarrow PbO + H_2O$$

The oxide is stable when heated, but it is readily reduced to the metal by carbon (p. 63), carbon monoxide, or hydrogen. Lead (II) oxide is also called lead monoxide and litharge.

Lead (II) chloride

This chloride is soluble in hot water, but insoluble in cold water. It can therefore be made either by precipitation from a cold solution of a lead (II) salt:

$$Pb^{2+}{}_{(aq)} + 2Cl^-{}_{(aq)} \rightarrow PbCl_{2(s)}$$

or by dissolving lead oxide, hydroxide, or carbonate in hot hydrochloric acid.

Lead (II) nitrate

This can be made by the action of nitric acid on the metal, or its oxide, hydroxide, or carbonate. It is soluble in water. When heated it, decomposes into lead (II) oxide, nitrogen dioxide, and oxygen (see p. 171).

Lead (II) acetate

Test papers for hydrogen sulphide consist of paper which has been soaked in a solution of lead acetate and then dried. They turn brown when exposed to hydrogen sulphide, owing to the formation of lead sulphide:

$$Pb^{2+}{}_{(aq)} + S^{2-}{}_{(aq)} \rightarrow PbS_{(s)}$$

Lead (IV) oxide, PbO$_2$

This is a brown powder commonly called lead dioxide. It can be made by the action of nitric acid on red lead (see below). It can also be made by oxidizing a solution of a lead (II) salt to the lead (IV) state, in the presence of an alkaline solution. Assuming that the reactions are ionic, they can be represented:

$$Pb^{2+} \rightarrow Pb^{4+} + 2e^- \quad \text{oxidation}$$
$$Pb^{4+}{}_{(aq)} + 4OH^-{}_{(aq)} \rightarrow PbO_{2(s)} + 2H_2O_{(l)} \quad \text{precipitation}$$

Lead (IV) oxide dissolves in alkalis to form plumbates:

$$PbO_2 + 2NaOH \rightarrow Na_2PbO_3 + H_2O$$

Lead (IV) oxide is an oxidizing agent: it oxidizes concentrated hydrochloric acid to chlorine:

$$PbO_2 + 4HCl \rightarrow PbCl_2 + Cl_2 + 2H_2O$$

Compare this reaction with that of manganese dioxide on concentrated hydrochloric acid:

$$MnO_2 + 4HCl \rightarrow MnCl_2 + Cl_2 + 2H_2O$$

The oxidation state of both metals is reduced from IV to II by the hydrochloric acid.

Red lead Pb₃O₄ (Trilead tetroxide)

Like tri iron tetroxide (Fe₃O₄), red lead acts as if it were composed of two oxides—PbO₂.2PbO. With dilute nitric acid it forms a solution of lead (II) nitrate and a residue of lead (IV) oxide:

$$PbO_2.2PbO + 4HNO_3 \rightarrow 2Pb(NO_3)_2 + PbO_2 + 2H_2O$$

It can be made by heating lead (II) oxide in air at about 500°C:

$$6PbO + O_2 \rightarrow 2Pb_3O_4$$

Silicon

Silicon is in Group IV of the Periodic Table, like carbon and lead. In the third period of the Periodic Table it lies between aluminium and phosphorus. Either vertically or horizontally it seems to be a sort of bridge element between the metals and the non-metals. On balance, it is more of a non-metal and resembles carbon rather than lead. It is interesting to note that both silicon and germanium are semi-conductors. The main features of silicon and its compounds may be summarized as follows:

Structure

Giant covalent resembling diamond, but not as hard and with a lower melting point.

Bonding

Covalent.

Oxidation state

IV, but it does not form ionic compounds.

Chloride (SiCl₄)

Covalent bonds between silicon and chlorine. Molecular structure and liquid at room temperature. Reacts readily with water.

Oxide, Silica (SiO₂)

This is a very abundant compound of silicon, occurring in various degrees of purity as sand. Unlike carbon dioxide it is not molecular, having a giant covalent structure with oxygen atoms linking silicon atoms (Si—O—Si). As a result silica is very hard and has a high melting point.

Like carbon dioxide, the oxide of silicon is weakly acidic; but because of its strong physical structure it reacts much less readily with alkalis than carbon dioxide does. With hot concentrated solutions of sodium hydroxide or with fused sodium hydroxide silica reacts to form sodium silicate. Silicates can have a complex structure, but the following equation represents the reaction in a simple form and shows the resemblance to carbonates.

$$SiO_{2(s)} + 2NaOH_{(l)} \rightarrow Na_2SiO_{3(l)}$$

Silicates

Silicates of many kinds are very common in the earth's crust in rocks, clays, and many minerals. Glass is a mixture of silicates made by fusing sodium and calcium carbonates with sand (see p. 273).

Problems

(1) Reduce some of the solid A on a carbon block to form the metal B. Heat some of A in a dry tube to form the residue C; test for oxygen. Add concentrated hydrochloric acid to A and test for chlorine. Identify A, B, and C, and give equations for all the reactions.

(2) To 4 drops of a solution of lead nitrate add 10 drops of bromine water followed by 4 drops of aqueous sodium hydroxide. Warm the mixture, but do not boil it. Centrifuge; pipette off the liquid; add 4 drops of concentrated hydrochloric acid to the residue; warm gently and test for chlorine. Record and explain your observations.

(3) Put one small measure of red lead into a small test tube. Add one-third of a tube of dilute nitric acid and warm it gently until all the orange colour disappears. Centrifuge; pipette off the liquid and add a few drops of hydrochloric acid to it. Record and explain your observations.

(4) You are given a solution of a lead salt. Put 10 cm³ of the solution into a boiling tube and add 1 cm³ of dilute hydrochloric acid. Heat the contents of the tube to boiling point and cautiously smell the vapour. Allow the tube to cool. Record and explain your observations.

(5) Weigh $\frac{1}{100}$ g-formula of lead nitrate in a dry boiling tube. Add 20 cm³ of water and shake the tube gently until the solid dissolves—take care that no liquid spills. Weigh a piece of zinc foil—not less than 1 g—add it to the solution and set it aside for twenty-four hours.

Pour the contents of the tube into a beaker. Pick out the piece of zinc; wash it; dry it; and reweigh it. Calculate the fraction of a g-atom of zinc which has reacted. Deduce an equation for the action between zinc and lead (II) ions.

Section 26
Carbon compounds (organic chemistry)

Before starting this section, you should revise the work on carbon and its compounds in Section 7.

Sources of carbon compounds

The number of carbon compounds which find a use in industry, the household, and medicine, is very large and steadily increasing. Fortunately carbon compounds are abundant in nature. Some of them can be put to use as soon as they have been extracted and purified; others provide starting material for more useful compounds.

Most of the naturally-occurring carbon compounds have their origin in living organisms. Plants and animals are largely built up of carbon compounds and in every living thing chemical changes are continuously taking place. Starting from carbon dioxide, water, and simple minerals, plants synthesize a multitude of carbon compounds. Many of these compounds are of such complexity that they have defied the efforts of chemists to synthesize them.

In past ages plants and animals have died and further changes in their chemical composition have been caused by micro-organisms (bacteria, etc.) in the process of decay. Vast deposits of the decayed remains of plants and animals have been laid down and finally buried under layers of sedimentary rock. An early stage of this process can be seen in peat bogs, where successive generations of vegetation have accumulated in a partly decayed state.

These deposits or organic material, after being buried, have undergone further changes caused by high pressures and temperatures. When we now find them, the substances of which they are composed are very different from those of the original organisms; nevertheless, these carbon compounds are of great value to us. The deposits are of two main types, petroleum and coal, and they are widely scattered throughout the earth's crust. Both these deposits contain gaseous carbon compounds trapped in them; petroleum frequently contains many times its own volume of this natural gas.

Of course, not all petroleum, natural gas and coal, is used as a source of carbon compounds; much of it is simply burned to provide energy for heating or for driving machines. At the moment the supplies are plentiful, but it should be remembered that they are not limitless. There is a danger that we may burn away, in a few hundred years, deposits of carbon compounds which have taken hundreds of millions of years to form. When they are burned, these complex substances are changed back into the carbon dioxide and water from which they were formed, and there is no way of replenishing them in the same large quantities. Soon, it may be advisable for us to seek other sources of energy and to retain the deposits of these carbon compounds as starting material for the chemical industry.

The natural synthesis of carbon compounds continues in plants and animals living today. They, too, are a source of compounds which are themselves useful to us or which can be converted into other useful compounds. Each year enormous quantities of starch and sugar, produced in crops as a result of photosynthesis, are harvested. Much of the starch and sugar, like petroleum, natural gas and coal, is burned to provide energy: energy for our bodies, not for machines. But some of this starch and sugar can be converted into useful chemicals, particularly ethanol and carbon dioxide (Experiment 26.1). Although more and more drugs are now synthesized in the laboratory, many are still extracted from the plants in which they were first discovered.

Experiment 26.1

To prepare ethanol from sugar (C or D)

Dissolve 30 g of black treacle (molasses) in 150 cm³ of warm water in a conical flask. Cool the solution to 30°C; add 1 cm³ of a suspension of yeast in water and put the conical flask aside in a warm place for four or five days. Note the effervescence of carbon dioxide.

Filter off the yeast and distil the filtrate from a 250 cm³ flask fitted with a thermometer. Note the temperature at which distillation starts and continue distillation until the temperature reaches 96°C.

Pour a few drops of the distillate on to a crucible lid and warm it with a bunsen flame until it catches fire.

Fermentation

The formation of ethanol and carbon dioxide from sugar when yeast is added is typical of many such actions in which useful compounds are made with the aid of micro-organisms. Yeast is a tiny single-cell organism which assimilates sugar and excretes alcohol and carbon dioxide as waste products. The energy produced by this chemical change helps it to grow and reproduce. This particular process, which is called *fermentation*, is an essential part of the production of alcoholic liquors.

To convert sugar into ethanol in the laboratory by normal chemical methods would be difficult and expensive. It is fascinating to think that some of the smallest and simplest of living things can cause chemical changes beyond the powers of the most advanced laboratory. They do so with the aid of minute quantities of natural catalysts called *enzymes*; these enzymes themselves have very complex chemical structures. Our own bodies contain many enzymes which bring about the multitude of chemical changes required to keep our bodies functioning correctly.

Distillation of aqueous ethanol

The distillate (the liquid which distils over) obtained in Experiment 26.1 is a mixture of ethanol (an alcohol) and water. Ethanol, like water, is a colourless liquid and the two liquids mix with each other in any proportions—they are said to be completely miscible. Ethanol has a lower boiling point than that of water, and, when dilute solutions of ethanol in water are distilled, the vapour, and hence the distillate, contains a greater proportion of ethanol than does the original solution.

If the distillate were distilled again, the first sample of liquid which distilled would contain a still greater proportion of ethanol. And, if these distillations were repeated over and over again, a sample of ethanol containing very little water would be obtained. The process of collecting the distillate and redistilling several times is not only time-wasting, it also give a progressively smaller yield of distillate. By the use of a fractioning column (*figure 104*), however, the effect of several distillations can be brought about in one operation.

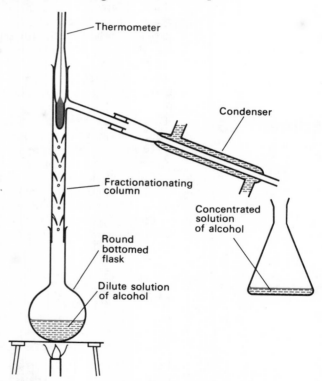

Figure 104

Fractional distillation

As the vapour rises into the fractioning column, it cools and condenses on the projecting glass points. Some of the condensed liquid falls back into the flask, but some of it is evaporated by the continuous stream of hot vapour coming up the column. Thus the vapour is evaporated and condensed several times on its way up the column. This has the effect of several distillations, so that the vapour which first passes into the condenser contains a much higher proportion of ethanol than it would have done after one distillation.

Fractional distillation is used extensively in industry. Very large quantities of dilute aqueous ethanol are distilled to produce either more concentrated solutions or almost pure ethanol. Even larger quantities of petroleum are distilled in this way to produce various liquid petroleum products (p. 255). Industrial fractioning columns (p. 256) are more complicated than that shown in *figure 104*. Liquids can be run out from many different levels of the column and either collected or fed back into the column at a lower level. This enables more complex mixtures of liquids to be separated and gives a greater yield of each.

The formula of ethanol

Molecular formula

Ethanol has the empirical formula C_2H_6O. 22·4 litres of ethanol vapour at s.t.p. weigh 46 g. This indicates that 1 g-molecule (1 mole) of ethanol weighs 46 g and therefore that 1 molecule of ethanol weighs 46. It follows that each molecule of ethanol contains two carbon atoms, six hydrogen atoms, and one oxygen atom; its molecular formula is the same as its simplest formula, C_2H_6O.

Structural formula

So far in this book, each of the compounds which we have studied has a formula different from that of any other compound; but for ethanol and many other carbon compounds this is not so. There is another compound, dimethyl ether, which has molecules of exactly the same composition as ethanol (C_2H_6O). Yet dimethyl ether resembles ethanol only in its composition and molecular weight; its chemical and physical properties are different. Different compounds having the same molecular formula are called *isomers*; so ethanol is said to be *isomeric* with dimethyl ether. It follows that the simple molecular formula, C_2H_6O, is an inadequate model of the molecules of these two compounds, because it does not show any difference between them.

This difficulty can be overcome if we assume that the atoms in the molecules of the two compounds are arranged differently. Both compounds are non-ionic, which indicates that all the bonds are covalent; if it is assumed that each atom forms its usual number of covalent bonds —carbon 4, oxygen 2, and hydrogen 1—it appears that a molecule of the composition C_2H_6O could be constructed in two ways:

$$
\begin{array}{cc}
\begin{array}{c}
\quad\ \text{H}\ \ \text{H} \\
\quad\ | \quad | \\
\text{H---C---C---O---H} \\
\quad\ | \quad | \\
\quad\ \text{H}\ \ \text{H} \\
\text{(I)}
\end{array}
&
\begin{array}{c}
\quad\ \text{H} \qquad \text{H} \\
\quad\ | \qquad | \\
\text{H---C---O---C---H} \\
\quad\ | \qquad | \\
\quad\ \text{H} \qquad \text{H} \\
\text{(II)}
\end{array}
\end{array}
$$

Each line represents one covalent bond (one pair of shared electrons). A formula in which each bond is shown is called a *structural formula*.

247

For a fuller understanding of structural formulae, three-dimensional models, showing the relative position of each atom, are valuable.

We can assume that one of these formulae represents a molecule of ethanol and that the other represents a molecule of dimethyl ether. Evidence to indicate which formula corresponds to which compound comes from the properties of the compounds and the manner in which they can be made. For example, consider the action of sodium on the two compounds: sodium has no action on dimethyl ether, but it reacts with 1 g-molecule of ethanol to form 1 g-atom of hydrogen. This indicates that in each molecule of ethanol there is one atom of hydrogen attached differently from the other five atoms of hydrogen. Thus, of the two possible structural formulae, the better model for an ethanol molecule is (I).

This structural formula is often abbreviated to either $CH_3.CH_2OH$ or C_2H_5OH, and the reaction with sodium can be represented by the equation:

$$CH_3.CH_2OH + Na \rightarrow CH_3.CH_2ONa + \tfrac{1}{2}H_2$$

This is a very simple example, and usually more than one piece of experimental evidence is required; but from experimental evidence of this type the most appropriate structural formula of a compound can be deduced.

Some properties of alcohols

Ethanol is one of a series of compounds called alcohols; these share a similar structure and similar properties. Two other common alcohols are methanol (CH_3OH) and propanol (C_3H_7OH). You will notice that the groups CH_3, C_2H_5, and C_3H_7, occur repeatedly in the formulae of the compounds which are studied in this section. These groups are respectively called the methyl, ethyl, and propyl groups.

The action of sodium on alcohols

Experiment 26.2

To investigate the action of sodium on ethanol and propanol (**C** or **D**)

Set up the apparatus shown in *figure 105*. If the boiling tube is wet, rinse it with a little alcohol to remove the water. Pour 10 cm³ of ethanol into the tube; add a piece of sodium about the size of a pea and quickly replace the stopper.

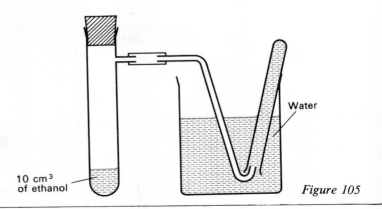

10 cm³ of ethanol

Water

Figure 105

Wait about a minute for most of the air to be swept from the apparatus and then collect the evolved gas over water in a test tube. Apply a light to the gas. The experiment can be performed with propanol.

When the reaction is complete, put one or two drops of the remaining solution on to a watch glass or microscope slide and evaporate them by holding the slide about 4 cm above a warm gauze. Note the formation of a white residue.

All the common alcohols react with sodium to form hydrogen and a sodium compound:

$$methanol-CH_3OH + Na \rightarrow \underset{\text{sodium methoxide}}{CH_3ONa} + \tfrac{1}{2}H_2$$

$$ethanol-C_2H_5OH + Na \rightarrow \underset{\text{sodium ethoxide}}{C_2H_5ONa} + \tfrac{1}{2}H_2$$

$$propanol-C_3H_7OH + Na \rightarrow \underset{\text{sodium propoxide}}{C_3H_7ONa} + \tfrac{1}{2}H_2$$

From this and other reactions, such as the oxidation of alcohols it seems that the alcohols are similar in properties and structure:

methanol

$$\begin{array}{c} H \\ | \\ H-C-O-H \\ | \\ H \end{array} \quad \text{or} \quad H.CH_2OH$$

propanol

$$\begin{array}{c} H \ \ H \ \ H \\ | \ \ \ | \ \ \ | \\ H-C-C-C-O-H \\ | \ \ \ | \ \ \ | \\ H \ \ H \ \ H \end{array} \quad \text{or} \quad CH_3.CH_2.CH_2OH$$

Functional groups and general formulae

You will notice that each of the alcohols contains the group—CH_2OH. This group of atoms is common to all alcohols of this type. It is this group of atoms, called a *functional group*, which gives rise to most of the properties which the alcohols have in common.

If we let R represent all the rest of the molecule, a general formula, $R.CH_2OH$, can be used to represent all the alcohols.*

Other series of carbon compounds, such as aldehydes and acids, contain their own funtional groups and each series can be given a general formula. The elementary study of organic chemistry can be largely concerned with the general properties of a series of compounds rather than the properties of individual members.

Burning of alcohols

Alcohols, like most other carbon compounds, burn readily; they are oxidized to carbon dioxide and water. Try small quantities in a crucible lid (an apparatus shown on p. 31 is suitable for identifying the products).

Work our equations for the burning of ethanol and propanol.

* There are other types of alcohols. These are examples of *primary* alcohols.

Carboxylic acids

Carboxylic acids can be made by the oxidation of alcohols. The oxidation can take place in two stages: first by the removal of two hydrogen atoms from each molecule to form one of a group of compounds called aldehydes

$$\underset{\underset{H}{|}}{\overset{\overset{H}{|}}{R-C}}-O-H + [O] \rightarrow R-\overset{\overset{H}{|}}{C}=O + H_2O$$

and then by the addition of oxygen to form a carboxylic acid

$$R-\overset{\overset{H}{|}}{C}=O \ +[O] \rightarrow R-\overset{\overset{OH}{|}}{C}=O$$

Three simple carboxylic acids are:

formic acid $H.COOH$, acetic acid $CH_3.COOH$, propionic acid $CH_3.CH_2.COOH$

Some properties of carboxylic acids

Like all other acids, carboxylic acids can give a hydrogen ion (a proton) to a base to form a salt. Only the hydrogen of the carboxyl group can be given in this way. They are weak acids, so that in aqueous solution they are only slightly ionized:

$$R.COOH \rightleftharpoons R.COO^- + H^+$$

The formulae of the salts of carboxylic acids are usually written as follows:

$\underset{\text{sodium formate}}{HCOONa} \qquad \underset{\text{sodium acetate}}{CH_3.COONa} \qquad \underset{\text{sodium propionate}}{CH_3.CH_2.COONa}$

The acids are readily displaced from these salts by the action of stronger acids:

$$R.COONa + HCl \rightarrow R.COOH + NaCl$$
$$\text{or} \qquad R.COO^- + H^+ \rightarrow R.COOH$$

Acetic acid

Like alcohol, acetic acid has been manufactured for thousands of years by making use of a chemical change brought about by a micro-organism. When dilute solutions of ethanol are allowed to run slowly through woody material which contains the micro-organism called *Mycoderma aceti*, the micro-organism—with oxygen from the air—oxidizes the alcohol to acetic acid and uses the energy provided by this reaction to grow and reproduce. The dilute, impure solution of acetic acid which results from this process is vinegar.

Esters

A reaction between an alcohol and a carboxylic acid results in the formation of an ester. Esters can be made by other methods, but only the direct action between acids and alcohols will be considered here.

Experiment 26.3

To prepare ethyl benzoate
(C)

Put about 3 g of benzoic acid (C_6H_5COOH) into a dry boiling tube add 12 cm³ of ethanol and 1 cm³ of concentrated sulphuric acid. Fit up the apparatus shown in *figure 106*

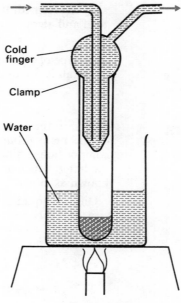

Figure 106

The hot vapours condense on the cold finger and the liquid so formed drops back into the boiling liquid. This process is called *boiling under reflux*; it enables reacting liquids to be kept at their boiling point without evaporating.

Boil the mixture under reflux for 1 hour. Remove the cold finger and leave the boiling tube in the beaker of boiling water for a further 30 minutes to evaporate the excess alcohol. The liquid which remains is impure ethyl benzoate.

Add to the ethyl benzoate about an equal volume of water; then add anhydrous sodium carbonate until effervescence ceases. The sodium carbonate neutralizes any remaining acid. Smell the ester cautiously.

The reaction between ethanol and benzoic acid can be represented by the following equation:

$$C_6H_5.CO\boxed{OH + H}O.C_2H_5 \rightleftharpoons C_6H_5.CO.O.C_2H_5 + H_2O$$

←benzoate→ ←ethyl→

(note that the reaction is reversible).

In the formation of esters by this method, it appears that the hydrogen of the alcohol forms water with the OH group of the acid and that the ester is formed from the remains of the two molecules.

Some properties of esters

Ethyl benzoate is typical of many esters. They are immiscible in water and most of them have distinctive smells. Some of these smells are pleasant and esters are manufactured for use as perfumes or flavouring substances.

The most important reaction of esters is the reverse of that by which they are formed. If esters are boiled with water, they slowly re-form the acid and alcohol from which they were derived:

$$R.CO.OR + H_2O \rightarrow R.CO.OH + R.OH$$

This type of reaction, called *hydrolysis*, is much quicker if aqueous acid or alkali is used instead of plain water (Experiment 26.4).

Natural esters

Esters, in the form of the oils and fats of plants and animals, are one of the main groups of naturally-occuring carbon compounds. Their composition is different from that of the oils obtained from petroleum; the latter, which are almost completely composed of hydrocarbons, are known as mineral oils.

Oils are liquid at room temperature; fats are solid at room temperature. But oils and fats are similar in chemical composition; they are esters of an alcohol called *glycerol* and a variety of acids called *fatty acids* (from now on both are called fats). Glycerol has the formula:

$$
\begin{array}{l}
CH_2OH \\
| \\
CH\,OH \\
| \\
CH_2OH
\end{array}
$$

It behaves like the alcohols we have already studied but, unlike them, it contains three OH groups per molecule and one of the OH groups is part of a —CH.OH (secondary alcohol) group. Each OH group can react with a molecule of an acid to form an ester.

The fatty acids all contain a carboxyl group, but their molecules are much larger than those of acetic and propionic acids. Here are the formulae of some of the most abundant fatty acids:

lauric acid	$CH_3\,(CH_2)_{10}.COOH$
myristic acid	$CH_3.(CH_2)_{12}.COOH$
palmitic acid	$CH_3.(CH_2)_{14}.COOH$
stearic acid	$CH_3.(CH_2)_{16}.COOH$
oleic acid	$CH_3.(CH_2)_7.CH = CH.(CH_2)_7.COOH$

You will see that the molecules of all the acids contain long chains of CH_2 groups, and that oleic acid differs from the others in that it is *unsaturated*; this is shown as a —CH=CH— group in the middle of the molecule. Unsaturated means that it can combine with other substances without losing any part of itself; such a reaction is called an *addition* reaction.

In a fat each molecule of glycerol, because of its three OH groups, can be associated with three molecules of an acid. For example, glyceryl tristearate (usually shortened to tristearin):

$$CH_3.(CH_2)_{16}.CO.O.CH_2$$
$$|$$
$$CH_3.(CH_2)_{16}.CO.O.CH$$
$$|$$
$$CH_3.(CH_2)_{16}.CO.O.CH_2$$

←————tristearate————→glyceryl

Any single natural fat is made up of several esters. All the esters are derived from glycerol, but the glycerol is combined with a variety of acids. For this reason, an analysis of a fat includes the relative quantities of the fatty acids of which it is composed. Here is the acid composition of one oil and one fat:

palm kernel oil   52% lauric, 15% myristic, 7% palmitic, 16% oleic, and smaller quantities of other acids.

beef fat   32% palmitic, 14% stearic, 48% oleic, and smaller quantities of other acids.

The physical properties of a fat are largely governed by its acid composition. A fat with a high proportion of stearic acid is likely to be a solid at room temperature. A fat with a high proportion of acids of lower molecular weight (lauric and myristic) or of unsaturated acids (oleic) is likely to be a liquid at room temperature.

In general, the body fats of warm-blooded animals are solids and the fats of fish and plants are liquids. Plants and animals reared under standard conditions show very little variation in the composition of their fats, but within the body of one organism there are various fats; for example, the milk fat of a mammal has an acid composition different from that of its body fat.

Hydrogenation of fats

In recent years, with the intensive cultivation of the oil-bearing plants such as palm, coconut, groundnut and olive, the liquid fats have become more abundant. The main demand, however, is for solid fats for the manufacture of soap and margarine. By a process known as hydrogenation, a part of the unsaturated esters in the fat can be made into saturated esters of higher melting points.

Hydrogenation consists of passing hydrogen into a liquid fat at about 2 atm pressure and 180°C, in the presence of a finely-divided nickel catalyst. The hydrogen combines with the unsaturated parts of the fat and makes them saturated:

$$\begin{array}{ccc} H\ H & & H\ H \\ |\ \ | & & |\ \ | \\ -C=C- & \rightarrow & -C-C- \\ \uparrow + \uparrow & & |\ \ | \\ H-H & & H\ H \end{array}$$

Thus, oleic acid would be converted into stearic acid:

$$CH_3.(CH_2)_7.CH = CH.(CH_2)_7.COOH + H_2 \rightarrow CH_3.(CH_2)_{16}.COOH$$

A fat is rarely completely hydrogenated. By careful control of conditions, just sufficient unsaturated fat can be hydrogenated to produce the desired change in physical properties. Of course, hydrogenation is not the only process in the making of margarine: purification, blending, and the addition of vitamins, all play their part in the making of an edible, solid fat.

Soap

Most soaps are the sodium salts of those acids which form a part of fats. The formation of an ester is a reversible process; if esters are boiled with water they are hydrolysed to re-form the alcohol and acid from which they were derived (p. 250). If aqueous alkali is used instead of water, the reaction is much quicker, but the sodium salt of the acid is formed instead of the acid itself.

This is the chemical reaction which takes place in the manufacture of soap. Fats are boiled with aqueous sodium hydroxide to form glycerol and a mixture of sodium salts of the fatty acids. The hydrolysis of glyceryl trilaurate will serve as an example:

$$CH_3.(CH_2)_{10}.CO.O.CH_2$$
$$CH_3.(CH_2)_{10}.CO.O.CH + 3NaOH$$
$$CH_3.(CH_2)_{10}.CO.O.CH_2$$
glyceryl trilaurate

$$\rightarrow 3CH_3.(CH_2)_{10}.COONa + \begin{matrix} CH_2.OH \\ | \\ CH.OH \\ | \\ CH_2.OH \end{matrix}$$
sodium laurate (a soap)   glycerol

The mixture of sodium salts forms a solution (p. 222) in the water, from which it can be precipitated by adding common salt. Further purification, and sometimes colouring and scenting, are necessary before the soap is ready for sale. The glycerol can be recovered by distillation of the remaining solution.

Experiment 26.4

To prepare a soap (C)

Pour into a boiling tube 2 cm³ of olive oil, 8 cm³ of aqueous sodium hydroxide solution, and 5 cm³ of ethanol. Fit up the apparatus shown in *figure 107*; add some small pieces of broken porcelain and boil the mixture under reflux for 1 hour. (The ethanol assists the oil and aqueous alkali to mix and the pieces of porcelain help the mixture to boil smoothly).

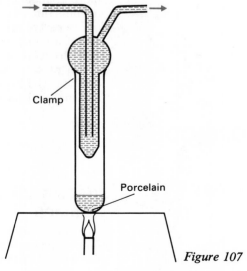

Clamp

Porcelain

Figure 107

After an hour, remove the cold finger and continue the heating for another five or ten minutes in order to boil off the alcohol. Remove the bunsen; add 10 cm³ of a saturated solution of common salt; shake the tube and cool it under the tap.

The crude soap should now separate as a solid which can be filtered off. Wash the soap while it is still in the filter paper by adding a further 10 cm³ of salt solution a little at a time.

The soap can be purified as follows: put it into a boiling tube; add 10 cm³ of water and boil for two or three minutes. Allow the tube to cool and note the viscous solution of soap. Separate the soap by shaking it with 10 cm³ of salt solution. Filter the soap, then wash it with 10 cm³ of salt solution followed by 10 cm³ of water. Allow the soap to drain, then dry and press it between filter papers.

In olive oil it is oleic acid which is largely present (80%) as the glycery ester, so the soap made in Experiment 26.4 is largely sodium oleate:

$$CH_3.(CH_2)_7.CH{=}CH.(CH_2)_7\,COONa$$

Detergents

There are many substances other than soap which have a detergent action, that is, the power to loosen oil and dirt and remove them from a surface by making them into an emulsion with water. Some of these detergents can be made synthetically and their manufacture has increased greatly during the past twenty years.

Detergents have a similar molecular structure. Soap molecules are large; one part of the molecule resembles a hydrocarbon and is covalent and the other part resembles a salt and is ionic. For example, sodium laurate:

$$\underset{\text{covalent}}{CH_3(CH_2)_{10}.COO^-}\cdots\underset{\text{ionic}}{Na^+}$$

Both the covalent part and the ionic part can be varied to give a number of detergents. For example:

$$CH_3.(CH_2)_{15}.SO_4{}^-\cdots Na^+$$

and
$$CH_3.(CH_2)_{13}.SO_3{}^-\cdots Na^+$$

The last two formulae are typical of synthetic detergents.

Hydrocarbons

These compounds, which contain carbon and hydrogen only, occur abundantly in coal, petroleum, and natural gas.

Natural gas

Natural gas consists mainly of methane (CH_4) and smaller quantities of ethane (C_2H_6), propane (C_3H_8), and butane (C_4H_{10}).

Petroleum

Petroleum is a more complex mixture of hydrocarbons. It contains liquid hydrocarbons, which have from five to seventeen carbon atoms

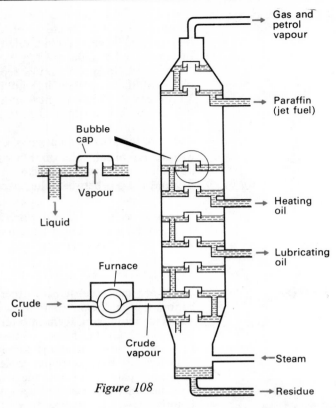

Figure 108

per molecule, and solid hydrocarbons, which have up to sixty or seventy carbon atoms per molecule.

Individual hydrocarbons have been obtained from petroleum but, for most purposes, it is sufficient to distil the crude petroleum into several fractions according to their boiling points, each fraction containing many different hydrocarbons. *Figure 108* is a simplified diagram of the fractional distillation of petroleum.

The trays become filled with liquids which have condensed from the vaporized petroleum. The hot vapours, as they push through the bubble caps, partly condense and at the same time cause some of the liquid in the trays to vaporize and move up to a higher tray. As the trays fill with liquid, some of it overflows and falls to a lower tray. In this way the vapours are continually being condensed and re-vaporized. At intervals up the column liquids can be led off, the higher-boiling liquids coming off near the bottom and the lower-boiling liquids near the top.

The main fractions—in order of ascending boiling point—are (i) petroleum ether (ii) motor spirit (petrol or gasoline) (iii) paraffin oil (kerosene) (iv) light lubricating and diesel oils (v) heavy lubricating and fuel oils.

Each fraction may be subjected to further fractional distillation and purification. For example, fractions (iv) and (v) can be further divided into various grades of lubricating oil, medicinal paraffin, and paraffin wax.

Saturated hydrocarbons

The detailed composition of petroleums and natural gases varies from one oilfield to another, but most of them contain a much great proportion of saturated hydrocarbons than of unsaturated hydrocarbons.

The carbon atoms of these saturated hydrocarbons are arranged in chains, either straight chains or branched chains. Here are some examples of their formulae:

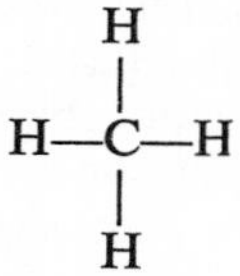

methane
(I)

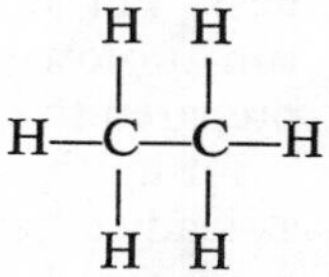

ethane
(II)

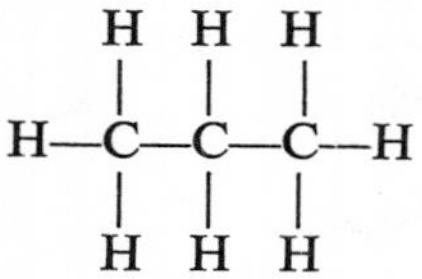

propane
(III)

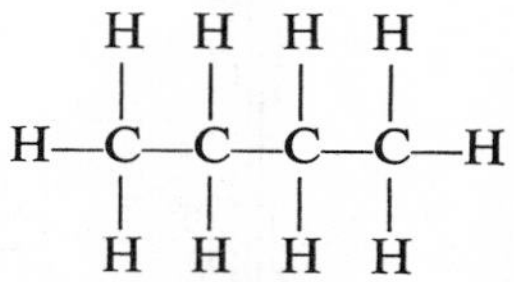

butane (C_4H_{10})
(IV)

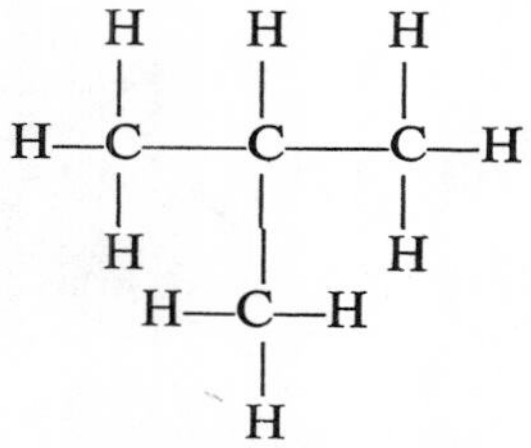

2-methyl propane (C_4H_{10})
(V)

(i)–(iv) are straight chains, (v) is a branched chain. You may find it amusing to construct all the possible isomers of pentane (C_5H_{12}), hexane (C_6H_{14}), and heptane (C_7H_{12}). Octane (C_8H_{18}) has as many as 18 isomers.

These saturated hydrocarbaons form part of a series of hydrocarbons called the *alkanes*. They are chemically unreactive and are not a convenient starting point for making other substances. Being saturated, their molecules cannot add other atoms or groups without first losing some part of themselves. They do, however, burn readily, some of them explosively when vaporized with air; it is as fuels that they find their main use.

Unsaturated hydrocarbons

In these compounds the combining capacity of the carbon is not fully used in combining with hydrogen. For example, the simplest unsaturated hydrocarbon, ethylene* (C_2H_4), contains two less hydrogen atoms per molecule than the corresponding saturated hydrocarbon ethane (C_2H_6). This unsaturation is shown in the structural formula as a double covalent bond between two carbon atoms:

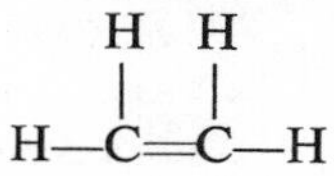

* Also called ethene.

Unsaturated hydrocarbons are important raw materials in the petrochemical industry (p. 269). The natural supply is insufficient and large quantities are made by removing hydrogen from saturated hydrocarbons (p. 269). In the laboratory ethylene is conveniently made from ethanol:

Experiment 26.5

To prepare ethylene and to investigate some of its properties (D)

Put one measure of anhydrous aluminium sulphate (this prevents excessive frothing) and 25 cm³ of ethanol into a dry 250 cm³ distillation flask. Put 50 cm³ of concentrated sulphuric acid into a tap funnel and run it slowly into the flask; swirl the contents of the flask and be prepared to cool it under the tap if it gets too hot.

Fit up the apparatus shown in *figure 109* and warm the flask so that a steady effervescence occurs (about 160°C). Collect the resulting gas in gas jars.

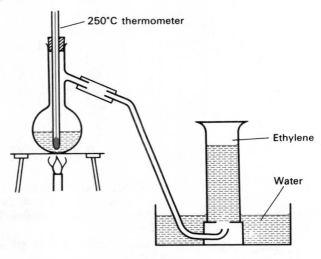

Figure 109

When three or four gas jars have been collected, remove the flame and take the delivery tube out of the trough so that water does not suck back.

To one gas jar apply a light; to another add bromine water and shake it; to another add a few drops of potassium permanganate in dilute sulphuric acid and shake it.

Some properties of ethylene

(i) It burns:
$$C_2H_4 + 3O_2 \rightarrow 2CO_2 + 2H_2O$$

(ii) It combines readily with bromine:

$$
\begin{array}{ccc}
\text{H} \quad \text{H} & & \text{H} \quad \text{H} \\
| \quad\ | & & | \quad\ | \\
\text{H—C=C—H} & \rightarrow & \text{H—C—C—H} \\
\uparrow + \uparrow & & | \quad\ | \\
\text{Br—Br} & & \text{Br} \ \ \text{Br} \\
& & \text{1,2-dibromoethane}
\end{array}
$$

This is another example of an addition reaction which is typical of unsaturated hydrocarbons. This reaction with bromine is a good test for unsaturated compounds which contain the —C=C— group, because the disappearance of the orange colour of the bromine, as it reacts, is easily observed.

(iii) It readily undergoes other addition reactions. Construct equations for the action of ethylene on (i) chlorine (ii) hydrogen (iii) hydrogen iodide. .

(iv) It is readily oxidized in the presence of water to form glycol:

$$
\begin{array}{ccc}
\text{H} \quad \text{H} & & \text{H} \quad \text{H} \\
| \quad | & & | \quad | \\
\text{H—C=C—H} & \rightarrow & \text{H—C—C—H} \\
| \quad | \\
+\text{H}_2\text{O}+[\text{O}] & & \text{OH} \quad \text{OH}
\end{array}
$$

This explains why it decolorizes potassium permanganate solution.

Glycol contains two alcohol groups —(CH.OH)— and has the typical properties of alcohols. It is made in large quantities for use as 'anti-freeze'; the industrial process, however, is not based on the reaction just described.

Compounds resembling ethylene

Unsaturated hydrocarbons resembling ethylene are called *alkenes*. They all contain the —C=C— group in their formulae and have similar properties. There are many compounds other than hydrocarbons which contain the characteristic —C=C— group and they too resemble ethylene, particularly in addition reactions.

Two addition reactions of this type of compound have great industrial importance. The first, the addition of hydrogen to unsaturated fats, has already been described (p. 253). The second is the formation of polymers.

Polymers

Polymers are substances of very high molecular weight, each molecule being composed of hundreds or even thousands of small identical units. Natural polymers—rubber, cotton, wool, etc.—and the industrial importance of natural synthetic polymers, are discussed on p. 269. The process by which identical units of small molecular weight are built up into a polymer is called *polymerization*.

Polythene

We have seen that molecules of ethylene will readily undergo addition reactions with those of other substances. Under suitable conditions, molecules of ethylene can be made to undergo an addition reaction with each other. The result can be a giant molecule consisting of long chains of CH_2 units.

As molecule after molecule of ethylene is added, the total unsaturation—two spare bonds—remains the same. In a general equation this can be shown as:

$$n\text{CH}_2{=}\text{CH}_2 \rightarrow -(\text{CH}_2{-}\text{CH}_2)_n-$$

where n is a variable number which can be thousands.

The substance which results from the polymerization of ethylene is called *polyethylene* or *polythene*. It was first made in the laboratories of I.C.I. and went into commercial production in 1939. Polythene is a typical plastic. At room temperature it is hard, strong, and light, but it softens readily on warming so that it can be moulded into a great variety of useful articles. Furthermore, it has excellent electrical insulating properties when used as a thin coating on wire. It was this last property, together with its lightness, which made it so useful in radio and radar devices during World War II—particularly in aircraft.

The conditions for the first polymerization of ethylene were a temperature of about 200°C and a very high pressure—over 1000 atm. The manufacture was improved by the use, as catalysts, of some metallic derivatives of organic compounds. These are usually called Ziegler catalysts. They enable polymerization to take place at much lower pressures; by careful choice of catalyst and conditions, greater control is now possible over the size of the polymer molecules. This means that a range of plastics, with differing physical properties, can be made from the same starting material.

Other polymers related to ethylene

Polythene was not the first synthetic polymer. Vinyl chloride ($\text{CH}_2{=}\text{CHCl}$) was polymerized to polyvinyl chloride (PVC) in the laboratory as early as 1917.

A molecule of vinyl chloride differs from that of ethylene in that one chlorine atom is present in the place of one hydrogen atom. But the group essential to this sort of polymerization, $-\text{C}{=}\text{C}-$, is still present:

$$n\text{CH}_2 = \text{CH.Cl} \rightarrow -(\text{CH}_2{-}\text{CH}_2)_n-$$

Here are the formulae of some substances which have been successfully polymerized for commerical purposes:

$$\begin{array}{ll}
& \text{CH}_3 \\
& | \\
\text{CH}_2{=}\text{C}{-}\text{COOCH}_3 & \text{methyl methacrylate} \\
\text{CH}_2{=}\text{CH.CH}_3 & \text{propylene} \\
\text{CH}_2{=}\text{CH.C}_6\text{H}_5 & \text{styrene} \\
\text{CH}_2{=}\text{CH.CH} = \text{CH}_2 & \text{butadiene} \\
\text{CH}_2{=}\text{CH}{-}\text{CCl} = \text{CH}_2 & \text{chloroprene}
\end{array}$$

The last three are used for making synthetic rubbers.

Organic bases

Most basic carbon compounds are related to ammonia:

$$H-N\diagdown^{\displaystyle H}_{\diagdown H} \quad \text{ammonia}$$

$$CH_3-N\diagdown^{\displaystyle H}_{\diagdown H} \quad \text{methylamine}$$

$$C_6H_5-N\diagdown^{\displaystyle H}_{\diagdown H} \quad \text{aniline}$$

Like ammonia, they are classified as bases because they can accept hydrogen ions (protons) from an acid, thus forming a salt:

$$NH_3 + HCl \rightarrow NH_4{}^+Cl^-$$
(ammonium chloride)

$$CH_3NH_2 + HCl \rightarrow CH_3 . NH_3{}^+Cl^-$$
(methylamine hydrochloride)

$$C_6H_5NH_2 + HCl \rightarrow C_6H_5NH_3{}^+Cl^-$$
(aniline hydrochloride)

These salts bear the same relationship to ammonium salts as the bases themselves do to ammonia.

Amino acids

These are carbon compounds whose molecules contain both the basic amino group (NH_2) and the acidic carboxyl group (COOH). The simplest of the amino acids is *glycine*:

$$\overset{\displaystyle H}{\underset{\displaystyle H}{\diagup}}N-\overset{\displaystyle H}{\underset{\displaystyle H}{C}}-\overset{O}{\overset{\|}{C}}-O-H \qquad (H_2N . CH_2 . COOH)$$

Glycine can form salts with bases and with acids; it is amphoteric.

Proteins

Proteins are a group of substances of great importance in the structure of living things. These substances all contain carbon, hydrogen, oxygen, and nitrogen, and they usually have very large molecules. They differ widely in structure and function: hair, wool, egg white, feathers, blood, silk, skin, and many other parts of living things, contain proteins.

The molecules of most proteins are very complex and research work of a very high order is required to determine their structure. The structure of some well-known proteins such as insulin have been worked out in recent years; many more are being studied. This field of research is thought to be particularly useful in helping to understand the workings of the human body.

When proteins are hydrolysed by boiling them with aqueous acids they break down into amino acids, which have much smaller molecules and a simpler structure than the proteins themselves. It appears that proteins are built up of hundreds or thousands of these amino acid units.

The peptide link

The way in which amino acids can link together is described as the peptide link. The combination of two molecules of glycine can be used as an illustration:

$$H_2N—CH_2—C—\boxed{OH+H}—N—CH_2—COOH$$
$$\underset{O}{\|} \qquad \underset{H}{|}$$

peptide link

$$H_2N—CH_2—\boxed{\underset{\underset{O}{\|}}{C}—\underset{\underset{H}{|}}{N}}—CH_2—COOH+H_2O$$

As there is still an amino group at one end and a carboxyl group at the other, further peptide linkages can be made at both ends of the molecule until a giant molecule resembling a protein is built up.

It seems likely that proteins are built up in this way, but most of them contain more than one amino acid built up in a very complex pattern. The synthetic manufacture of a natural protein has not yet been achieved.

Nylon

It is interesting that this well-known synthetic fibre is a polymer built up in a manner very similar to that of proteins. It is made not from a single amino acid but from two units: (i) adipic acid, $HOOC.(CH_2)_4.COOH$, which contains two acidic groups per molecule, and (ii) hexamethylene diamine, $H_2N.(CH_2)_6.NH_2$, which contains two basic groups per molecule. On heating these two substances together, they form a polymer in the following way:

$$HOOC—(CH_2)_4—\underset{\underset{O}{\|}}{C}—\boxed{OH+H}—\underset{\underset{H}{|}}{N}—(CH_2)_6—NH_2$$

$$HOOC—(CH_2)_4—\boxed{\underset{\underset{O}{\|}}{C}—\underset{\underset{H}{|}}{N}}—(CH_2)_6—NH_2+H_2O$$

peptide link

As there is still an acidic and basic group at each end of this molecule, further peptide links can be formed until giant molecules of weights up to 25 000 are obtained. This polymer is melted and forced through tiny holes to make it into filaments. The filaments are then stretched to give fibres of various diameters.

By using other similar compounds as starting material, many varieties of fibres of the nylon type have been made.

Terylene

Terylene, like nylon, is a polymer which is built up from two units. In terylene, however, the units are joined by an ester link (p. 314), not a peptide link:

$$\underset{\text{terephthalic acid}}{\text{HOOC—C}_6\text{H}_4\text{—CO}}\boxed{\text{OH+H}}\underset{\text{glycol}}{\text{O—CH}_2\text{—CH}_2\text{—OH}}$$

$$\downarrow$$

$$\text{HOOC—C}_6\text{H}_4\text{—}\underset{\text{ester link}}{\boxed{\text{CO—O}}}\text{—CH}_2\text{—CH}_2\text{—OH+H}_2\text{O}$$

As the acid has two carboxyl groups and the alcohol has two OH groups, ester links can continue to be formed at both ends of the molecule until a long chain is formed. This type of polymer is sometimes called a *polyester*.

Chemicals from coal

When coal is heated in the absence of air, the main products are coke, coal gas, ammonia, hydrogen sulphide, benzene and coal tar.

Coke

Coke remains as a solid residue in the retorts in which the coal has been heated. It consists almost entirely of carbon and is used either as a fuel or to reduce the ores of metals. Coal gas was the principal fuel gas until the discovery of natural gas. It consists largely of hydrogen, methane, and carbon monoxide. Coal tar is a complex mixture of carbon compounds many of which are very useful; they can be isolated by further distillation and purification.

Summary

(1) The main sources of carbon compounds are petroleum, coal, natural gas, and the starch and sugar made by plants.
(2) The chemical reactions in living things are assisted by complex natural catalysts called enzymes.
(3) The micro-organism, yeast, assimilates sugar and produces ethanol and carbon dioxide as waste products. This is one of the many natural chemical processes which produce chemicals useful to man.
(4) Fractional distillation has the same effect as several separate distillations. It is used to separate mixtures of liquids.
(5) Isomers are substances which have the same molecular formula but different properties.
(6) A structural formula shows the arrangement of atoms and groups of atoms within a molecule.

(7) Carbon compounds can be classified into series. In each series there is a group which is common to the structure of all its members. This is called the functional group of the series and its presence explains many of the properties which the compounds have in common.

(8) Alcohols can be oxidized first to aldehydes:

$$R.CH_2OH + [O] \rightarrow R.CHO + H_2O$$

and then to carboxylic acids:

$$R.CHO + [O] \rightarrow R.COOH$$

(9) A saturated compound is one which cannot combine with anything else without losing a part of itself.

(10) Unsaturation in a compound is indicated by a double or a treble covalent bond in its structural formula.

(11) Alcohols react with carboxylic acids to form esters:

$$R.COOH + HOR \rightleftharpoons R.COOR + H_2O$$

The reaction between an ester and water to re-form the acid and alcohol is an example of hydrolysis; it is quicker if acid or alkali are present.

(12) Fats are esters of glycerol and fatty acids.

(13) When fats are boiled with aqueous sodium hydroxide, they are hydrolysed to glycerol and the sodium salts of the fatty acids (soap).

(14) The melting point of a fat can be raised by hydrogenation. Hydrogen combines, in the presence of a catalyst, with the unsaturated parts of the fat.

(15) Alkane hydrocarbons are saturated and their carbon atoms are arranged in chains.

(16) Ethylene is one of a series of unsaturated hydrocarbons called alkenes. It readily undergoes addition reactions, for example with bromine. Many compounds with molecular structures resembling that of ethylene readily form polymers.

(17) Amines are organic bases which resemble ammonia.

(18) Amino acids are amphoteric; they contain both the amine (NH_2) and the carboxyl (COOH) groups. Their molecules can combine with each other by means of the peptide link to form much longer molecules. It is thought that protein molecules are built up in this way.

Section 27
The chemical industry

Scientific method in industry

The manufacture of new substances for the use of mankind is as old as civilization. Metals, glass, dyes, alcohol, and vinegar, are but a few which have been made by men for thousands of years.

This primitive chemical industry, however, was founded on craft rather than on science. The processes were evolved by a mixture of experience, trial and error, and pure chance. The men engaged in this work, skilful though they were, had not the aid of tested chemical principles or scientific methods; as a result, much time, labour and material were wasted and the products were often crude and unreliable. These rule-of-thumb methods remained, little changed, until the middle of the eighteenth century.

The revolution in the methods of the chemical industry sprang not only from the discovery of new materials and practical techniques in laboratories, but also from the new scientific approach to chemical problems. There is a tendency to think that theoretical chemistry and practical chemistry have little connection with each other. This is not so; chemical theories not only attempt to explain practical discoveries, they can also be used to suggest further research and to forecast the likely results of the research. A successful chemical industry is one which applies theoretical chemistry to improve and develop its chemical processes and to suggest research which will lead to the manufacture of new and useful substances.

You may have thought that the work you have done on chemical formulae and equations was rather academic and of no immediate practical value. But once an equation which accurately represents a reaction has been deduced, it can be used to calculate the relative weights of the reactants and the products. It does not necessarily follow that, if an industrial chemist always uses the ratio of reacting weights shown in an equation, he always obtains the yield of the product which the equation indicates; but at least he has the equation as a guide. Before the conception of the simple theories of quantitative chemistry—the law of constant composition, the law of conservation of matter, atomic weights, reacting weights, and formula weights—an industrial chemist had no such guide. As a result, the ancient recipes frequently contained wasteful proportions of some ingredients and even ingredients which were unnecessary. This is just one example of how the expansion and increased efficiency of the chemical industry was made possible by the simultaneous growth of chemical theory.

The purpose of the chemical industry

Efficiency and increased production are not ends in themselves. It is understandable that they are uppermost in the minds of those people who are responsible for maintaining the economic prosperity of industry and those who work in it; but it is valuable to consider the uses to which the products of the industry are put.

Men have continually sought to control their natural surroundings; and, from earliest times, the chemical industry has provided substances which helped them to do this. In general, this is the purpose of the chemical industry. Control over nature has increased rapidly since scientific methods were applied to the chemical industry, so that now there are few parts of our lives which are not influenced by its products.

A summary of the main products of the chemical industry is given below. No one can doubt the power which they have given us over our own lives and those of most living things. Such power must be used with caution. The first supposedly easy chemical remedy to a problem may have other harmful effects not immediately apparent; and to apply those remedies without careful investigation into their long-term effects can cause other problems worse than those they seek to remedy. The effects of the lavish use of new chemical insecticides on seeds, crops and the soil has, in some places, resulted in an appalling killing of other creatures, particularly birds. Such practices could result in an imbalance in nature and a sterile countryside which profits no one.

(1) Structural materials

Since the industrial revolution, the discovery of methods of extracting new metals—aluminium for example—and the increased efficiency of the methods of extracting the old metals has led to a great increase in the production of metals for building, engineering, and domestic articles. The last thirty years has also seen the sudden increase in the manufacture of plastics, glass, and fibre glass; all three are extensively used in the place of the more traditional materials, metal and wood. Plastics are discussed again on p. 269 and glass on p. 273.

(2) Fertilizers

The growth of plants depends not only on the process of photosynthesis (p. 33) but also on the assimilation through their roots of mineral nutrients from the soil. The most important nutrients are compounds of nitrogen, phosphorus, and potassium. The natural sources of these three essential elements—animal manure, compost, wood ash, and minerals such as sodium nitrate and calcium phosphate—are insufficient for modern agriculture. The chemical industry now makes large quantities of the compounds of these elements for use as fertilizers. By far the greatest demand is for compounds of nitrogen: it is this demand which makes the industrial conversion of atmospheric nitrogen into ammonium compounds and nitrates so important.

(3) Pharmaceutical chemicals

The application of chemicals either externally or internally to the human body is not new; many substances have been made and used for thousands of years, frequently with unpredictable and hazardous effects. Many chemicals of this type occur naturally in plants; for example, morphine and codeine occur in opium, which is made from poppies. These natural substances are either extracted from their natural sources or, if their structure is known, they can sometimes be synthesized from simpler and more readily available substances; vitamin C can be synthesized in this way.

Other pharmaceutical chemicals do not occur in nature and have to be made synthetically. The anaesthetic diethyl ether and the sulphonamide antibiotics are examples of this.

The by-products of some micro-organisms are a source of pharmaceutical chemicals which have yielded several new and useful drugs in recent years; for example, penicillin and streptomycin. Alcohol, a by-product of the micro-organism yeast (p. 245), has been made and consumed, at least since the beginning of civilization, because of its effect on the human mind and body.

The chemical industry produces a large and rapidly increasing number of compounds which can be taken into the human body in addition to normal diet. The main functions of these compounds can be summarized as follows:

(i) *To cure disease.* These are the compounds which kill the bacteria and other micro-organisms that cause disease. They are usually given the general name of antibiotics.

(ii) *To prevent pain.* These range from aspirin (acetylsalicylic acid), for the relief of minor pain, to morphine, used for the severe pain which results from accidents or from some diseases. Anaesthetics have taken much of the terror out of surgery.

(iii) *To enable the body to function more efficiently.* Compounds called vitamins are essential for the correct functioning of our bodies. They are only required in minute quantities and there is usually sufficient of them in a normal, balanced diet. But if they are not in the diet, their absence can result in ailments known as deficiency diseases; scurvy, for example, is caused by a deficiency in vitamin C. Many vitamins can now be either extracted or made synthetically and used to supplement an imperfect diet.

Under this heading could come compounds used as sedatives or stimulants. Sedatives are substances which have a calming effect and can be used, for example, to induce sleep or treat mental disease. Stimulants have the opposite effect and for short periods they can cause people to become more alert or energetic; it is not unusual for astronauts to take a stimulant just before they face the arduous task of re-entering the earth's atmosphere.

(iv) *For pleasure.* Alcohol is the most ancient of the compounds deliberately made for this purpose. But many new compounds, most of which have a legitimate and useful medical function, can be used for the effects on the body which some people find pleasant. These pleasant effects are, of course, only temporary and they tend to wear off more rapidly the more frequently the drug is taken. Furthermore, most of them have harmful after-effects which can be disastrous when a person becomes addicted to the drug.

(4) Heavy chemicals

This name has no connection with the density of the chemicals. It is a name given to chemicals produced in very large quantities, usually for use in other sections of industry. Sodium hydroxide, sodium carbonate and sulphuric acid, are all classified as heavy chemicals.

To produce chemicals in bulk, there must be a plentiful supply of raw material and good facilities for transporting this raw material into the factory and the finished products out. Thus, the choice of sites for the heavy chemical industry is important. A good example is the alkali industry in mid-Cheshire, which requires enormous quantities of common salt and limestone; the Cheshire salt beds provide the former and the Derbyshire quarries the latter. Customers for sodium hydroxide and sodium carbonate, the soap and glass industries, lie nearby in the Wirral and South Lancashire respectively, and a large port, Liverpool, is conveniently placed for exporting the products. The proximity of these places, and the good rail and water transport system which linked them, made mid-Cheshire an ideal site for Brunner and Mond when they started to make sodium carbonate by the Solvay process (p. 273) in the last century and thus founded the modern alkali industry in Great Britain.

(5, Fine chemicals

This is the name given to all chemicals produced in quantities which are small compared with those of the heavy chemical industry and which generally have a more complex structure. The chemical changes required to make them are often more complex, so they are usually made in small batches rather than by a continuous process (p. 271).

All the pharmaceutical chemicals can be included under this heading and there are many others: dyestuffs, pigments, synthetic perfumes, and flavouring essences.

(6) Explosives

Until the mid-nineteenth century gunpowder was the only explosive in common use. There had been some refinements in its manufacture, otherwise it remained basically the same as it had been for centuries. With the growth of the chemistry of carbon compounds came the discovery of several new compounds which could be exploded; they included guncotton (cellulose nitrate), nitroglycerine, mercury fulminate, and—a little later—TNT (trinitrotoluene). These four were used in the first world war; some others were used in addition in the second world war. As raw materials for all these compounds, nitric acid and a source of carbon compounds are needed.

As the number of explosive compounds grew, it became possible to classify them according to their function. Most explosives are used either as high explosives, propellants, or initiators. High explosives (e.g. TNT) provide the main filling for bombs and shells; they are required in large quantities and their function is to explode very rapidly—the explosion causing maximum damage by its blast wave and fragments. Propellants (e.g. cordite—a mixture of guncotton and nitroglycerine) explode relatively slowly and steadily, so that they exert a uniform thrust to force a projectile out of a gun barrel without shattering the gun itself. Initiators (e.g. mercury fulminate) are more sensitive than high explosives and propellants; they can be exploded by striking them with a firing pin and the explosion wave thus set up will detonate a propellant or a high explosive. Initiators are very dangerous to handle and are used in small quantities at a time.

(7) Petro-chemicals

The manufacture of chemicals on a large scale from petroleum and natural gas is one of the youngest of the chemical industries; but it has expanded so rapidly that petroleum and natural gas are now the most important source of carbon compounds.

Many of the compounds in petroleum are saturated hydrocarbons (p. 256), which have little value as starting material for the synthesis of useful carbon compounds. Fortunately, methods have been discovered for converting them into more suitable compounds for this purpose. By subjecting the natural substances to increased temperature and pressure in the presence of catalysts, the following reactions can be brought about:

(i) *Cracking*. This is a reaction in which compounds of high molecular weight are decomposed to compounds of lower molecular weight. This not only produces compounds useful to the chemical industry, but also more volatile compounds useful as motor fuels.

(ii) *Dehydrogenation*. This is a reaction in which compounds lose hydrogen. It converts saturated hydrocarbons into the more useful unsaturated hydrocarbons (p. 257) and the hydrogen is a valuable by-product. Here are three examples:

$$CH_3.CH_3 \rightarrow CH_2{=}CH_2 + H_2$$
ethane   ethylene (ethene)

$$CH_3.CH_2.CH_3 \rightarrow CH_3.CH{=}CH_2 + H_2$$
propane   propylene (propene)

$$CH_3.CH_2.CH_2.CH_3 \rightarrow CH_3.CH_2.CH{=}CH_2 + H_2$$
butane   butene

and

$$CH_2{=}CH.CH{=}CH_2 + 2H_2$$
butdiene

(iii) *Re-forming*. In this reaction, chain hydrocarbons can be converted into ring hydrocarbons of the benzene type. This is particularly useful, because in most petroleums hydrocarbons of the benzene type occur only in small quantities and the reaction provides a source of these compounds alternative to coal tar.

At one time, it was not possible to have much control over the nature and yield of the products of these reactions; but now, by careful research into the effects of temperature, pressure, and catalysts, it has become possible to produce much greater yields of the more valuable compounds.

(8) Polymers

Polymers (p. 259) are substances of very high molecular weight, each molecule being composed of hundreds or even thousands of small identical units. Naturally-occuring polymers include rubber, cotton, and wool.

Rubber molecules are built up of C_5H_8 units, so that they can be represented by the formula $(C_5H_8)n$, where n is a number of many hundreds.

Plant fibres such as cotton consist of cellulose, which is a polymer built up of $C_6H_{10}O_5$ units. The formula for cellulose can be written $(C_6H_{10}O_5)n$.

The structural material of animals' hair, horn, nails, wool, etc., consists of giant molecules of protein (p. 261).

Many natural polymers have physical properties which make them useful to man. The functions of rubber, cotton, and wool need not be stressed here; attempts to produce artificial polymers to replace them have been made for some time. Useful synthetic polymers can now be made at a price which enables them to compete with the natural polymers. The synthetic polymers do not have exactly the same physical properties as the natural products, but this very difference has made available a much greater variety of material for the manufacturers of clothing and what are loosely described as consumer goods.

For commercial purposes synthetic polymers can be classified into three main types: plastics, synthetic rubbers, and synthetic fibres. Of the three, plastics are the least like natural substances. Either during or after its manufacture plastic material can be softened and moulded—hence the name. Being easily shaped, and reasonably strong after they have hardened, plastics are particularly useful for containers, thin sheets, and films. If your laboratory has been built recently, it is quite likely that the waste pipes are made of plastic.

Chemical engineering

The manufacture of chemicals on a large scale is not simply a matter of repeating a laboratory preparation, using larger quantities of starting material. The new problems which arise in designing and constructing equipment (generally called the plant) used in industrial chemistry and the problem of controlling a process once it has started, are the concern of the chemical engineer. It is he who makes a chemical reaction economically profitable on a large scale.

It is not possible here to describe everything that must be considered if an industrial chemical process is to run smoothly. Perhaps the following summary will serve to show what a complex operation it is and what a high degree of skill and organization it requires:

(1) Raw materials

Obviously those cheapest and closest to hand are preferred. If materials come from abroad, cost, mode of transport, and even the political changes in the country of origin which might interfere with supply and cost, must all be considered.

(2) The chemical reactions

These will have been thoroughly investigated in the laboratory beforehand. But the industrial chemist must continually be searching for improved conditions which will give him better yields more quickly and also for completely different, and possibly better, ways of making the same material.

(3) The physical conditions of the process

The chemical engineer seeks to use energy, labour, space, material, and time, with the minimum of waste. To do so, he must look for the most efficient methods of applying heat (heat transfer), moving substances from place to place, evaporating, subliming, filtering, centrifuging, drying, mixing, extracting, etc. All these things concern not only the man who builds and operates a chemical plant but also the research workers who are investigating these problems.

(4) Structural material

Material which comes into contact with chemicals is liable to corrosion and must be chosen with care. This problem is particularly acute in dealing with radioactive chemicals by remote control. It is sometimes necessary to operate these processes without inspecting or replacing the chemical plant for years. Fortunately some of the newer materials, including some of the plastics, are suitable for these extreme conditions.

(5) Type of process

Generally, a process which can be run for long periods without stopping is preferred to one which has to be stopped while the products are being removed and a new lot of raw material added. The first type is called a continuous process and the second a batch process.

(6) Control

This includes control of the physical conditions—temperature, pressure, rate of flow, etc.—and chemical composition. The latter may include analysis of the raw materials, analysis during the process, and analysis of the products. The more these things can be done without interrupting the process, or wasting man-power, the better. For this reason automatic control is increasingly used in the industry.

(7) Research, development, pilot plants, patents

In a competitive world few industrialists can afford to neglect the search for new processes and for improvements to existing ones. When a new idea comes from a research laboratory, much work remains to be done before it reaches its final industrial form. The development of new ideas occupies much of a chemical engineer's time. Usually, a pilot plant will precede the building of a complete new factory. This pilot plant will probably be on a much larger scale than the laboratory process but smaller than the ultimate industrial process; it should enable the engineers to discover and remedy faults and generally improve the process before it goes into full production.

A new process is usually protected by a patent to prevent it from being copied by a competitior. At the same time, an industrialist is continually on the look-out for the new processes of his competitors. If they are much better than his own, he may be able to pay for the privilege of copying them under licence.

(8) General administration

Not everyone in the chemical industry is a chemist or a chemical engineer—far from it. Many considerations, which may seem far removed from chemistry—transport, safety, the working conditions of the employees, sales, building, etc.—require the attention of the industry.

Some individual processes

Ammonia – the Haber process

The fundamental reaction of this process is:

$$N_2 + 3H_2 \rightleftharpoons 2NH_3$$

The raw materials, therefore, are nitrogen and hydrogen. They are used in the ratio shown in the equation: 1:3 by moles, which is the same as 1:3 by volumes. One of the many ways in which nitrogen and hydrogen can be produced is to mix air with a volume of hydrogen so calculated that, when the mixture is burned to remove the oxygen in the form of water, the remaining hydrogen is in the correct proportion. The water is removed by condensation.

The hydrogen for this process used to be made from water; but nowadays much of it is obtained as a by-product of the dehydrogenation of petroleum (p. 269). Because of this, a Haber process is frequently established near a plant for the catalytic processing of petroleum.

The conditions for the process vary in different parts of the world; typical conditions are 500°C and 200 atm. The mixture of gases under these conditions is passed over a catalyst, usually iron to which oxides of other metals have been added.

The nitrogen and hydrogen are not completely converted into ammonia by passing them once over the catalyst, because the reaction is reversible. A typical yield for the conditions given above is 5–10%. The uncombined nitrogen and hydrogen are recirculated over the catalyst, after the ammonia has been condensed out in liquid form by cooling the gas to about $-20°C$.

Nitric acid

Much of the ammonia which is made by the Haber process is converted directly into nitric acid by a process of catalytic oxidation. The principles of this process are given on p. 164 and are illustrated in Experiment 17.9.

Sodium carbonate

The raw materials are sodium chloride in the form of brine, carbon dioxide made by heating limestone ($CaCO_3 \rightarrow CaO + CO_2$), and ammonia.

The main impurities in brine, calcium and magnesium ions, are removed by precipitating them as their carbonates.

Ammonia gas is dissolved in the brine thus forming ammonium hydroxide:

$$NH_{3(g)} + H_2O_{(l)} \rightarrow NH_4OH_{(aq)}$$

The ammoniated brine is then passed down towers against a counter-flow of carbon dioxide. The carbon dioxide first forms ammonium hydrogen carbonate:

$$NH_4OH_{(aq)} + CO_{2(g)} \rightarrow NH_4HCO_{3(aq)}$$

and the hydrogen carbonate ions so formed then form a precipitate of sparingly soluble sodium hydrogen carbonate with the sodium ions from the dissolved sodium chloride:

$$Na^+_{(aq)} + HCO_{3(aq)}^- \rightarrow NaHCO_{3(s)}$$

The sodium hydrogen carbonate is filtered off, washed, and heated to form anhydrous sodium carbonate (soda ash):

$$2NaHCO_3 \rightarrow Na_2CO_3 + H_2O + CO_2$$

The remaining solution contains ammonium ions and chloride ions (ammonium chloride) and some unprecipitated sodium hydrogen carbonate.

The action of heat on the sodium hydrogen carbonate recovers half of the carbon dioxide, which is then recirculated. Most of the ammonia is recovered from the filtrate by heating it with the lime which is left after heating the limestone:

$$2NH_4Cl + Ca(OH)_2 \rightarrow CaCl_2 + 2NH_3 + 2H_2O$$

The chief uses for sodium carbonate are in the manufacture of glass, soap, sodium hydroxide, sodium hydrogen carbonate, and general chemicals.

Glass

Glass consists of the silicates of sodium and calcium plus smaller quantities of the silicates of other metals. A mixture is made of sand, soda ash (sodium carbonate), limestone (calcium carbonate), and dolomite (a double carbonate of calcium and magnesium). This is heated in a furnace together with scrap glass which assists the melting. The furnace is heated in the same way as the open hearth furnace (p. 280) to a temperature of about 1500°C.

$$Na_2CO_3 + SiO_2 \rightarrow Na_2SiO_3 + CO_2$$
$$CaCO_3 + SiO_2 \rightarrow CaSiO_3 + CO_2$$

This is a simplified explanation of the reactions which take place during the making of glass.

The presence of other silicates can modify the physical properties of glass. Lead silicate, for example, increases the refractive index of the glass and potassium silicate raises its melting point. Small quantities of the oxides of metals which form coloured silicates, copper and cobalt for instance, can be added to make coloured glass.

Borates, which are compounds of the element boron (group III of the Periodic Table), are added to the mixture in the making of resistance glass. This is the glass which is widely used for laboratory apparatus and kitchen ware; it is more resistant to shock and sudden changes in temperature than ordinary glass.

Sulphuric acid the contact process

The raw materials are sulphur dioxide and oxygen. The sulphur dioxide is obtained from a variety of sources:

(i) by burning sulphur: $S + O_2 \rightarrow SO_2$

(ii) by burning ores which contain sulphur; iron pyrites (FeS_2) and zinc blende (ZnS) are commonly used

(iii) by burning the hydrogen sulphide which occurs in some natural gas:

$$2H_2S + 3O_2 \rightarrow 2SO_2 + 2H_2O$$

(iv) from anhydrite ($CaSO_4$) by heating it strongly with a mixture of coke, sand, and aluminium oxide. The overall reaction can be represented by:

$$2CaSO_4 + C \rightarrow 2CaO + 2SO_2 + CO_2$$

The clinker which remains is a valuable by-product, because it can be used to make cement.

The sulphur dioxide is dried and purified and mixed with pure, dry air. The mixture is heated to about 450°C and then passed into two converters containing a catalyst (either vanadium pentoxide or platinum). The sulphur dioxide is oxidized by the oxygen of the air to sulphur trioxide:

$$2SO_2 + O_2 \rightleftharpoons 2SO_3$$

The temperature rises, because the reaction is exothermic; on leaving the first vessel the temperature of the gases may have risen to nearly 600°C. Before entering the second converter, the gases are cooled to 450°C again by passing them through a heat exchanger in which some of their heat is used to raise the temperature of the sulphur dioxide about to enter the first converter. This is an example of how energy is conserved in an industrial process.

When the gases leave the second converter, 95–98% of the sulphur dioxide has been oxidized to sulphur trioxide. The sulphur trioxide is first dissolved in concentrated sulphuric acid and then changed into sulphuric acid by mixing the solution with water:

$$SO_3 + H_2O \rightarrow H_2SO_4$$

There is another important method for making sulphuric acid, the Lead Chamber process, in which sulphur dioxide, in the presence of water, is oxidized to sulphuric acid; nitrogen dioxide is used as a catalyst.

Sulphuric acid is used in enormous quantities; about 2 000 000 tons a year are made in the United Kingdom alone. Its chief use is in making the fertilizers calcium superphosphate and ammonium sulphate, and in making rayon by the viscose process. There are many other uses, including the making of explosives, detergents, dyestuffs, sodium sulphate and accumulator acid.

Experiment 27.1

To prepare sulphur trioxide
(D)

Set up the apparatus shown in *figure 110*. The heated tube should be made of resistance glass. Pass a steady flow of oxygen over the heated platinized asbestos for about 15 minutes, so that the asbestos is completely dry (the tube should not be connected with the receiving vessel while this is being done). Then pass sulphur dioxide and oxygen, at about the same rate, over the heated platinized asbestos for about 10 minutes.

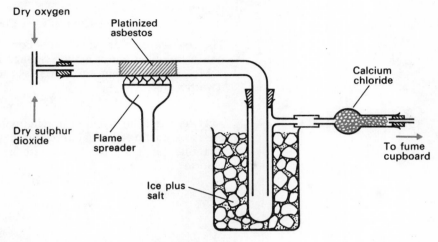

Figure 110

Notice the white smoke of sulphur trioxide. This is dangerous and should not be inhaled. Put a small quantity of the solid sulphur trioxide, which·collects in the cooled tube, into water. Notice the vigorous reaction and the acidic solution so formed.

Sodium hydroxide

Most sodium hydroxide is now made by the electrolysis of brine, using a graphite anode and an iron cathode. At the anode chlorine is formed, and at the cathode hydrogen and sodium hydroxide are formed. It is important that the products at the two electrodes are kept separate from each other; one method of doing this is to place an asbestos diaphragm between them. A possible explanation of the process is as follows:

Action at the anode:

$$Cl^-_{(aq)} \rightarrow \tfrac{1}{2}Cl_{2(g)} + e^-$$

Action at the cathode:

Sodium ions move to the cathode.

Water ionizes slightly:

$$H_2O_{(l)} \rightleftharpoons H^+_{(aq)} + OH^-_{(aq)}$$

Hydrogen ions are discharged:

$$H^+_{(aq)} + e^- \rightarrow \tfrac{1}{2}H_{2(ag)}$$

This leaves sodium ions and hydroxide ions (sodium hydroxide) at the cathode.

275

Sodium hydroxide is used in large quantities in many industries: general chemicals, rayon, petroleum, soap, and paper. Chlorine and hydrogen are by-products of this process.

Calcium carbide

Calcium oxide and coke are heated in an electric furnace at a temperature of about 2000°C:

$$CaO + 3C \rightarrow CaC_2 + CO$$

The calcium carbide, which is a liquid at this temperature, is cooled until it solidifies and it is then crushed into small fragments.

Most of the calcium carbide is used to make acetylene gas by mixing it with water:

$$CaC_2 + 2H_2O \rightarrow Ca(OH)_2 + C_2H_2$$

Acetylene is a highly unsaturated hydrocarbon ($CH \equiv CH$) which is used as a starting material in the synthesis of carbon compounds. Large quantities of it are combined with hydrogen chloride to make vinyl chloride (p. 260).

$$\begin{array}{ccc} H-C \equiv C-H & \rightarrow & H-C=C-H \\ + & & | \quad | \\ H-Cl & & H \quad Cl \end{array}$$

Ethanol

The fermentation of sugar or starch is used to make alcoholic drinks, and some ethanol for industrial use is also made in this way (p. 245). Since large quantities of ethylene have become available as the result of the cracking and dehydrogenation of petroleum, it is now an important starting material for making ethanol. The ethylene is absorbed in concentrated sulphuric acid, with which it undergoes an addition reaction:

$$\begin{array}{ccc} \overset{H}{\underset{|}{}} \ \overset{H}{\underset{|}{}} & & \overset{H}{\underset{|}{}} \ \overset{H}{\underset{|}{}} \\ H-C=C-H & \rightarrow & H-C-C-H \\ + & & | \quad | \\ H-SO_4-H & & H \quad SO_4-H \end{array}$$

The resulting compound, ethyl hydrogen sulphate, is then hydrolysed with water to form ethanol:

$$\begin{array}{ccc} \overset{H}{\underset{|}{}} \ \overset{H}{\underset{|}{}} & & \overset{H}{\underset{|}{}} \ \overset{H}{\underset{|}{}} \\ H-C-C-SO_4H + H.OH & \rightarrow & H-C-C-OH + H_2SO_4 \\ \underset{|}{} \ \underset{|}{} & & \underset{|}{} \ \underset{|}{} \\ H \ H & & H \ H \end{array}$$

Ethanol is also the starting material for many useful carbon compounds; acetaldehyde, ether, chloroform, butadiene (for synthetic rubber), and various esters and solvents, are just a few of them. Carbon dioxide, a by-product of the fermentation process, finds a ready sale; it is used in the solid form (Dry Ice) as a refrigerant, as a compressed gas in fire extinguishers, and in solution in some drinks—soda water, mineral water, bottled beer, etc.

The extraction of metals

Occurrence of metals

Few metals are found as free elements; most of them occur in compounds with non-metallic elements. Oxides, sulphides, carbonates and chlorides are the ores from which metals are most frequently extracted.

Many ores must undergo a preliminary treatment before the main extraction process. Some must be separated from large quantities of earth; others must undergo chemical purification (e.g. the aluminium ore, bauxite); and others must be roasted in air to convert them to oxides (e.g. the zinc ore, zinc blende). The following table shows the chemical nature of the principal ores of some important metals and the methods used to extract them.

Table 17

Metal	Ore	Method
sodium	chloride	electrolysis of molten chloride
magnesium	chloride (sea water)	electrolysis of molten chloride
aluminium	oxide	electrolysis of molten oxide
zinc	sulphide and carbonate	
iron	oxide and carbonate	heating oxide with coke
lead	sulphide	
copper	sulphide	heating without coke

Methods of reduction

The essential reaction in the extraction of a metal is reduction. The metals, being in the combined state, are in the form of ions and these must be reduced to atoms (e.g. $Na^+ + e^- \rightarrow Na$).

The position of a metal in the electrochemical series is a good indication of the ease with which this reduction will take place. The metals high in the series (e.g. sodium) are the most difficult to form from their compounds, those low in the series are easiest to form from their compounds. This is important in deciding the method of reduction.

Sodium, magnesium, and aluminium ions are difficult to reduce with chemical reducing agents. All three are made by the reduction of their ions at a cathode during the electrolysis of their molten compounds. They cannot be made by electrolysis of aqueous solutions because hydrogen—and not the metal—is then formed at the cathode.

Zinc, iron, and lead compounds are more readily reduced, so it is economical to produce the metals by using a cheap reducing agent, coke.

Copper, which is the lowest of these elements in the electrochemical series, can be produced by controlled heating of the ore in oxygen without any reducing agent.

Purity of the metal

Electrolytic methods produce the purest metal and some, e.g. zinc and copper, are purified by electrolysis after the first crude extraction.

Quantity of the metal

The need to produce very large quantities of a metal can influence the choice of a method of extraction. For this purpose a process which can be worked for long periods, continuously adding the raw materials and removing the metal and waste products, is the most suitable. The production of iron in a blast furnace is an example.

The use of by-products

By-products can help considerably in reducing the cost of a metal. One of the most abundant by-products is sulphur dioxide, formed when ores containing sulphur are roasted in air. Whenever possible this sulphur dioxide is collected and converted into sulphuric acid (p. 274).

Aluminium

Bauxite, which contains 50–70% aluminium oxide, is the chief ore of aluminium. It is converted into pure aluminium oxide which is then dissolved in molten cryolite (sodium aluminium fluoride—Na_3AlF_6) and electrolysed. Aluminium oxide alone is too difficult to melt.

At the cathode:

$$Al^{3+} + 3e^- \rightarrow Al \quad \text{(reduction)}$$

At the anode:

$$O^{2-} \rightarrow \tfrac{1}{2}O_2 + 2e^- \quad \text{(oxidation)}$$

A diagram of the cell is shown in *figure 111.*

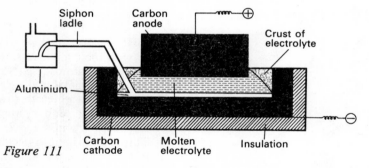

Figure 111

Zinc

(i) Zinc ore (zinc blende) is roasted in air to convert it to the oxide:

$$2ZnS + 3O_2 \rightarrow 2ZnO + 2SO_2$$

The oxide is then mixed with powdered coke and heated with producer gas. This reduces it to zinc:

$$ZnO + C \rightarrow Zn + CO$$

Zinc has a low boiling point compared with metals such as iron and under these conditions it boils and is collected by condensing its vapour. Until recently the extraction was done by a batch process in which rows of retorts, closed at one end, were heated in a furnace. But a continuous process has now been developed in which the mixture of zinc oxide and carbon is fed into the top of a vertical retort. The retort is open at the bottom so that the residue of the raw material can be continuously removed.

(ii) The use of an electrolytic method for producing zinc is increasing. The ore is converted to zinc sulphate, which is then electrolysed in aqueous solution. Zinc is formed by reduction at the cathode:

$$Zn^{2+}_{(aq)} + 2e^- \rightarrow Zn_{(s)}$$

Iron and steel
The extraction of iron

Three typical ions ores are haematite Fe_2O_3, magnetite Fe_3O_4, and siderite $FeCO_3$. After a preliminary roasting, the ore is smelted with limestone and coke in a blast furnace by blowing hot air into the mixture.

The approximate ratio by weight of the raw materials which are fed into the furnace is 1 limestone: 2 coke: 3 iron (III) oxide: 9 air. *Figure 112* is a simple diagram of the blast furnace.

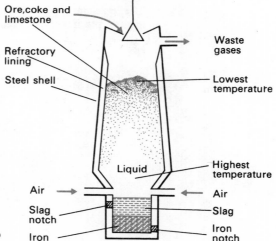

Figure 112

The chemical reactions in the furnace can be summarized as follows.

(1) The coke is oxidized to carbon monoxide:

$$2C + O_2 \rightarrow 2CO$$

(2) The iron oxide is reduced to iron by the carbon monoxide:

$$Fe_2O_3 + 3CO \rightarrow 2Fe + 3CO_2$$

(3) The limestone reacts with impurities in the ore to form a liquid called slag. For example, with sand (silica or silicon dioxide) it forms calcium silicate (p. 303):

$$CaCO_3 + SiO_2 \rightarrow CaSiO_3 + CO_2$$

The heat of these exothermic reactions is sufficient to keep the slag and iron molten and they run to the bottom of the furnace. Liquid slag and iron do not mix; the slag floats on the iron and the two can be separated by running them out of different holes (the slag notch and iron notch). The furnace is much hotter at the bottom than it is at the top. The hot gases pass out of the top of the furnace and are used to heat the air before it is blown into the furnace. The solid raw materials are continually fed into the top of the furnace.

This is a typical continuous smelting process. One furnace, running continuously, can produce up to a million tonnes of iron and some can operate for three years before their lining has to be renewed.

The iron and slag are tapped off from time to time and the iron is either run into moulds or used immediately for making steel. This iron, called pig iron, is impure: it may contain sulphur, phosphorus, silicon, manganese, and up to 4% carbon.

Steel making

To make steel from iron the carbon content must be reduced to below 1·5% and the other impurities removed as far as possible. There are two main processes:

(i) *The Bessemer process*
The Bessemer converter (*figure 113*) is tilted to receive a charge of molten pig iron. It is returned to the vertical position and air is blown

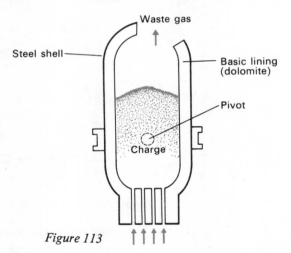

Figure 113

through the molten iron. The impurities burn and the acidic oxides so formed either pass off as gases or combine with the basic lining of the furnace to form a slag. By watching the flame, an experienced steel melter can judge the carbon content of the molten steel.

If this has fallen too low, a high-carbon steel is added to raise the carbon content after the air blast has stopped. The converter is then tilted to pour out the steel.

(ii) *The open hearth process*
Heat for the Bessemer process is produced by the exothermic reaction between the impurities and oxygen. In the open hearth process (*figure 114*) heat is produced by burning a gaseous fuel.

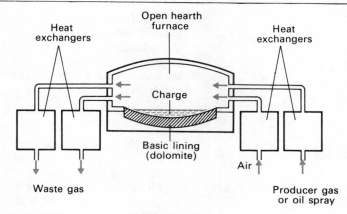

Figure 114

Both gas and air are preheated and from time to time their flow into the furnace is reversed so that they can pick up the heat which the waste gases have left in the heat exchanger.

The raw materials for this furnace are usually pig iron, scrap steel, limestone, and iron (III) oxide which acts as an oxidizing agent. Steel-making by the open hearth process takes much longer (about 12 hours) than by the Bessemer process, but the composition of the steel is more easily controlled.

The use of oxygen in steel making

Pure oxygen has two advantages over air in steel making; it increases the speed and prevents the formation of small quantities of nitrogen compounds. The latter make the steel brittle and their presence is difficult to avoid when air is used.

A modified Bessemer converter, which has recently come into use, uses a blast of oxygen delivered through an oxygen 'lance' on to the surface of the molten iron (*figure 115*). The blast forces oxygen into the molten iron and is sufficiently strong to keep the contents of the converter mixed. A still more recent modification is to use an oxygen lance together with a converter which is rotated to speed up the mixing.

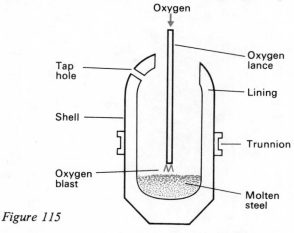

Figure 115

Electric furnaces in steel making

Electric furnaces, in conjunction with an oxygen lance, are being increasingly used to make steel. At the moment they do not produce large quantities but they are particularly useful for special steels which are melted under vacuum to assist the removal of gaseous and volatile impurities.

Coda

The study of chemistry goes back to the beginnings of civilization. It has developed from a primitive craft, in which knowledge was accumulated slowly and by chance, to a science which is expanding so rapidly that new facts are discovered almost daily. The crude chemical products of the past have given way to a vast number of substances produced by an ever-growing chemical industry. These products are causing a revolution in all our lives; their use, for good or evil, affects us all. It is essential, therefore, that some study of chemistry should be a part of everyone's education.

It has been the object of this book to introduce some of the elementary principles of chemistry and to give some idea how chemical theory can develop from observation in the laboratory. Many of you will continue with this subject and possibly add to our store of knowledge. Do not be discouraged by the seemingly endless accumulation of facts: these can be recorded in books and looked up when needed; there is much more to chemistry than this. Chemistry is a way of using our minds and skill to help us to understand the universe and its creatures. A mind well stocked with facts is useful, but it is more important to cultivate a flexible, scientific attitude which will enable you to judge wisely when faced with unfamiliar problems not only in chemistry but in life generally.

Appendix A

Volumetric analysis

If the volumes of two solutions which exactly react with each other—an acid and an alkali for example—are measured, the concentration of one can be calculated if the concentration of the other is known. This is called *volumetric analysis*.

Titration

Titration is the technique for determining the volumes of two reacting solutions.

The volume of one solution, an alkali for example, is measured with a pipette. There are various sizes of pipette, a common one being 25 cm³. The pointed end of the pipette is put at the bottom of the solution, which is then sucked up until it is above the mark on the top stem of the pipette. The forefinger is placed firmly over the top of the pipette and then gently released, so that the level of the solution slowly drops until it reaches the mark on the stem (always measure from the bottom of the meniscus). At this moment the pressure of the forefinger is increased to prevent further loss of solution from the pipette. The pipette is transferred to a conical flask into which the solution is discharged by removing the forefinger. The last drop of solution is not blown from the pipette; it can be removed by touching the surface of the liquid with the tip of the pipette.

The other solution is poured through a small filter funnel into a burette, which has previously been rinsed with one or two cm³ of the solution. A little of the solution is then allowed to run to waste by opening and closing the burette tap quickly; this removes air from the jet. The level of the solution in the burette is measured by holding a piece of white paper behind it and looking at the bottom of the meniscus.

Three or four drops of indicator solution—methyl orange is commonly used—are put into the solution of the alkali. The acid solution is then slowly run from the burette into the conical flask, the contents of which are swirled gently and continuously. This is titration.

The solution in the flask will be yellow and the titration must stop as soon as it turns orange. At this point, the *end point*, the two solutions have exactly reacted with each other and the level in the burette is again measured. The difference in the levels in the burette before and after the titration measures the volume of the acid which has been run into the alkali. Thus, the reacting volumes of the two solutions are known.

Standard solutions

One solution in titration must be of *known concentration*: this is called the *standard solution*. It is usual to dissolve a known weight of solute in water in a 250 cm³ graduated flask and then to make the solution up to the mark (the technique is described on p. 80).

The concentration of a standard solution is expressed either as the number of g-formulae per litre or g-equivalents per litre. Molarity, expressing g-formulae per litre, has already been discusesd in Section 9.

Equivalents

When substances react quantitatively, the equation indicates the reacting quantities exactly. Thus:

$$NaOH_{(aq)} + HCl_{(aq)} \rightarrow NaCl_{(aq)} + H_2O_{(l)}$$

1 g-formula reacts with 1 g-formula
40 g reacts with 36·5 g

We can say that *in the reaction* 40 g of sodium hydroxide are equivalent to 36·5 g of hydrogen chloride (aqueous). In short: 40 g NaOH ≡ 36·5 g HCl.

G-equivalent of an acid

This can be defined as *the weight of an acid which gives rise to 1 g-ion of hydrogen ion.*

Thus, 1 g-equivalent of nitric acid, HNO_3 (formula weight $1 + 14 + 48 = 63$) = 63 g.

Sulphuric acid can react in two ways:

(1) $H_2SO_{4(aq)} \rightarrow H^+_{(aq)} + HSO_4^-_{(aq)}$
(2) $H_2SO_{4(aq)} \rightarrow 2H^+_{(aq)} + SO_4^{2-}_{(aq)}$

In (1) 1 g-equivalent = 1 g-formula = 98 g.
In (2) 1 g-equivalent = 1 g-formula ÷ 2 = 49 g

A substance can have more than one equivalent weight, but only one formula weight.

G-equivalent of a base

This is the *weight which in a stated reaction reacts with a g-equivalent of an acid.*

In the reaction: $NaOH + HCl \rightarrow NaCl + H_2O$ 40 g of NaOH react with 36·5 g of HCl.

The g-equivalent of HCl = 36·5 g.

∴ in this reaction the g-equivalent of sodium hydroxide = 40 g

In the reaction: $Na_2CO_3 + 2HCl \rightarrow 2NaCl + CO_2 + H_2O$, 106 g of Na_2CO_3 react with $2 \times 36·5$ g of HCl.

∴ in this reaction the g-equivalent of sodium carbonate
= g-formula ÷ 2
= 53 g

Milligramme-equivalents

In actual titrations work is usually in volumes of cm³ rather than in litres. Therefore, it is sometimes useful to calculate in milligramme-equivalents (mg-equivalents), this being $\frac{1}{1000}$ of a g-equivalent.

Normality of solutions

The normality of a solution is the number of g-equivalents of the solute per litre of solution for use in a stated reaction.

Example 1 Calculate the normality of a solution containing 5 g of sodium hydroxide per litre, when reacting with acid.

$$1 \text{ g-equivalent of sodium hydroxide} = 40 \text{ g}$$

$$\text{Normality} = \frac{\text{grammes of solute per litre}}{\text{g-equivalent of solute}}$$

$$= \frac{5 N}{40} = 0 \cdot 125 N$$

Example 2 Calculate the concentration of a 2 N solution of nitric acid, when reacting with alkali.

$$1 \text{ g-equivalent of nitric acid} = 63 \text{ g}$$

$$\text{Concentration (g/1)} = \text{normality} \times \text{g-equivalent}$$

$$= 2 \times 63$$

$$= \underline{126 \text{ g/1}}$$

Calculations from titration readings

Suppose that at the end point of a titration V_I and V_2 are the reacting volumes of the two solutions and N_I and N_2 are their respective normalities. The number of g-equivalents of each solute in the reacting volumes is $N_I \times V_I$ and $N_2 \times V_2$ if V is measured in litres. If V is measured in cm³ the same expressions give the number of mg-equivalents of each.

At the end point the number of g-equivalents or mg-equivalents of each reacting substance must be equal. Therefore,

$$N_I \times V_I = N_2 \times V_2$$

This expression can be useful in routine calculation, but it is advisable to understand the various steps in a volumetric calculation rather than blindly apply the expression. The following example is worked in three different ways to help you to understand these steps.

Example 3 In a titration using methyl orange as indicator 50 cm³ of hydrochloric acid had reacted with 25 cm³ of sodium carbonate solution at the end point. The hydrochloric acid contained 3·65 g/litre; calculate the concentration of sodium carbonate solution. ($Na_2CO_3 + 2HCl \rightarrow 2NaCl + CO_2 + H_2O$)

(i) *In Molarities*

Formula weight of HCl = 36·5

$$\therefore \text{ Molarity of HCl} = \frac{3 \cdot 65}{36 \cdot 5} = 0 \cdot 1 \text{ M}$$

$$\text{In 50 cm}^3 \text{ of } 0 \cdot 1 \text{ M HCl there are } \frac{50 \times 0 \cdot 1}{1000} \text{ mole HCl}$$

$$= 0 \cdot 005 \text{ mole HCl}$$

From the equation, 2 moles HCl ≡ 1 mole Na_2CO_3

$$\therefore \quad 0.005 \text{ moles HCl} \equiv 0.0025 \text{ moles Na}_2\text{CO}_3$$

$$\therefore \quad 25 \text{ cm}^3 \text{ Na}_2\text{CO}_{3(aq)} \text{ contain } 0.0025 \text{ moles}$$

$$\therefore \quad 1000 \text{ cm}^3 \text{ Na}_2\text{CO}_{3(aq)} \text{ contain } 0.0025 \times \frac{1000}{25} \text{ moles}$$

$$= 0.1 \text{ mole}$$

$$\therefore \quad \text{molarity of Na}_2\text{CO}_3 = 0.1 \text{ M}$$

$$\therefore \quad \text{concentration of Na}_2\text{CO}_3 = 0.1 \times \text{g-formula weight per litre}$$

$$= \underline{10.6 \text{ g/l}}$$

(ii) *In Normalities*

Equivalent weight of hydrochloric acid $= 36.5$

$$\therefore \quad \text{Normality of acid} = \frac{3.65}{36.5} = 0.1 \text{ } N$$

In 50 cm³ of 0·1 N HCl there are $\dfrac{50 \times 0.1}{1000}$ g-equivalents HCl

$$= 0.005 \text{ g-equivalents HCl}$$

At an end point the number of equivalents is equal.

$$\therefore \quad \text{Number of g-equivalents in 25 cm}^3 \text{ Na}_2\text{CO}_{3(aq)} = 0.005$$

$$\therefore \quad \text{Number of equivalents in 1000 cm}^3 = 0.005 \times \frac{1000}{25}$$

$$= 0.2 \text{ equivalents}$$

$$\therefore \quad \text{Normality of Na}_2\text{CO}_3 = 0.2 \text{ } N$$

Equivalent weight of Na$_2$CO$_3$ *in this reaction* $=$ formula wt. $\div 2$
$$= 53$$

$$\therefore \quad \text{Concentration of Na}_2\text{CO}_3 = 53 \times 0.2 \text{ g/l}$$

$$= \underline{10.6 \text{ g/l}}$$

(iii) *Applying the equation $N_1 V_1 = N_2 V_2$*

$$N_1 \times 25 = 0.1 \times 50$$

$$\therefore \quad N_1 = 0.2 \text{ then proceed as above.}$$

Example 4 3·6 g of iron were reacted with 25 cm³ M sulphuric acid until all the acid was used up. 2·2 g of iron remained. Deduce the equation for the reaction.

$$\text{Weight of iron which reacted} = 3.6 - 2.2 = 1.4 \text{ g}$$

$$1.4 \text{ g of iron} = \frac{1.4}{56} \text{ g-atoms of iron} = 0.025 \text{ g-atom}$$

$$25 \text{ cm}^3 \text{ M H}_2\text{SO}_4 \text{ contain } \frac{25}{1000} \text{ moles H}_2\text{SO}_4 = 0.025 \text{ moles.}$$

$$\therefore \quad 0.025 \text{ moles Fe react with } 0.025 \text{ moles H}_2\text{SO}_4$$

$$\therefore \quad 1 \text{ mole Fe reacts with } 1 \text{ mole H}_2\text{SO}_4$$

$$\therefore \quad \text{Left hand side of the equation is Fe} + \text{H}_2\text{SO}_4$$

It is reasonable to assume that the full equation is:

$$Fe + H_2SO_4 \rightarrow FeSO_4 + H_2$$

Problems

(1) 25 cm³ of a solution containing 5·6 g/l of potassium hydroxide exactly reacted with 30 cm³ of nitric acid. Calculate the concentration of nitric acid in g/l.

(2) A solution of barium hydroxide contains 17·1 g/l. Calculate (a) its molarity (b) its normality when reacted with hydrochloric acid (c) calculate the volume of the barium hydroxide solution which would be required to react exactly with 25 cm³ of a solution containing 12 g of acetic acid per litre.

(3) 25 cm³ of a solution containing 1·86 g of a metal carbonate in 250 cm³ exactly reacted with 27·0 cm³ of hydrochloric acid containing 3·65 g/l of hydrogen chloride.

$$X_2CO_3 + 2HCl \rightarrow 2XCl + H_2O + CO_2$$

Calculate (a) the formula weight of X_2CO_3 (b) its equivalent weight in this reaction (c) the atomic weight of X.

(4) 25 cm³ of a solution containing 10·6 g/l of anhydrous sodium carbonate exactly reacted with 25 cm³ of hydrochloric acid containing 3·65 g/l of hydrogen chloride, when titrated using phenolphthalein indicator. Use these figures to suggest an equation for the reaction.

Appendix B
The periodic table of the elements

Groups \ Periods	I	II											III	IV	V	VI	VII	O
1	1 H 1·00																1 (H) 1·00	2 He 4·00
2	3 Li 6·94	4 Be 9·01											5 B 10·8	6 C 12·0	7 N 14·0	8 O 16·0	9 F 19·0	10 Ne 20·2
3	11 Na 23·0	12 Mg 24·3				Transition Elements							13 Al 27·0	14 Si 28·1	15 P 31·0	16 S 32·0	17 Cl 35·5	18 Ar 39·9
4	19 K′ 39·1	20 Ca 40·1	21 Sc 45·0	22 Ti 47·9	23 V 51·0	24 Cr 52·0	25 Mn 54·9	26 Fe 55·9	27 Co 58·9	28 Ni 58·7	29 Cu 63·5	30 Zn 65·4	31 Ga 69·7	32 Ge 72·6	33 As 74·9	34 Se 79·0	35 Br 79·9	36 Kr 83·8
5	37 Rb 85·5	38 Sr 87·6	39 Y 88·9	40 Zr 91·2	41 Nb 92·9	42 Mo 96·0	43 Tc 99	44 Ru 101	45 Rh 103	46 Pd 107	47 Ag 108	48 Cd 112	49 In 115	50 Sn 119	51 Sb 122	52 Te 128	53 I 127	54 Xe 131
6	55 Cs 133	56 Ba 137	*57 La 139	72 Hf 178	73 Ta 181	74 W 184	75 Re 186	76 Os 190	77 Ir 192	78 Pt 195	79 Au 197	80 Hg 201	81 Tl 204	82 Pb 207	83 Bi 209	84 Po 210	85 At 211	86 Rn 222
7	87 Fr 223	88 Ra 226	89 Ac 227	90 Th 232	91 Pa 231	92 U 238												

Atomic number is the number above the symbol
Atomic weight is the number below the symbol

* This is the position allotted to fourteen elements which are known collectively as the Lanthanide Series.

Appendix C

Symbols –atomic numbers–approximate atomic weights

Element	Symbol	Atomic number	Atomic weight
aluminium	Al	13	27
argon	Ar	18	40
arsenic	As	33	75
barium	Ba	56	137
boron	B	5	11
bromine	Br	35	80
calcium	Ca	20	40
carbon	C	6	12
chlorine	Cl	17	35·5
chromium	Cr	24	52
copper	Cu	29	64
fluorine	F	9	19
gold	Au	79	197
helium	He	2	4
hydrogen	H	1	1
iodine	I	53	127
iron	Fe	26	56
lead	Pb	82	207
lithium	Li	3	7
magnesium	Mg	12	24
manganese	Mn	25	55
mercury	Hg	80	201
neon	Ne	10	20
nitrogen	N	7	14
oxygen	O	8	16
phosphorus	P	15	31
potassium	K	19	39
radium	Ra	88	226
rubidium	Rb	37	85·5
selenium	Se	34	79
silicon	Si	14	28
silver	Ag	47	108
sodium	Na	11	23
strontium	Sr	38	88
sulphur	S	16	32
tin	Sn	50	119
uranium	U	92	238
zinc	Zn	30	65

Appendix D
Valencies

Valency 1		Valency 2	
Metallic	*Non-metallic*	*Metallic*	*Non-metallic*
sodium Na	chloride Cl	magnesium Mg	carbonate CO_3
potassium K	bromide Br	calcium Ca	sulphate SO_4
silver Ag	iodide I	zinc Zn	sulphite SO_3
	hydroxide OH	barium Ba	sulphide S
	nitrate NO_3	copper (II) Cu	oxide O
copper (I) Cu	hydrogen carbonate HCO_3	iron (II) Fe	
		lead (II) Pb	
	hydrogen sulphate HSO_4	mercury (II) Hg	
ammonium NH_4	hydrogen sulphite HSO_3	tin (II) Sn	
	hydrogen sulphide HS		
	chlorate ClO_3		
Valency 3		**Valency 4**	
Metallic	*Non-metallic*	*Metallic*	*Non-metallic*
aluminium Al	phosphate PO_4	lead (IV) Pb	carbon C
iron (III) Fe		tin (IV) Sn	silicon Si

Index